CENTRAL AMERICA IN CRISIS

WASHINGTON INSTITUTE TASK FORCE ON CENTRAL AMERICA

Marcelo Alonso, Chairman
Rolando Bonachea
Rolando Castaneda
Sergio Diaz-Briquets
Jorge Guardia
Jorge Perez-Lopez
Emilio Adolfo Rivero
Eduardo Ulibarri

Foreword By
Manuel Lujan Jr.

Commentary By
Paul E. Sigmund

CENTRAL AMERICA IN CRISIS

WASHINGTON INSTITUTE TASK FORCE REPORT

Marcelo Alonso
Task Force Chairman

Revised 1984 Edition

WI — The Washington Institute for Values in Public Policy

Washington

The Washington Institute for Values in Public Policy is an independent, nonprofit research and educational organization that provides nonpartisan analyses exploring the ethical values underlying public policy issues. The Washington Institute seeks to promote democratic principles which affirm the inherent value, freedom, and responsibility of the individual, the integrity of the family and the interdependence of the community of man. The Institute researches a broad range of public policy options, recognizing that the individual, the government and private social institutions share the responsibility for the common welfare—including the maintenance of a strong national defense. Policy options are generally viewed in light of their impact on the individual and the family. To encourage more informed decision-making on public policy issues, the Institute offers its research and resources to scholars, policymakers and the public.

© 1983, 1984 by Washington Institute for Values in Public Policy. All rights reserved. Except for use in reviews, no part of this book may be reproduced or utilized in any form or by any means mechanical, including photocopying, recording, or by any information storage and retrieval system.

Printed in the United States of America

Library of Congress Catalogue Card Number: 83-061052

International Standard Book Number: 0-89226-022-X

The views expressed in this book are those of the contributors and do not necessarily reflect the views of the officers, staff and trustees of the Washington Institute.

The Washington Institute for Values in Public Policy, 1333 New Hampshire Ave. NW, Suite 910, Washington, DC 20036

Design by Stephanie D. West, West & Wohler Associates, Inc.

CONTENTS

Map of Central America—Basic Data	vi
Publisher's Note	viii
Contributors	ix
Acronyms	x
Acknowledgments	xii
Preface	xiii
Foreword	
Manuel Lujan Jr.	xv
Introduction	
Eduardo Ulibarri	1
Chapter 1 Historical Context	12
Chapter 2 Social Context	40
Chapter 3 Economic Context	90
Chapter 4 Political Conflict and Violence	158
Chapter 5 Basic Elements of a Program for Action	192
Commentary on the Kissinger Commission Report	
Paul E. Sigmund	215
Appendix 1 Summary of the Report of the National Bipartisan Commission on Central America	237
Appendix 2 Caribbean Basin Initiative	253
Appendix 3 Recommendations of the Contadora Group	255
Appendix 4 Resolution AG/551 (XI-0/81) of the General Assembly of the Organization of American States	259
Index	261

CENTRAL AMERICA BASIC DATA

Country	Area, km² (Sq. Mi.)	Population	Per Capita Product ($)	Export Crops	Major Industries
Guatemala	108,890 (42,000)	7,053,000	1,199	coffee, meat, sugar, bananas, cotton	food processing, textiles, mining
El Salvador	21,040 (8,120)	4,813,000	681	coffee, corn, sugar, cotton	food processing, textiles
Honduras	112,090 (43,280)	3,691,000	639	coffee, meat, timber, bananas	food processing, textiles, mining
Nicaragua	130,000 (50,200)	2,422,000	897	coffee, cotton, meat	food processing, chemicals
Costa Rica	50,700 (19,580)	2,223,000	1,527	coffee, bananas, beef, sugar, materials	food processing, textiles, construction materials
Panama	77,080 (29,760)	1,837,000	1,918	bananas, sugar, shrimp, coffee	food processing, shipping, oil trans-shipment
Belize*	22,970 (8,870)	145,000	1,030	sugar, timber, citrus	

Source: IDB, *Social and Economic Progress Report*, 1980-81
*Became independent on September 22, 1981. Presently member of the British Commonwealth but claimed by Guatemala.

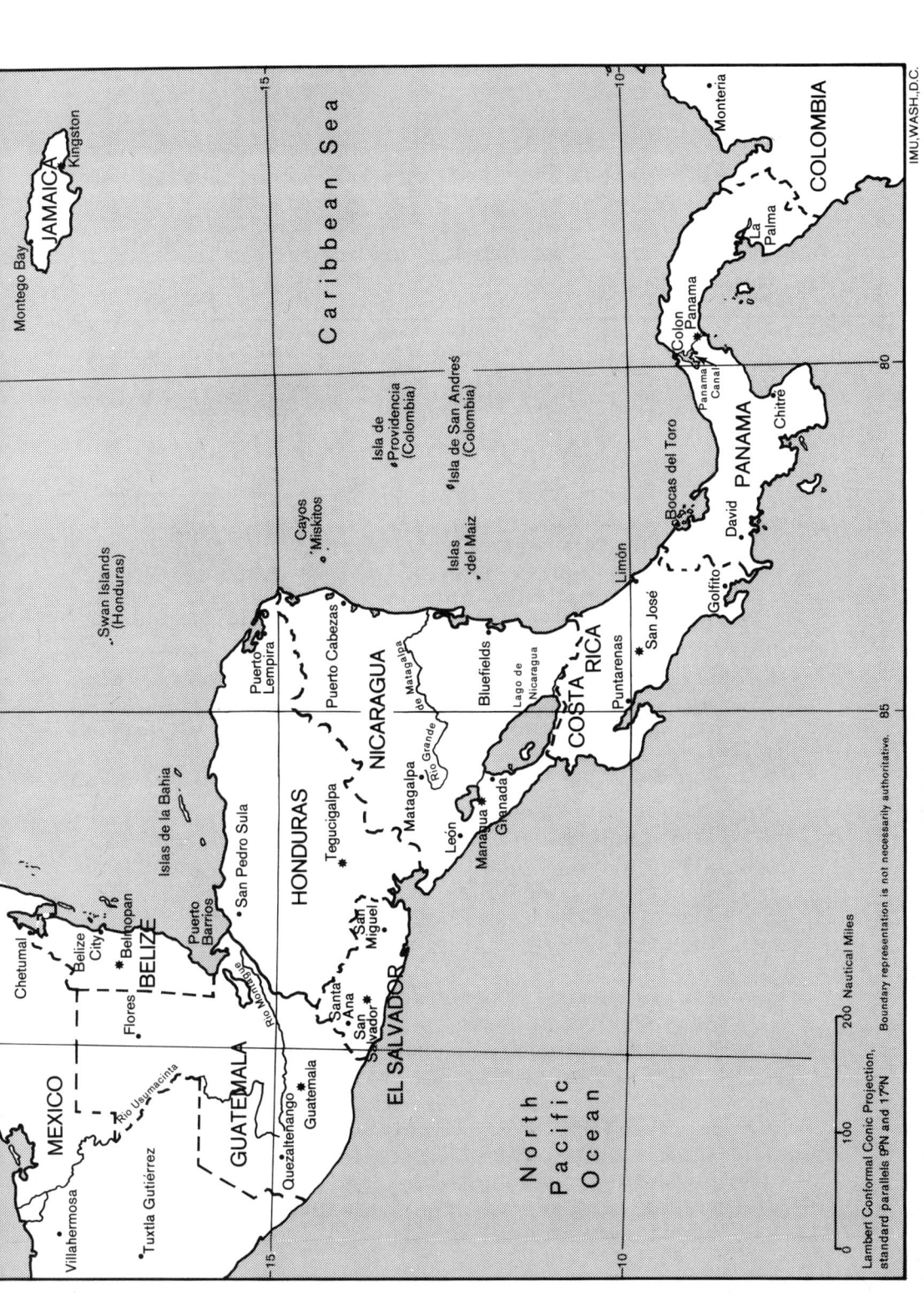

PUBLISHER'S NOTE

This report is the concluding document of the Task Force on Central America. The Task Force is a research project initially commissioned by the Professors World Peace Academy—US (PWPA-US) as an outgrowth of its 1981 annual conference "United States Foreign Policy Options for the 80s" which was chaired by Professor Morton A. Kaplan of the University of Chicago. The Central America Task Force became a project of the Washington Institute for Values in Public Policy in late 1982.

As a result of the wide critical acclaim for *Central America in Crisis* after it was published in May 1983, the Washington Institute commissioned the Task Force to revise and update the first edition. For this updated edition, Congressman Manuel Lujan Jr. (R-NM) has written a Foreword which places the crisis in Central America within the context of the current policy debate presently underway in Congress. Eduardo Ulibarri, editor-in-chief of Costa Rica's largest daily newspaper, *La Nacion*, contributed an original introduction from the unique perspective of someone intimately involved with the current state of affairs in Central America. Professor Paul E. Sigmund of Princeton University provided a commentary on the final report of the National Bipartisan Commission on Central America, the so-called Kissinger Commission, which follows the last chapter. Also added to the revised edition are four appendices containing valuable reference documents on Central America.

CONTRIBUTORS

The members of the Washington Institute Task Force on Central America:

Marcelo Alonso, Task Force Chairman, is Executive Director of the Florida Institute of Technology Research and Engineering (FITRE), Melbourne, Florida.

Rolando Bonachea is Associate Professor of Latin American History, and Dean, College of Arts and Sciences, University of St. Louis; and Commissioner, Commission of Human Rights, St. Louis, Missouri.

Rolando Castaneda is Senior Loan Officer, Central America Division, Inter-American Development Bank, Washington, DC.

Sergio Diaz-Briquets is President of BD International, a Washington consulting group.

Jorge Guardia is Professor of Law and Economics at the University of Costa Rica, and General Manager of Counsel, a private consulting firm.

Jorge Perez-Lopez, an international economist, is a private consultant specializing in Latin American affairs in Washington, DC.

Emilio Adolfo Rivero is a lawyer and journalist in Washington, DC.

Eduardo Ulibarri is Editor-in-Chief, *La Nacion*, San Jose, Costa Rica; and Associate Professor, Mass Communication School, University of Costa Rica.

Foreword to the revised 1984 edition:
Manuel Lujan Jr. is a Republican Congressman from New Mexico.

Commentary on the Kissinger Commission Report:
Paul E. Sigmund is Professor of Politics, and Director, Latin American Studies Program, Princeton University, Princeton, New Jersey.

ACRONYMS

AID	Agency for International Development (US)
APRA	Alianza Popular Revolucionaria Americana (Peru)
ARENA	National Republican Alliance Party (El Salvador)
CABEI	Central American Bank for Economic Integration
CACM	Central American Common Market
CBI	Caribbean Basin Initiative (US)
CDS	Sandinista Defense Committee (Nicaragua)
CEPAL	Commission Economica para America Latina (UN; same as ECLA)
COMECON	Council for Mutual Economic Assistance
DAC	Development Assistance Committee (part of the OECD)
ECLA	Economic Commission of Latin America (UN; same as CEPAL)
EGP	Guerrilla Army of the Poor (Guatemala)
FAO	Broad Opposition Front (Nicaragua)
FAR	Revolutionary Armed Forces (Guatemala)
FDR	Democratic Revolutionary Front (El Salvador)
FMLN	Farabundo Martí Movement (El Salvador)
FPN	National Patriotic Front (Nicaragua)
GDP	Gross Domestic Product

IBRD	International Bank for Reconstruction and Development; also known as World Bank
ICAITI	Central American Institute of Technological and Industrial Research
ICAP	Central American Institute of Public Administration
IDA	International Development Agency
IDB	Inter-American Development Bank
IFC	International Finance Corporation
IMF	International Monetary Fund
INCAP	Institute of Nutrition in Central America and Panama
INRA	Instituto Nacional de Reforma Agraria (Nicaragua)
PAC	Authentic Constitutional Party (El Salvador)
PCN	Party of National Conciliation (El Salvador)
PGT	Partido Guatemalteco del Trabajo (Guatemala)
PLN	National Liberation Party (Guatemala)
PLN	National Liberation Party (Costa Rica)
PRAM	Revolutionary Party of April and May (El Salvador)
PREALC	Regional Employment Program of Latin America and the Caribbean
PRN	National Republican Party (Costa Rica)
PRUD	Revolutionary Party of Democratic Union (El Salvador)
PUN	National Union Party (Costa Rica)
OAS	Organization of American States
OECD	Organization for Economic Cooperation and Development
ODECA	Organizacion para el Desarollo Economico de Centro America
OPIC	Overseas Private Investment Corporation
ORPA	Organization of the People in Arms (Guatemala)
SDR	Special Drawing Rights
SIECA	General Treaty of Central American Economic Integration
UNDP	United Nations Development Program

ACKNOWLEDGMENTS

The authors wish to recognize the Professors World Peace Academy-US, the Washington Institute for Values in Public Policy, and the International Conference on the Unity of the Sciences for supporting this work. In particular we wish to recognize the constant encouragement and interest expressed by Professors Morton Kaplan and Richard Rubenstein, past Presidents of PWPA-US and Mr. Neil Salonen, Director of the Washington Institute. Our work would not have reached completion without the dedication and logistic assistance of the ICUS and PWPA staffs, particularly of Richard Wojcik, General Manager of ICUS, and Hugh Spurgin, Secretary-General of PWPA-US, the former during the earlier and more difficult stages of our work, and the latter during the second and rather delicate phase. To all these people the authors convey their deepest gratitude.

In the preparation of this report many persons in Central America, Mexico, and the United States were interviewed or read portions of the manuscript. Their contribution was critical to our study. The list of commentators includes heads of state, ministers, church authorities, persons in the military, university professors, bankers, professionals, and industrialists. Listing their names would be too long for reproduction here, but to all of them the authors convey their most sincere thanks and appreciation.

PREFACE

We who have prepared the chapters of this book know how fluid the situation in Central America can be. While we have kept our contributions as current as possible, we recognize how difficult it is to keep a document of this kind completely up to date. Nevertheless, we believe this study can serve as a valuable reference work to those who wish to understand Central America or who must make policy decisions regarding that area.

It is very difficult to make any decision regarding Central America without understanding the complexity of its present crisis—and that, in turn, requires some familiarity with the history and political evolution of the region and a full grasp of the socioeconomic factors in each of the countries. So the historical, social and economic contexts are examined first.

Next, two critical elements that have become particularly relevant in recent years are examined. These two elements, ideological polarization and violence, give an international character—and sometimes, unfortunately, a radical flavor—to the struggle for democratization of the region and for redressing the social and economic grievances of large segments of the population. Time is short and resources are limited, and that makes solutions even more difficult. Thus, in the final chapter, we offer some basic elements for a program of action. In that context we examine the Caribbean Basin Initiative President Reagan proposed on February 24, 1982, the report of the National Bipartisan Commission on Central America, released on January 14, 1984, and the recommendations of the Contadora Group.

It is not too late to redress the social claims of the people of Central America and to bring democratic institutions into full operation. But action must be taken quickly and decisively.

The United States under the present administration has shown great concern for contributing to a solution of the crises afflicting the region. We hope there will be similar participation by Mexico, Venezuela and Colombia, who are more closely tied to Central America than are the rest of the countries in the Western Hemisphere. If this document serves in any way to assist individuals, organizations and governments in finding the ways and means to help, we will feel more than rewarded for our modest efforts.

M.A., R.B., R.C., S.D.-B., J.G., J.P.-L., E.A.R., E.U.
Washington, DC
January 1984

FOREWORD
By Manuel Lujan Jr.

War and terrorism wrack the Middle East. Pawns and players maneuver on the chessboard of Europe. Slowly the sleeping giant of China awakes and emerges into the midday of world politics. The arms race, the space race, the nuclear threat—with such global tremors commanding our attention almost daily, it is not surprising that this country sometimes overlooks events in Central America, right at our doorstep. For many decades, journalists, political leaders, and other opinion shapers in both Mexico and Central America have tried to attract the attention of the United States to what is happening in its own hemisphere. But until recently, this country's foreign policy has all too often been preoccupied with events beyond its oceans.

Today the United States is awakening more and more to the fact that Central America is of global importance, its future strategically vital to our own. On April 27, 1983, when President Ronald Reagan spoke to a joint session of Congress on "Central America: Defending Our Vital Interests," he reminded his listeners that two-thirds of all our foreign trade, including petroleum, passes through the Caribbean sealanes and the Panama Canal. Thus nothing less than our national security is at risk in this sinuous isthmus between Colombia and Mexico. In President Reagan's view, Soviet military theorists would like nothing better than to gain control of the Caribbean and the Panama Canal, for then they could cripple our capacity to resupply Western Europe and tie down the forces that we might otherwise use to counter Soviet moves in other parts of the world. And many of us in Congress agree with him; so do many informed citizens throughout the land.

But it is more than self-interest that moves us. In these small and struggling nations we see chronic, endemic poverty and a growing need for social and economic change. And, sadly, we see these ills being exploited by those who pursue political goals through violence. Human suffering and the tragedies of terrorist killings and guerrilla attacks are a constant threat to the region's peace and freedom.

It is not easy for thoughtful observers in this country to understand at a distance the myriad forces pushing and pulling at the fabric of Central America. In *Central America in Crisis*, first published in May of 1983, the authors strove to assemble an objective, concise policy analysis and reference work for those who seek a better understanding of the region, and for those who make or shape policy decisions that affect it. In this the authors have already succeeded; the book's first edition was used by the Kissinger Commission as a rich source of information on the history, social structure, political forces, and economy of the region.

In this revised edition, the authors carry forward the central theme that policy decisions require a sound understanding of the area's history and its political and economic evolution. Thus the historical, social, and economic factors are examined first; then the political and ideological conflicts; and finally violence. An analysis of the Kissinger Commission report follows the final chapter.

The authors have recognized that two of these elements—ideological polarization and violence—tend to give "a radical and international character to the struggle for democratization of the region." These two elements, in fact, are the main reasons why it is especially difficult to find solutions to the other problems, the social and economic needs, of the Central American people. This constraint has been carefully taken into account in the concluding chapter, where the authors offer the basic framework of a Program for Action.

Throughout the book, the authors identify and examine many aspects of United States policy toward Central America. In particular, an appendix which summarizes the Kissinger Commission report and excerpts of the Caribbean Basin Initiative have been included. Together they place the crisis in Central America in a hemispheric context.

The Kissinger report is an especially pivotal document. It emphasizes that the crisis is acute—made even more so by worldwide economic recession and Cuban-Soviet-Nicaraguan intervention—and that the roots of the problem are indigenous in the poverty and closed political systems that have long characterized the region. The report weighs the prospects for economic and political development, explores the security issues, and probes the diplomatic nuances. It then offers recommendations—among them a program of assistance designed to reduce poverty through economic growth, to foster social equity through democratization and self-determination, and to help stabilize economies and societies plagued by violence. This program is an integral part of the proposed Central America Democracy, Peace, and Development Initiative Act of 1984, which President Reagan transmitted to Congress in February.

As Congress—and concerned citizens everywhere—debate this bill and the crisis it addresses, both the Kissinger Commission report and *Central America In Crisis* can be of immense value. For both embody the central aim of United States policy toward Central America: to sustain the independence and freedom of the region by strengthening the security of its threatened nations as a "shield for democratization," and to put an end to violence and terrorism.

The issues are complex, the problems are enormous—and the time is short. Only when lawmakers and opinion leaders are informed and the whole spectrum of perceptions and perspectives is brought to light can freedom and peace be served. And in so doing, we serve our own national interests as well.

INTRODUCTION

By Eduardo Ulibarri

As the crisis worsens in Central America and its ripples are felt abroad, there is a natural tendency for the outside observer to oversimplify, to apply alien analogies, to fit the situation's round peg into the square hole of his own experience. The result is not understanding but distortion or historical metaphors. The urgency and seriousness of the crisis call for a different approach.

For decades, US policymakers and opinion leaders tended to see the area's problems in the context of a fight between communism and democracy. And although some leaders quickly saw that the situation was more complex and called for social and political reform, most simply equated democracy with American interests and labeled as communist all actions against the establishment. Dissatisfaction, questioning of the status quo, or genuine attempts at democratic change were viewed as part of an international conspiracy, and so it became legitimate to support those fighting such an alleged conspiracy, even if they were bloody dictators not really facing a communist menace. The US attitude toward the Somoza regime in Nicaragua up to the early 1970s was a clear example of this attitude.

In recent years this one-sided perspective has been losing ground in the US government, in favor of a more balanced approach. However, a nearly opposite—and equally inadequate—view has been gaining ground among politicians and opinionmakers. This posture underplays the communist totalitarian menace and blames all of Central America's current conflicts on injustices, backwardness, and abuses inherent to military-oligarchic regimes supported by the United States, against which people have rebelled. And while it concedes that rebellion may be linked to external forces, it defines revolt as fundamentally nationalistic, accepting outside Marxist aid only for the lack of support from other sources. Thus US attempts to affect the outcome are seen as irrelevant, hypocritical, or harmful. This has led to the Vietnam analogy.

What this analogy states is that US involvement in the area will end as it did for Americans in Vietnam, with open war, severe human losses, and, in the end, virtual defeat. The comparison usually ends at this point; it does not consider what happened to Vietnam and Cambodia once the United States decided to end its role. For those living in Central America and involved in promoting democracy, it is valid to feel terrified at the prospect of being abandoned by a democratic ally such as the US, and then being ruled by governments like those that precipitated the bloodbaths in Vietnam and Cambodia, no matter how "national" they are. As Mexican poet Octavio Paz has said, it is not enough to "nationalize" revolutions; it is more important to attain their "democratization."

Any of these simplistic approaches distorts reality. This can lead to policies that resort to violence in support of factions calling themselves anti-communist—or, at the other extreme, can paralyze US conduct abroad and lead to communist takeovers. Either way, the prospects for democracy suffer. So, rather than looking for shallow explanations or one-sided analogies, it is paramount to realize how many-sided the situation is.

Current Central American crisis can be traced to three basic roots: (1) a heritage of injustice, underdevelopment, and dictatorship in many of its countries; (2) the crumbling of traditional power alliances that long maintained the status quo; and (3) Cuban and Soviet manipulation of these problems, with the aim not of advancing people's legitimate aspirations, but of promoting their own strategic and ideological aims and of undermining US security. The first two roots are closely related, although not always dependent on each other. Both are national in character, so they differ from country to country and demand tailored solutions. The third root, though fostered by the other two, has not only a regional but also a global nature. The way Soviet-Cuban manipulation affects each country at a given moment depends not only on the internal situation, but also on the strategies and opportunism of the Soviet Union and Cuba. For in facing this threat, solutions that are national in scope just won't work; responses must be regional or even global in scope.

Injustice, underdevelopment, and dictatorship have worsened the human condition in many Central American nations. People have been denied individual rights and a fair chance for economic progress, and that has made them ripe for polarization, violence, and Marxism. Instead of flexible political partnerships determined by elections, most of Central America was ruled in the past by obstinate power alliances, usually divorced from people's aspirations, with the oligarchy and the military as their core. The most obdurate of these developed in the northern reaches of Central America, where El Salvador and Guatemala had consistently refused to widen their base by incorporating emerging groups, mainly from the middle classes. In Nicaragua there used to be a symbiosis between the military and a sector of the oligarchy, both represented by the Somoza family, partial owner and total ruler of the country. In Honduras, where the strong influence of foreign companies and the lack of national integration prevented development of a strong national oligarchy, the military-economic alliance was based on more flexible patterns, and a competition for power by two traditional parties stimulated greater popular involvement in politics. Panama has no strong oligarchy either, but this is due to its peculiar development as a nation and its dependence on a foreign-controlled canal. The main permanent source of power here—the National Guard—has demonstrated a high degree of flexibility.

History offers but one lasting example of a true "civilian society" of free individuals sharing basic democratic values and having a voice in the decision-making process: Costa Rica. The Costa Rican system, because of its democratic evolution, social mobility, and absence of a military elite, has been able not only to absorb, but also to promote change and emerging groups.

4
CENTRAL AMERICA

In the past the ruling elites in Central America had usually been adept at managing the state apparatus, satisfying conflicting interests inside the power alliance, and using rewards and repression to keep things stable. In such cases the precarious condition of the people wasn't enough to create a critical situation. The 1932 rebellion in El Salvador, for example, although deeply rooted in social unrest, was quickly controlled by a small but effective ruling group.

Then, almost 50 years later, the government of General Carlos Humberto Romero found it could not control street demonstrations. His removal in 1979 opened the way for a period of rapid change in El Salvador. In Nicaragua, the Somoza dictatorship lost command not so much because people's conditions worsened, but because it tried to increase control beyond what it could manage and lost the loyalty of traditional allies. So, even if we just look at the local ingredients of the Central American problem, we see that injustice, underdevelopment, or dictatorship lead most readily to crisis when coupled with a ruling elite's ineffectiveness in managing power. And once a regime collapses, it is vital to create new power alliances that can fill the power vacuum and, at the same time, promote democracy. Since differences are so great from country to country, it would be a serious mistake to use general rules and forget the particular interplay of actors and situations and their roots in local history and tradition. This does not mean, however, ruling out basic democratic goals for all these countries—goals such as economic development, social reform, and the creation and progression of new power alliances, centered around democratic and reform-minded groups, that can pave the way to stability based on democratic institutions and practices.

If we look at Central American countries and compare their current situation with previous years, we can see positive forces at work despite the violence and instability. Amid a deadlocked crisis, a new power alliance is struggling for change and democracy in El Salvador, with the US government as its main supporter. In Guatemala, despite terrorism and political abuse there is presently at least a more promising political environment than during General Fernando Romeo Lucas' government. In Honduras, the process of democratic reconstitution has been completed, and the nation is now struggling for consolidation in a difficult environment. Costa Rica has remained stable and, through a working democracy, is trying to surmount its deep economic crisis and deal with foreign hazards, while Panama has taken important steps toward full democracy. It is in Nicaragua that the prospects for democracy appear dim, due to the dominance of a Marxist regime.

It is not a simple and straightforward process to overcome a stubborn and durable power alliance based on injustice, ignorance, and political paralysis. Because new coalitions cannot be based on a vacuum, democratic sectors striving for influence and power will usually have to compromise and even cooperate for a while with some members of previous ruling elites. This is why Christian Democrats shared government with the military in El Salvador, and why Honduran liberals have had to compromise with the armed forces at a time of foreign menace. What is vital as alliances realign is that the democratization process continues so that a real civilian society starts to develop. Unfortunately, it is at this point that non-traditional political groups often act without concern for the previous power structure.

Only in Nicaragua, despite a successful insurrection in the name of democracy which had the support of several Latin American countries and, in the end, of the United States, is the trend backward. A totalitarian regime committed to Marxism is well advanced in controlling independent sources of influence; the economy is in collapse; and promises for social development have not come true. How did this happen?

The Somoza regime in Nicaragua began to totter in the late '70s, at a moment when there was a vacuum, or at least a fuzziness, in US policy toward the area. By then, Cuba had changed its revolutionary tactics, stressing the importance of unity among guerrilla groups as a first step toward a wider alliance with democratic sectors that could legitimize their movement and make access to power easier. The sum of these two elements produced tragic results.

During the months immediately before Somoza's collapse in 1979, the Carter Administration lost the kind of influence the US government had usually had over affairs in Nicaragua. Previous administrations had not put enough pressure on Somoza to advance democracy; this time the error was to place strong emphasis on the national problems and downplay the global ingredients of the crisis (i.e., Soviet and Cuban influence and strategy). Many Latin American democratic governments and leaders—mainly Costa Rica, Panama, Colombia, Mexico, and Venezuela—made the same error by acting on a limited analysis or wrong perceptions of what was really happening and what were the priorities at the time. The irony is that, had the Soviet and Cuban menace been closely considered, a Marxist takeover in Nicaragua might have been averted by limiting the Sandinistas' strong influence in the opposition alliance. The Sandinistas could have been disarmed and a multi-national force assigned to occupy Nicaragua until a democratic government had been established and consolidated. Instead, promises were accepted from the Sandinistas as guarantees—some to the Organization of American States (OAS), some to a group of Latin American democratic leaders. Initially moderates were even included in the official power structure. But Marxists remained as the main controllers of military power. With no effective competition within the anti-Somocist alliance, they easily filled the vacuum left by Somoza and became the holders of real power and the architects of a new totalitarian society.

The Nicaraguan experience has taught Central American democrats that, despite the urgency of local problems, it would be disastrous not to look beyond them and consider the Marxist menace. We cannot remain passive toward Soviet and Cuban strategies or underestimate their effectiveness in transforming valid popular demands into vehicles for advancing their purposes. For them, popular frustration is just an ingredient in their strategies, not a condition for action.

It would also be dangerous to think we can neutralize such a menace merely by solving the most acute national problems. Social justice, economic development, and democracy are precious achievements, and upon them stability rests. But they are not a vaccine against communist interference. At times, the Soviet-Cuban strategy may call for destabilization of a democratic country or the undermining of a political system in order to interrupt democracy. Given no "objective" conditions for revolution, the strategists may well create "subjective" ones, such as terrorism by small groups of radicals. The effectiveness of such a strategy may depend not so much on social or economic conditions as on the terrorists' ability to manage violence. This is the kind of menace that, for example, many Costa Ricans feel, especially since recent terrorist acts by small groups without roots in society seem to have the aim not of immediately seizing power, but of disrupting a working democracy based on consensus.

So the best approach to analysis and policymaking toward Central America is to take into account both local, regional, and global problems. Paying attention to just one source of problems could mean either neglecting vital reforms or opening the way to totalitarianism. This means that, as Central American democrats and their allies work towards development, reform, and democracy, they should meet the communist challenge wherever it appears.

To keep such a balanced approach, especially in highly polarized societies, is a very difficult task. This is evident in El Salvador, where so frequently the US government and public opinion face the decision of whether to increase aid to a regime that is facing the guerrillas' totalitarian menace and trying to make democracy work, but at the same time is unable, so far, to control death squads or conduct reliable judicial processes in cases involving US citizens. But to opt for single-minded analyses or decisions, no matter how consistent they may look at a given time, will be worse than acknowledging the contradictions, compromising, and making, at times, not the best but the least-worst decisions. It will help to remember that, although any dictatorship is reprehensible, traditional oligarchic-military regimes and the alliances that have succeeded them in some countries can evolve into democracy, while communist-totalitarian regimes will end any hope of attaining it. National oligarchies and armed forces, although generally inflexible and accustomed to privilege, are easier to influence than communist groups. Communists are part of an international movement, respond to international strategies, and have international loyalties and alliances aimed at increasing power, not developing justice or democracy. Once Marxists are in firm control, democratic countries and groups are almost impotent in influencing them. Traditional oligarchic regimes do not belong to any international "movement" that shares their aims and provides support; rather, they depend on national strategies and forces in keeping power and privilege. And they usually lack a comprehensive doctrine for providing some sort of legitimacy to their control. So they are easier to influence, both by emerging national groups and by foreign democratic countries. Again El Salvador is an example of how such an influence can smooth and pave the way for transition to democracy, while the Sandinistas' peculiar responses against calls for democratization show how difficult it is to make a Marxist regime change its plans for total control of a society. The Salvadoran government conducted free elections for a Constitutional Assembly in March 1982; it recently called for presidential elections in March 1984; and it has taken steps to at least meet with guerrilla leaders—yet the Sandinista regime has disregarded the value of "bourgeois" elections and has rejected all serious attempts at political compromise. The Nicaraguan government made some "good-will" gestures by the end of 1983, but they had nothing to do with loosening its closed political regime. They might temporarily ease tensions with Central American countries and the United States, perhaps only to buy time for consolidating the internal dictatorship. But even such symbolic acts as reducing the number of Cuban personnel or setting a date for elections in 1984 came about not by political persuasion but by strong military pressure, both by the *Contras* and by the presence of US forces in Honduras.

It is a real pity that polarization from within and interference and stratagems from without have led Central America not to the danger of war but to war itself. The presence in Nicaragua of a virtual totalitarian regime dependent on Cuba and the Soviet Union, although not the cause of internal conflicts in neighbor countries, is the main instrument for manipulating them toward communist goals, and that has led to the regionalization of violence. The fighting sputters across a wide front and is conducted by mostly unconventional means.

Peace is a precious goal, but it should not be bought at the price of democracy. For democracy is even more precious, not only because of its sheer importance to the human condition, but because the lack of functioning and respected democratic institutions has been one of the main reasons for violence in Central America. Development and consolidation of democratic institutions cannot be accomplished through one-sided solutions, appeasement, or naivete, but through intelligent strategies at the least possible cost. A starting point to such an approach is to strip away simplistic analogies and theories that may have worked somewhere else in the past but that are not relevant for the region.

This book, through a multidisciplinary approach, faces Central American problems from the most relevant viewpoints. It focuses on the current crisis, but also looks at its historical development and future projections. The picture that emerges shows there are no simple ways to come to grips with the crisis, but there *are* ways out of it. Democracy has been mainly a fiction to the majority of Central American people, yet it *can* be achieved through internal political decision, intelligence, and flexibility teamed with external support by countries, governments, groups, and individuals sharing democratic values.

CHAPTER 1
HISTORICAL CONTEXT

1.1 BACKGROUND

Central America bridges the North and South American continents, spanning some 1,300 miles from Guatemala to the Republic of Panama. During the Spanish colonial period that began in the 16th century, the region was known as the Captaincy General of Guatemala. Three hundred years of Spanish colonial rule came to an end in 1821, and after efforts at political unity failed, the area was divided into small nation-states (Guatemala, Honduras, El Salvador, Costa Rica and Nicaragua) thus shaping the current geopolitical configuration of Central America.

In the precolonial era, the Central American peoples had simple economies that ranged from primitive food gathering, fishing, and hunting to more advanced agricultural economies. Some groups produced manioc and arrowroot (tubers); others grew beans, maize, and squash—staples even in the diet of today's population. The village was the principal form of land tenure, and a village council closely monitored the allocation of arable land to each family. Other plots of arable and wooded land were held communally by the villages. In addition to agricultural production, these cultures had developed craft skills and trade and transport networks. Both in agriculture and trade, the Indian himself served as the beast of burden, since the civilization lacked draft animals and, because of the terrain, could make little use of the wheel except on children's toys.

With the arrival of the Spanish conquistadores in the early 16th century, conquest and disease took a heavy toll of the indigenous population, and the process of colonization clashed with established indigenous patterns. This collision of cultures laid the foundations for later ethnic features and socioeconomic problems, such as the dominant power groups that still are characteristic of present-day Central America.

Throughout the colonial period, the Spanish conquistadores were delighted to find gold in the streams and an easily subdued local labor force to gather it. However, as in other parts of the Caribbean and Mexico, forced labor and European diseases took a frightful toll. The native populations of Central America decreased from 12–15 million at the beginning of the conquest to about 2.5 million at the end of the first century of Spanish occupation. Warfare and enslavement, particularly in Nicaragua and Costa Rica, gradually decimated the native groups, and large numbers of Indians from Honduras and Nicaragua were shipped off as slaves to labor in Cuba, Panama, and Peru.[1] In addition, European diseases such as measles, typhus, and smallpox became the most feared cause of mortality among the native population. The introduction of African slaves and the subsequent racial miscegenation of blacks, Amerindians, and caucasians during the colonial period led to the mestizo population now predominant throughout modern Central America, with the exceptions of Costa Rica (predominantly white) and Guatemala (predominantly Amerindian). In the process, the Spanish language largely supplanted some 80 native dialects.

In the first part of the 16th century, the Spaniards rapidly exhausted the limited ores found in Central America, and thus a frantic search began for products that could be exported to bring wealth to the conquering group. Thus began the production of sugar cane, cacao, and indigo on large plantations. In the 19th century the production of bananas and coffee was introduced, thereby reinforcing the agricultural-export economies characteristic of present-day Central American nations.

During the colonial period, dominant power groups developed. Large landholding individuals, in order to advance their own economic interests, frequently organized into powerful associations which added to the disadvantages of the increasingly dispossessed natives. Since the beginning of the conquest and colonial periods, the clergy of the Roman Catholic Church, though frequently allied with the conservative oligarchy, became, in Central America as in the rest of Spanish America, an advocate and frequent defender of the rights of the native population. That brought the church into opposition with powerful land associations, the Spanish crown, and later, Central America's established governments.

When the Captaincy General of Guatemala declared its independence from Spain on September 15, 1821, Guatemala, Honduras, El Salvador, Nicaragua, and Costa Rica were provinces under its jurisdiction. Initial attempts to become part of Mexico had been unsuccessful, for Iturbide's Empire in that country collapsed in March 1823. That same year, on June 24, the Federation of United Provinces of Central America was created. Each province was to have a chief of state while the Federation itself had a president. Provisional juntas and presidents tried to rule and to hold the precarious Federation together amid civil strife and schisms which dragged on until 1840. Elected in 1830, the Honduran patriot Francisco Morazan tried unsuccessfully to instill new life into the collapsing Federation, but by 1840 local loyalties and intra-regional rivalries were insurmountable. Nevertheless, efforts at political integration stretched over more than a century, and even today the reunification of Central America is mentioned in the constitutions of Nicaragua, Honduras, and Guatemala as a political objective to be pursued.

With the proclamation of independence from Spain the military became an important force in the area,[2] while the plantation system continued to be the basic socioeconomic factor. An incipient labor movement began to lay organizational foundations in the latter part of the 19th century.[3] Eventually the ideas of the anarcho-syndicalist movement, which began in Europe in the 19th century, became influential in the labor organizations of Central America.

The political fragmentation of the region during the post-independence period, which gave rise to the present political structure, was due in large measure to the traditional isolation of the provinces and the resulting local loyalties among the dominant groups. The revolutionary factions which had successfully challenged the domination of Spain in 1821 acted on the heels of the South American and Mexican wars of independence, with the ideological influences of the American and French revolutions serving as catalysts. However, the grievances that troubled most of Spanish America's inhabitants of Spanish origin were excessive taxation and the lack of political opportunities for those not born in the mother country. Their concerns emerged as a resolution to enhance the power of emerging socioeconomic groups—not one that advocated social justice for the large masses of the dispossessed.

The Catholic Church was an important factor in the declaration of independence in Central America. Many Central American clerics, who had received at least part of their education in Europe, had absorbed the ideas of liberty associated with the French Revolution and the work of the Encyclopedists. Besides, the Spanish revolution in 1820 was strongly anticlerical, which made the Central American priests eager to get rid of a government that in Spain was hostile to the church. Of the 29 signatories to the Act of Independence, 13 were members of the clergy.

After 1821 a pattern was established by which landowners, and military and business groups became the dominant factors that disputed and held political power. Throughout the 19th century, conservative and liberal groups patterned after those in the mother country competed for political dominance. The conservatives gained support primarily from the wealthiest landholding families, who were unenthusiastic supporters of independence and advocates of a strong centralist state that would preserve the social stratification of their respective countries. The liberals, not having their wealth tied to landholding patterns, favored ideas of laissez-faire capitalism and federalism, ideas which were popular in 19th-century Europe. Between 1821 and 1840 both groups supported the elusive idea of Central American reunification.[4] The church also entered the political sphere during the postindependence period, mainly due to its conflict with liberals over anticlericalism.

In the 20th century, anarchists, Marxists, social democrats, and right- wing coalitions also entered the political arena. Further, the rise of the banana industry during this period, with substantial involvement of US companies, increased US interests in the socioeconomic and political events of the region.

The United States has considered Central America an important strategic area to US national security interests. Economically, the area provides agricultural products and other raw materials and is an important outlet for US manufactured goods, food, and fuel. Perhaps more than any economic consideration, the United States has considered the geography of the area to be of paramount importance. The Caribbean is one of the most strategic sea lanes in the world, and the Panama Canal has traditionally been considered crucial to the trade and defense of the United States. As a result, the United States has continued, in its own interest, to establish a dominant presence in the Caribbean islands and Central America. However, the United States entered the political arena of Central America in the late 19th century without an understanding of the region's history of political fragmentation, factionalism, social and economic inequities, and use of violence as a means for the acquisition of political power. As we shall see, more recent political instability, along with the developing threat from the Soviet Union and the international communist movement which began in the 1930s, led increasingly to US efforts at consolidating a sphere of influence in Central America.

Besides US influence in Central America throughout the 19th and 20th centuries, manifested through investment in the Panama Canal, banks, plantations, and railway companies and at times through military intervention, a new factor has had some bearing on regional events during recent decades. This has been the international socialist movement that has provided financial and political support to the National Liberation Party in Costa Rica, to the Sandinistas in Nicaragua before and after their coming to power, and to revolutionary and guerrilla movements in El Salvador.

An element that has contributed to the shaping of events in Central America in the last decade has been the preaching of the theology of liberation to rural and urban masses by many members of the clergy. Some observers have expressed the idea that the liberation theologists, by advocating social confrontation, paved the way for insurgency, in many cases with direct communist involvement. Whether or not the liberation theologists, trying to redress legitimate grievances that had gone unheeded for generations, served the overall objectives of the Soviet Union is a question that future historians may long debate.

A recurrent theme in Central America has been the

struggle for power by or among the wealthy landowners, the emerging industrial and business classes, and the military. The succession of power has been determined by the strength and viability of the alliances proposed either at election times or when coups d'etat took place. Political contests have been, in the main, the occupation of privileged minorities, though Panama, Costa Rica, and Nicaragua offer examples of popular mobilizations achieving important national objectives.

The following discussion focuses on political development within each of the Central American countries. A summary of the governmental organizations of these nations appears in Table 1.1.

1.2 NICARAGUA

The political history of this country has been one of civil war, instability, factionalism, and foreign intervention. Internally, conservatives and liberals have battled one another since independence. A factionalized Nicaragua invited England's intervention in the 18th century—and got for their efforts the so-called "Mosquito Kingdom." By the middle of the 19th century, US private economic interests were in conflict with the British presence. In the mid-nineteenth century an American, William Walker, made repeated efforts to control Nicaragua. Walker was unsuccessful and was captured and executed in Honduras in 1860. Internal instability and conflicts set the stage for repeated military intervention in the 20th century, commencing with the overthrow of the repressive government of liberal president Zelaya (1893–1909) and ending with the establishment in 1936 of the Somoza dynasty, which lasted for several decades until 1979.

One interpretation of Zelaya's debacle is that it resulted from the corrupt and repressive nature of his presidency, which increasingly strained US-Nicaraguan private business and government relations. On the other hand, Zelaya's presidency brought several reforms to Nicaragua, including an emphasis on education and economic modernization. Subsequent years ushered in two periods of US military occupation—during the first period (1912–25) to keep the conservatives in power, and during the second period (1926–33) to prevent conservative-liberal confrontation from erupting into civil disorder. It was during the second American occupation of Nicaragua that both Cesar Augusto Sandino and Anastasio Somoza Garcia became important national figures—the former through his bitter fight against the occupation forces, and the latter through his leadership in the National Guard.[5]

Sandino was a man of action, not an ideologue. Early in the decade of the twenties he lived in Mexico, where he seems to have been influenced by the Mexican Revolution of 1910. When Sandino returned to Nicaragua in 1926, he joined the liberal insurrection against the conservatives. A year later when the liberals agreed to US mediation, he chose to continue the armed struggle against the conservatives, and eventually against the United States.

In 1934, after several years of guerrilla warfare, Sandino was prepared to sign a peace agreement with President Sacasa. However, Sandino's assassination by the National Guard eliminated the need for any conditional peace treaty, and secured General "Tacho" Somoza as the power behind the Sacasa presidency until he ran uncontested in an election in 1936. Thus the legacy of the Somoza dynasty began—a legacy of caudillo rule, characterized by broad-based support, nepotism, repression against all opposition, and personal aggrandizement of wealth and property.

The Somoza dictatorship suppressed the conservatives but promoted some social reforms, such as women's emancipation, public health, and education. However, the corruption and brutality of his rule, and that of his puppet regimes (i.e., his uncle Victor Remon y Reyes), increased political opposition during the 1950s. While campaigning for a fourth term in 1956, Anastasio Somoza was assassinated.

Replacing his father as a liberal nominee for president, Luis Somoza Debayle assumed office and installed his younger brother, Anastasio "Tachito" Somoza Debayle, as Commander of the National Guard. In 1967 Luis was replaced as president by Tachito. Both Luis Somoza Debayle (1957–67) and Anastasio Somoza Debayle (1967–79) continued the policies of their father—denying conservatives participation in government, increasing the family fortune, and implementing limited social and economic programs. During the 1970s, opposition to the

Somoza dictatorship increased as the public reacted against government corruption, inefficiency, and repression, and this led to popular support for armed opposition movements. Chapter 4 discusses the insurrection period and subsequent accession to power by the Sandinistas, with the support of other Latin American countries (Costa Rica, Panama, Venezuela, and Mexico) and a final push by the United States. The Sandinistas have gradually taken full control of the government and the military in Nicaragua. The internal policies adopted by the new revolutionary government seem to preclude the advent of democratic rule. Also there have been sustained efforts by the Sandinistas to strengthen the political and economic ties between Nicaragua and the Soviet bloc, resulting in the presence of thousands of communist technicians in Nicaragua, and in agreements that tie the future of the country to the communist world.

In the international arena the Sandinistas have voted consistently with the Soviet bloc in the United Nations and have cooperated in the campaign that the communist governments are staging in Europe against American nuclear rearmament.

The Nicaraguan rulers' cooperation with the Soviets appears to be gaining momentum and setting ambitious long-term goals. The official Nicaraguan newspaper *El Nuevo Diario* reported that the Soviets are preparing in Spain a huge dry dock (graving dock) large enough to hold an ocean liner and a coastal vessel at the same time. Supposedly the dry dock is to be installed 3 miles offshore of the little port of San Juan del Sur, on the Nicaraguan Pacific coast. It was stated in the newspaper that about 100 Soviet engineers, some of them with their families, will travel to Nicaragua and stay there for seven to ten years, teaching the Nicaraguans how to use and maintain the dry dock.

In connection with this project, there are reports of conversations between Soviet and Sandinista leaders regarding the construction of a transisthmian canal linking the Caribbean with the Pacific Ocean. The building of such a canal—envisioned by the US in the 19th and beginning of the 20th centuries—if placed under the control of the Soviet government and its surrogates, would be a new and destabilizing factor in the world equation of power.

1.3 EL SALVADOR

The 19th-century history of El Salvador, like that of the rest of Central America, can best be described as a struggle for political power between liberals and conservatives. For about 100 years the nation was torn by civil wars, instability, and chaos. The growth of coffee plantations toward the end of the century gave rise to an elite class of landowners and businessmen who demanded an orderly government. At the turn of the century, the armed forces of El Salvador, considered to be among the most effective in the area,[6] joined forces with this new economic elite. Between 1913 and 1927 one family of landowners, the Melendez family, succeeded by brother-in-law Alfonso Quiñonez, controlled the presidency, and they ruled the country with an iron hand.

The world depression of the '20s undermined the coffee market, and the economic hardships endured by the people led to civil unrest and peasant rebellions in the 1920s and '30s. During this period, rumors of communist incitement of the peasantry were widespread. In 1932 a peasant uprising took place in the Department of Sonsonate, led by an Indian "ladino," Augustin Farabundo Martí.[7] General Maximiliano Hernandez, serving then as vice president, led a successful coup against the president and proceeded mercilessly to crush the peasant rebellion. A conservative estimate is that no less than 10,000 people died, including Marti, who was captured and executed.[8]

Since the 1930s El Salvador's political history lists a series of coups and revolutions. General Martinez, known as "El Brujo" (the witch) for his involvement with secret potions, ruled as dictator-president between 1931 and 1944, at times through puppet presidents. A general workers' strike finally overthrew him. In 1948 his successor was deposed by another military uprising—a significant event because it laid the foundation for the nation's present political system. The military hierarchy in 1948 founded the Revolutionary Party of Democratic Union (PRUD) and succeeded in electing as presidents Colonel Oscar Osorio in 1948 and Jose M. Lemus in 1956. The elections of 1956 were denounced by the opposition as fraudulent, and Lemus' administrations met increasing opposition until he was removed from the presidency in October 1961, by the military who had put him in office.

One reason for Lemus' demise was that the military of 1948 had envisioned a moderate program of reforms to meet the basic needs of the people without alienating the traditional economic elite. But the elite successfully blocked Lemus' reform program. Powerful interest groups, such as the Coffee Growers Association, the Chamber of Commerce and Industry, and the Association of Stockmen and Farmers, have traditionally been effective in protecting their economic interests against reforms, even reforms supported by the military.

The new military junta formed the National Conciliation Party (PCN) and continued the efforts of their predecessors at moderate reforms. On April 29, 1962, the provisional military junta held elections that were boycotted by all major opposition parties. The candidate of the PCN, Julio Adalberto Rivera, won the election as expected. The new president pledged to support reforms and the Alliance for Progress. By the mid-60s the Christian Democratic Party had become the most important challenger to the PCN. The Authentic Constitutional Party (PAC) and the National Action Party (PAN), both of a conservative stance, entered the political arena in the 1960s, along with the Social Democrats. The Revolutionary Party of April and May (PRAM), politically of a Marxist orientation, was not allowed to participate in the electoral process.[9]

At the end of the 1960s, the tenuous internal political process of El Salvador became temporarily cohesive when war broke out with Honduras in 1969. The "Soccer War," as it became known (because it began after riots following a soccer match between the two countries), seems to have been rooted in tensions between the two countries as a result of Salvadoran peasant migration to Honduras. The war lasted only a few days and was mediated by the Organization of American States, but was not formally settled until 1978.

In the aftermath of the "Soccer War" El Salvador began to prepare for new presidential elections in 1972. Three opposition groups, the Christian Democratic Party (PDC), the National Revolutionary Movement (MNR) and the Nationalist Democratic Union (UDN) formed a unified front called Opposition National Union (UNO) and presented as its candidates Jose Napoleon Duarte for president and Guillermo Manuel Ungo for vice president. The Duarte-Ungo ticket ran on a platform of social and economic reforms. But the traditional party of the military, the PCN, supported Colonel Arturo Molina, who won the election allegedly through electoral fraud. And that touched off one of the worst political crises that has ever confronted the nation. Violence and unrest spread throughout the country.

In 1977, amid charges of still another electoral fraud, General Carlos Humberto Romero became president. Opposition groups, coalescing into revolutionary organizations, met severe repression. The cycle of violence rapidly escalated as leftist-oriented groups battled the military and right-wing paramilitary organizations.[10] Violations of human rights soon became a cause célèbre.

As 1979 came to an end, the military deposed General Romero and established a junta representing the private and professional sectors, including Manuel Ungo, who had widespread support as a reformist, was appointed to the junta. Three months later, in January 1980, the civilian members of the junta resigned, charging the military with responsibility for human rights abuses and for an unwillingness to carry out reforms. Ungo, president of the Democratic Revolutionary Front (FDR), an umbrella organization for many of the opposition armed groups, left the country and joined the ranks of the opposition in exile. Ungo's 1972 running mate, Jose Napoleon Duarte, the leader of the parties advocating a democratic-electoral solution, was appointed in March 1980 as a member of a new junta established by the military and later, in December 1980, was chosen to preside over the junta. Duarte, a moderate and widely respected centrist-reformist, rapidly became for many in El Salvador one last opportunity for reform. For the United States, Duarte provided a moderating force and a commitment to reform through democratic process. While readjustments in the composition of the government took place, violence continued unabated. The assassination of Catholic Archbishop Oscar Arnulfo Romero in March 1980 showed that the war would not allow safe haven to anyone.[11]

An important decision of the junta was to nationalize the banks and savings and loan institutions, giving the government a tight control on capital assets and financial transactions. A little after Duarte joined the ranks of the government, agrarian reforms were enacted. Large segments of the peasantry, for the first time in their lives, began to receive tangible benefits from official initiatives.

In March 1982—under pressure from the United States, which was anxious to expedite a democratic solution—El Salvador conducted yet another Constituent Assembly election. Duarte's party won the most votes, but got only 24 out of 60 seats in the Constituent Assembly. The actual winner was Major Roberto D'Aubuisson, leader of the right-wing National Republican Alliance (ARENA)[12] who, in coalition with the PCN and three other parties, had enough votes to control the majority of the Constituent Assembly. After intensive negotiations a moderate, technocrat President Alvaro Magaña, became chief of state. President Magaña is a respected banker and economist, and a graduate of the University of Chicago. Major D'Aubuisson was elected president of the Constituent Assembly and two other conservatives became vice presidents, along with a Christian Democrat.[13]

The right-wing victory at the Constituent Assembly hardened and emboldened the traditional elites, further solidified the opposition, and sent the US searching for new means to convince D'Aubuisson that reforms had to be undertaken. The coalition maintains that social reforms have led to economic inefficiencies, and therefore it is necessary to slow down and reformulate other social reforms to assure prompt economic recovery.

Initial concerns of the United States that the reforms might be undone have proved unfounded. There has been steady progress in the reorganizing of financial institutions and reallocation of credits to the general public. Hundreds of thousands of peasants have received benefits through the implementation of phases I and III of the agrarian reform.

The Apaneca Pact, signed in August 1982 by all the political parties represented in the Constituent Assembly, called for guarantees and consolidation of the reforms enacted and implemented by the Revolutionary Junta that ruled the country immediately before the Constituent Assembly, and asked for improvement and efficiency in the measures that had been established in the agrarian, banking, and external trade reforms (see Note 17).

1.4 GUATEMALA

In the 161 years since its declaration of independence, Guatemala has had 16 constitutions. This is in itself a reminder of the political turbulence that has plagued this country throughout its independent life. A population split into two different cultures aggravates an already unstable situation. There is on the one side the white population and the ladinos (culturally assimilated half-castes and Indians), mainly concentrated in the great cities of Guatemala, Quezaltenango and Escuintla, who have been the driving force in the economic, social, and political development of the country. On the other side are the Indians, who adhere to their own values, thus remaining outside the cultural mainstream that rules the nation; they live mainly in hamlets and small cities on the western highlands. This latter part of the population, which forms a majority of a little over 50 percent, has been alienated from any pursuit of national goals since the time of the Spanish colonial rule. As a corollary this group has had lower levels of longevity, education, income, and social progress than the other half of the Guatemalan population.

The political history of Guatemala has been described as centralized, personalistic, and headed by dictatorial governments. As in the other Central American nations, conflicts have revolved around controversies between liberal and conservative factions, and arbitrary and ruthless leadership has been the rule rather than the exception. Justo Rufino Barrios (1871–85) seems to have been one of Guatemala's most gifted leaders. During the 14 years of his administration, Barrios undertook such public works projects as the expansion of postal and telegraph services and the development of a national infrastructure. He also encouraged the growth of coffee and banana plantations, fostering a landed aristocracy and successfully crushing church power and political influence in the country. He was a liberal and a firm advocate of Central American integration. Trying to achieve reunification by force, he attacked El Salvador and died in battle.

During the 20th century, the dictator Jorge Ubico (1931–44) restored fiscal integrity to the government and established an efficient police state. His ruthless use of political power and his failure to deliver promised social reforms caused growing discontent, which finally led to a general strike that forced his resignation on July 1, 1944. Ubico's overthrow was eventually followed by the formation of a National Assembly, the enactment of a new constitution, and a general election in December of the same year. The elected president, Dr. Juán José Arévalo, is a rare example in Guatemala's history of a man who came to the presidency legitimately and surrendered power in the same way. The government headed by Arévalo ushered in a period in which some much-needed reforms were implemented while others were forestalled by the opposition of conservative elements among the military, landowners, and businessmen. The Guatemalan Institute of Social Security and the Labor Code stem from the reforms enacted at that time.

However, during President Arévalo's term (1945–51) several events took place that had a negative effect on later political developments. Not a communist himself, Arévalo allowed the communists to gain important positions in his administration and in the labor movement. Several of his appointees in the foreign service were declared persona non grata by various governments because of their involvement in communist activities while serving as ambassadors.

The two main contenders to succeed Arévalo in the presidency were Colonel Francisco Arana, chief of the armed forces, and Lieutenant Colonel Jacobo Arbenz, minister of defense. Both of them had been members of a ruling junta after Ubico's downfall and before Arévalo's coming to power, and as such enjoyed some popularity. Arana was assassinated in July 1949, and though the motives for his murder have never been ascertained, his death triggered a cycle of violence stretching to the present day. Arana's demise left Arbenz unopposed within the government ranks; he was nominated for president and won with considerable popular support, though members of the opposition termed the elections fraudulent.

Under Arbenz (1951–54) Guatemala fell deeper under communist influence, thus arousing the concern of both the Guatemalan army and the US government. Colonel Carlos Castillo Armas, backed by the US Central Intelligence Agency (CIA) and operating from Honduras, overthrew Arbenz in 1954 and was appointed president that same year. Castillo Armas was assassinated by a member of his guard in 1957. In 1958 General Miguel Ydígoras Fuentes was elected president in elections regarded as fair. President Ydígora's efforts to implement a reform program were blocked in the Guatemalan congress. Finally, in 1963, he was overthrown by the military.

This pattern of unrest continues today. From the early '60s on, leftist guerrilla activities and right-wing violence have added uncertainty to an already deteriorated political situation. It is remarkable that, in spite of an unstable political setting, Guatemala has made impressive economic progress during most of the last two decades.

The elections in 1974 and 1978, both called fraudulent by the opposition parties, brought to the presidency General Kjell Laugerud and General Romeo Lucas, respectively. Neither Laugerud nor Lucas attained the absolute majority of votes required by law to be proclaimed president-elect, and so their coming to power was decided by Congress.

Though efforts were made by the government in the last decade to improve the lot of the needy by means of new settlements, relocation processes, development of rural areas, and increase in minimum wages, overwhelming inequities continue in Guatemala. The economic upsurge of the '60s and early '70s was not accompanied by corresponding social and political progress.

On March 7, 1982, presidential elections named a successor to General Romeo Lucas. The popular turnout at the polls was higher than expected. The official results showed General Angel A. Guevara, the government candidate, as winner over three opposition leaders. Since General Guevara did not attain an absolute majority of the votes cast, a congressional vote designated him president-elect. However, General Guevara never became president. On March 23 a military coup overthrew General Romeo Lucas, and a military junta took power. The junta called the previous election fraudulent and void, and selected as president General Efrain Rios Montt, who allegedly had been deprived of his electoral victory when he ran for president in 1974. The new government placed several officials of the deposed regime under arrest, and promised to restore peace, put an end to corruption, and protect human rights.

The recent political situation in Guatemala is a

complex one, with numerous parties striving for power and influence. In the elections of March 7, 1982, eight political parties, forming four different coalitions, were represented at the polls. To the extreme left of the political spectrum, the communist party—*Partido Guatemalteco del Trabajo* (PGT)—did not participate in the elections. Of the right-wing parties, the National Liberation Party (PLN) was deemed the strongest, and went to the polls with a presidential candidate. And the Christian Democrats, forming a center-left party, seemed to be broadening its political following. But the present standing of the political parties must be reassessed, due to the new conditions created by the coup d'etat of March 23, 1983 and the subsequent overthrow on August 8 of General Ríos Montt by his Defense Minister, General Mejías Victores.

General Mejías, new Chief of State, has said that the government may call for elections for a Constituent Assembly as early as possible. A group of prominent lawyers has been assembled with the purpose of drafting a new constitution that eventually will be discussed and voted upon by the Constituent Assembly. The Bar Association, the University, the Supreme Court, the Council of State, and the Electoral Tribunal each nominated three of the lawyers that were to draft the new constitution, apparently with the purpose of assuring ideological and political balance in the composition of the group. On November 10, 1983, voter registration began. Since then, thousands of voters have been registered every day and the petitions for new voter cards have been increased by 30 percent. In Guatemala City alone, 750,000 voter cards have been issued. Thus an effort to restore the democratic process in Guatemala is apparently again on its way.

1.5 HONDURAS

The political history of Honduras from the mid-20th century to the present is an interesting account of both democratic evolution and setbacks. For example, from 1920 to 1966, Honduras experienced only two military coups, which would suggest that this period resulted in some democratic achievements. However, during this period, as in similar periods in the 19th century, the civilian government exercised power only as long as the military consented to its policies. Yet the Honduran internal political situation has not been immune to regional and international intervention, nor to the influx of business investors and individual adventurers, all of whom have complicated the post-Federation period of this country.

The two traditional political parties of Honduras, the Nationalists and Liberals, mirror Central America's conservative-liberal dichotomy. After a civil war in 1923, the Nationalists dominated the political scene through the leadership of Paz Baraóna, Tiburcio Carías, Juan Manuel Gálvez, and Júlio Lozano Díaz. In 1954, near the end of this period of conservative government, a banana plantation strike allowed the AFL-CIO (financed by AID and the CIA) to test their theory that they could gain control over the Honduran labor unions from the communists. They could and did; today the labor unions of Honduras continue to have close ties to the AFL-CIO.

Civilian government was interrupted by a military coup in 1957. President Lozano Diaz, whose government had become increasingly repressive, was replaced by a military junta. In 1958 the junta conducted free elections, and liberal candidate Ramón Villeda Morales was elected and served as president until 1963. Pragmatic and cautious, Villeda Morales undertook socioeconomic reforms such as the 1962 Agrarian Reform Law.

Another military coup in 1963 returned the government's leadership to the conservatives. Colonel Oswaldo López Arellano, who led this coup, established a populist dictatorship that lasted until 1975. During this period the "Soccer War" between El Salvador and Honduras took place (see the preceding discussion on El Salvador). As a result of the economic crisis aggravated by the war, the liberals and conservatives formed a coalition party and elected Ramón Ernesto Cruz as president in 1971. However, López Arellano again seized the presidency in December 1972. In 1975 another military coup, led by Colonel Juan Alberto Melgar Castro, overthrew López Arellano. In July of that same year, peasant uprisings were suppressed by the government.

The most recent military officer to hold power in Honduras was General Policarpo Paz Garcia, who was designated provisional president by the Constituent Assembly in April 1980. His administration was regarded as corrupt, inefficient, and unjust. On the other hand, he has been credited with trying to act as a transition president to democracy. In any case, as with previous military governments, the Honduran population does not perceive the military to be brutally repressive, as do the people of Nicaragua or Guatemala. The army continues, as in the past, to be the power behind the government.

The United States during the Carter Administration pressed for elections in Honduras. Eventually a Constituent Assembly was elected, controlled by the opposition. In accordance with the decision of the Constituent Assembly, national elections were held in November 1981. A high percentage of voters turned out at the polls, electing the opposition liberal candidate, Dr. Roberto Suazo Cordova, as president. The Honduran government is presently structured to permit a strong, centralized government. But in Honduras' 161 years of independence, there have been 385 armed rebellions, 126 governments and 16 constitutions. This suggests the fragile and vulnerable position the government of Honduras faces in the 1980s—at a time when it must contend with tension at the Nicaraguan border and the infiltration of Salvadoran guerrillas.

1.6 PANAMA

After proclaiming its independence from Spain in 1821, Panama became part of Colombia. Several attempts to form an independent nation were made during the 19th century. In 1840, General Tomas Herrera declared Panama's independence from Colombia, but it lasted for only 13 months and was followed by reunification.

In 1868 a French company under Ferdinand de Lesseps began the construction of a canal across Panama, connecting the Atlantic and Pacific Oceans. Financial difficulties and yellow fever brought the work to an end in 1889. Later on, in 1902, the United States decided to take over the construction of the canal. When the Colombian Senate refused to authorize the US to build the canal, the Panamanians revolted and declared independence from Colombia on November 3, 1903.[14] During that same month, the new Panamanian government and the United States signed a treaty designated as the Hay-Bunau-Varilla Treaty, granting the Americans the right to construct the canal. Since then a succession of treaties has been negotiated, modifying the original terms of the Hay-Bunau-Varilla Treaty. Efforts to modify the clauses of this treaty have become landmarks in Panama's political history. At times these efforts achieved significant results, as in 1936 when the United States gave up its right to intervene in the national affairs of Panama.

During the 1950s, industrial development began to play a role in the economic activities of the country, and that brought about an increase in political participation by the industrial and financial sectors, which soon began to challenge the hegemony of landowners and business groups.

During the 1960s, Panama's economic upsurge was heralded by the ideas of President Roberto P. Chiari (1960–64), who advocated incentives to international commerce, minimum wages, and the settlement of capital-labor conflicts through state intervention. In 1968 Arnulfo Arias became president for a third term in office, but was deposed by a military junta only 11 days after coming to power.

General Omar Torrijos, one of the leaders of the military coup that ousted President Arias, acquired full civil and military powers in 1972 for a term of six years. In 1977 Aristides Royo was elected president, but resigned the presidency in July 1982 for reasons of health and was succeeded by R. de la Espriella.

In 1977 President Carter and General Torrijos signed two treaties by which the United States agreed to transfer control of the canal to Panama in the year 2000. After the signing of the treaties a referendum was held in Panama in which 66 percent of the voters approved them. Likewise, the US Senate ratified the two treaties in March and April 1978.

Presently there is intense political activity in anticipation of general elections in June 1984. The Democratic Revolutionary Party, which is now in power, appears to be the favorite, though some observers think the government could be effectively challenged by a coalition of opposition parties. The main political parties in Panama, which cover both sides of the political spectrum, are the Liberal Party, the Christian Democratic Party, the Socialist Democratic Party, the Republican Party, and the Panamanian Popular Party which follows the Soviet communist party line.

Traditionally, opposition groups have focused on Panamanian-US tensions over control of the canal. The treaties negotiated by Carter and Torrijos have resolved this issue and should usher in a period of economic growth and political stability.

1.7 COSTA RICA

Costa Rica is a country justly proud of its democratic traditions, political pluralism, and orderly electoral process. In the 20th century the country's democratic process has been disrupted only twice. In 1917 General Federico Tinoco overthrew President Gonzalez Flores (1914–17) and ruled until 1919; then in 1948 the National Assembly declared fraudulent an election won by Otilio Ulate over the government's candidate, Rafael Calderon. The events of 1948 triggered a brief uprising led by Jose Figueres, who ruled the country provisionally for a year and restored Mr. Ulate to the presidency. The political history of Costa Rica has registered revolts and dictatorships but far less frequently than any of the other countries in Central America. Civilian governments and free elections, rather than strong-man rule and coercive violence, have been predominant traits of Costa Rican politics.

Today, the most important political entities are a moderate-centrist coalition named UNIDAD (Unity), with conservative leanings and close ties to the wealthy landowners, and the National Liberation Party (PLN) led by Jose Figueres, the hero of the 1948 revolution.[15] The PLN, to which the current President Luis Alberto Monge belongs, favors state participation in socioeconomic development, and has found ideological common ground with the International Socialist Movement (Social Democrats) as well as with APRA of Peru and *Acción Demócratica* of Venezuela.

The legislative, judicial, and executive branches of government are strong and operate in the tradition of checks and balances. The government places great emphasis on education and democracy. There are a police force and a civil guard for routine tasks of law and order, but no military armed force. In foreign policy, Costa Rica has been a strong supporter of Western democracies and a foe of dictatorial regimes of both the left and right. This anti-dictatorial posture may well explain Costa Rica's willingness to offer a safe haven to Nicaraguan Sandinista revolutionaries during their struggle against Anastasio Somoza.[16]

During his time in office, President Rodrigo Carazo Odio (1978–82) played an active role in the overthrow of General Somoza, ruler of neighboring Nicaragua. Costa Rican territory was used as a training ground for insurgents camped near the Nicaraguan border. Men and military equipment from Cuba, Panama, and Venezuela were channeled to the battlefields in Nicaragua through Costa Rica.

1.8 CONCLUSION

For the observer of Central America it is clear that these nations, viewed in a historical perspective, share many common characteristics. For example, they are Catholic, they share many cultural attitudes and values, and Spanish is the predominant language of the region. Moreover, they share some common historical processes, dating from the precolonial period through 300 years of Spanish colonialism that ended in 1821. These countries (except Costa Rica) have each experienced prolonged periods of political violence and instability. The military has been the most powerful institution, and frequently the final arbiter and decisionmaker. Another important force has been the large landowners. In some countries the pursuit of democracy has remained as elusive as the ideal of Central American reunification, and large portions of the populations have been excluded from the political process. Dependence on the export of agricultural products has made their economies very unstable and the countries very vulnerable to foreign intervention.

This is not to say that the area can be neatly categorized or that generalizations can explain the specific realities confronted by the policymaker or the layperson concerned about Central America's future. In any analysis the differences between the countries must be recognized. Political parties, an evolving military, and a radical and reformist-minded movement, now present simultaneously a challenge and a hope for the future; success will be measured in their ability to reconcile competing visions of their own countries' futures.

Democratic institutions in Central America have generally not functioned as intended. In most instances those ruling the countries have been the first to ignore or hinder their full play. In addition, vast portions of the population have lacked the political maturity, awareness, or education required for active and effective participation in a democratic process. There are signs, however, of positive changes in some countries.

The recent political events in Guatemala could be one of the rare occasions in which, in spite of such an expeditious means of seizing power, positive influence in the life of a country might be exerted. The unbridled violence practiced by government and terrorist groups alike, the corruption among officials, and the extreme social and economic imbalances are all evils that must be redressed if Guatemala is to switch from self-destruction to prosperity, justice, and progress. Presently the young army officers in the Guatemala army appear intent on achieving such an ambitious goal.

The high popular turnout at the polls in elections held in Honduras, Costa Rica, Guatemala, and El Salvador in late 1981 and early 1982 reflects a general trend in Central America toward a larger participation by the people in the shaping of their political future, and also a determination on the part of the people to look for solutions to their problems through democratic processes.

But for these encouraging trends to become permanent features it is imperative for democracy to work and deliver. The people of Central America must see proof that the democratic system is capable of redressing generations-old grievances and of creating social and economic well-being. The United States should encourage and reward democratic procedures by giving economic and technological aid to governments following a democratic path. This aid should be oriented so that ordinary citizens can participate as much as possible, at local levels, in carrying out development plans This, in itself, should work as a democratic education program.

It would be unrealistic to ignore the internal and external obstacles facing democratic development in Central America. As to internal obstacles, a long tradition of abuse of power and of squandering and pilfering of public funds must be reversed—and can be, though not easily. As to external problems, the Soviet Union—first through Cuba and then through Nicaragua and other proxies—seems intent on expanding the foothold it already has on the insular Caribbean and on Central America. The Soviet Union is manipulating legitimate grievances and long-standing economic and social imbalances that pervade the region, aggravating unfavorable conditions and creating new problems wherever possible. In answer to this attitude the United States should put into effect a mixed policy of containment and aid, holding back the Soviets and at the same time improving the living standards of the local population. In any case, firmness of decision is imperative. International retaliation in Soviet-controlled vulnerable areas should also be considered.

Besides unilateral measures that can be implemented by the United States, political stability in Central America requires the cooperation of its hemispheric allies. Mexico, Venezuela, and Colombia, because of their proximity to the region, could be highly influential in implementing necessary measures. Other Latin American nations could also offer positive support in the development of social, economic, and defense programs. In the region itself, the recently created Central American Democratic Community involving Honduras, El Salvador and Costa Rica offers a firm basis upon which workable programs could be elaborated and implemented.

Honduras, El Salvador, and Costa Rica share the same experience of opposition parties obtaining power through clean and free elections in recent months. All three countries are beset by economic difficulties that must be solved through the cooperation of national and international initiatives. This newly created democratic community could become a touchstone upon which the proposition of economic development through political stability can be tested. It is for the United States and its hemispheric allies to provide much-needed support and encouragement.

NOTES

1 For a more detailed account of Indian labor in Central America, see William L. Sherman, *Forced Native Labor in Sixteenth Century Central America* (Lincoln: University of Nebraska Press, 1979).

2 For a detailed study of militarism in Latin America, see Edwin Lieuwen, *Arms and Politics in Latin America* (New York: Frederick A. Praeger, Inc., 1960) and John J. Johnson, *The Military and Society in Latin America* (Stanford: Stanford University Press, 1964).

3 For a country-by-country political history, see Martin C. Needler, ed., *Political Systems of Latin America* (Princeton: D. Van Nostrand Company, Inc., 1965). For an analysis of Latin American labor movements, see Victor Alba, *Politics and the Labor Movement in Latin America* (Stanford: Stanford University Press, 1968).

4 For a detailed account of reunification attempts, see Thomas L. Karnes, *The Failure of the Union, Central America 1824–1975*, rev. ed., (Tempe: Arizona State University Center for L.A. Studies, 1976).

5 See J. Lloyd Mecham, *A Survey of United States-Latin American Relations* (New York: Houghton Mifflin Company, 1965), and Dana G. Munro, *Intervention and Dollar Diplomacy in the Caribbean, 1900–1921* (Princeton: Princeton University Press, 1964).

6 In El Salvador and Guatemala the military is considered to be the best organized institution, and therefore a dominant influence in the political arena. (See Johnson, 1964: 143).

7 Today one of the most powerful armed groups in the guerrilla war is a Marxist movement named after the communist leader, Marti.

8 A thorough study of the rebellion can be found in Thomas P. Anderson, *Matanza: El Salvador's Communist Party of 1932*, (Lincoln: University of Nebraska Press, 1971).

9 In fact, it was the governing junta's intention to permit PRAM's participation in the elections (following Lemus' overthrow) that prompted another coup in January 1961.

10 For an analysis of El Salvadoran opposition groups, see Gabriel Zaid, "Enemy Colleagues," *Dissent* (Winter 1982), pp. 13–40.

11 For a detailed discussion of the church's current role in Central America, see James V. Schall, "Central America and Politicized Religion," *World Affairs* (Fall 1981), pp. 126–149.

12 Major D'Aubuisson was accused by the US Ambassador to El Salvador, Robert White, of being a "pathological killer." In "Continued Salvadoran Aid Pledged," St. Louis *Post-Dispatch*, April 23, 1982, p. 1. The accusation has been repeatedly denied by D'Aubuisson.

13 Though international observers have claimed the elections were honest, others claim fraud. For opposing views, see Raymond Bonner, "Fraud is Reported in Salvador Vote," the New York *Times*, June 4, 1982, p. 4 and Raymond Bonner, "Salvadoran Leader Denies Vote Fraud," New York *Times*, June 6, 1982, p. 3.

14 For origins of US policy toward Panama, see Mecham, Chapters 4 and 5.

15 For additional information on the PLN, see Burt H. English,

Liberación Nacional in Costa Rica, The Development of a Political Party in a Transitional Society (Gainesville: University of Florida Press, 1971).

16 On May 14, 1981, a special commission of the Legislative Assembly charged Costa Rican President Carazo Odio (1978–82) with harboring Nicaraguan revolutionaries and allowing arms traffic. It should also be noted that Costa Rica assisted Fidel Castro during the Cuban insurgency in the 1950s.

17 On March 25, 1984, at press time, general elections were held in El Salvador. Despite some guerrilla efforts to sabotage the elections, about 1.3 million people voted, or 70% of those able to vote. According to the US Bipartisan Commission that witnessed the process, the elections were fair and honest, revealing the desire of the Salvadoran people for a truly democratic solution, and a repudiation of the guerrilla tactics. Also, while the final result is not yet known; it appears that Jose Napolean Duarte is the front-runner with about 45% of the votes, followed by Roberto D'Aubuisson with about 20% of the votes. The rest of the votes were distributed among several other candidates. A runoff election between Duarte and D'Aubuisson is scheduled.

TABLE 1.1
Government organization in Central America

	Executive Power	Legislative Power	Judicial Power	Observations
Panama Last Constitution enacted in 1972 and reformed in 1983.	The President and two Vice-Presidents are elected for a five-year term by a majority of the popular vote. No reelection is permitted for the next two presidential terms.	A Legislative Assembly, with a number of members according to population, elected by districts for a five-year period.	Headed by a Supreme Court, whose justices are named for a ten-year term by the Council of Ministers, with approval by the Legislative Assembly.	The 1983 Constitutional reforms will be fully implemented after the May, 1984 elections.
Honduras Last Constitution enacted in 1982.	The President and three "Designees to the Presidency" are elected for a four-year term by a majority of the popular vote. No reelection permitted.	A Congress of Deputies, with members elected for a four-year period. Number changes according to population.	Headed by a Supreme Court composed of nine permanent justices and seven substitutes, elected for a four-year term by Congress; reelection permitted.	There are still problems of limits with El Salvador.
Costa Rica Last Constitution enacted in 1949.	The President and two Vice-Presidents are elected for a four-year term, with reelection.	A Legislative Assembly formed by 57 Deputies elected for a four-year term by provinces, according to their population.	A Supreme Court whose members are elected for a term of eight years by the Legislative Assembly; reelection permitted.	Catholic religion is that of the State, which contributes to its maintenance. However, there is religious freedom.
Guatemala Last Constitution enacted in 1965.	The President and Vice-President are elected for a four-year term, by an absolute majority of popular votes. No reelection is permitted for the next term.	A Congress of Deputies. Each electoral district has two or more Deputies, according to population.	A Supreme Court with members elected for a four-year term by Congress.	Congress inactive since March, 1982 coup. President named by the military. Constitutional elections are scheduled for 1984.
Nicaragua A "Fundamental Statute", decreed in 1979, abolished the 1974 Constitution.	Originally a five-member junta, it has now only three.	Shared by the junta and a Council of State appointed by the Government.	Headed by a Supreme Court, with justices named by the junta.	The main source of real power is not the junta but the National Directorate of the Sandinist Front of National Liberation.

CHAPTER 2
SOCIAL CONTEXT

This chapter presents an overview of social conditions in Central America by examining selected social, cultural, and economic indicators, using the most recent data available. It concludes with recommendations for improving the living standards for the vast majority of the populations in most countries of the region.

2.1 ETHNIC COMPOSITION

The present ethnic and racial composition of Central America reflects both the colonial history of the region,[1] and later attempts to develop certain sectors of the economy by importing unskilled and mainly English-speaking Antillean labor. The largely mestizo population of the region evolved over the centuries as European settlers, mainly of Spanish origin, intermingled with the Amerindian population and the descendants of African slaves and black Antillean migrants. Relatively endogamous pockets of each of these groups still survive. In Costa Rica, for instance, a significant percentage of the national population is of unmixed Spanish descent. Within each country, however, these groups are culturally homogeneous with the mestizo population. In some countries, important differences still separate the culturally similar European-descent and mestizo population from the indigenous and/or Antillean-origin groups who have preserved a separate identity. The assimilation of these groups is a challenge to the region.

Guatemala faces the greatest difficulties because of its wider cultural diversity. More than half the population is partly or fully alienated from the dominant national culture; a quarter of the indigenous population, or close to a million people, are completely marginalized from the national economy (Table 2.1). Guatemalans define two major cultural groups: the ladino and the Indian. The distinction has little to do with race, since a person of pure indigenous stock can be called ladino as long as he speaks Spanish and generally follows Western ways. So-called Indians, on the other hand, have preserved significant elements of their native culture, such as dress and language. While many speak Spanish in addition to their own tongues, others do not, thereby presenting problems in becoming totally integrated into Guatemalan society.

Panama, Honduras, El Salvador, and Nicaragua also have sizable indigenous minorities. The Miskitos in Nicaragua, for example, have become well known in recent years. But these minorities comprise a smaller percentage of the total population than in Guatemala. Panama has the second highest percentage, yet the number there did not exceed seven percent in 1978.

Minorities primarily descendant from English-speaking Antilleans live in Panama, Costa Rica, Nicaragua, Honduras, and Guatemala, but they are a small segment of the population of Central America. Their ancestors either were forcibly brought into the region by colonial authorities, or chose to enter and seek work in the emerging plantation sector or in the construction of main communication links (e.g., the Panama Canal and railroads). Most of these colonies of Antillean origin are concentrated along the coastal areas bordering the Caribbean Sea. Gradual progress is being made to assimilate these groups, particularly among the younger generations.

With one exception, the Central American nations have not had severe difficulties arising from culture and language heterogeneity, although each country has minorities that have not been fully incorporated into the dominant culture. Guatemala, which is divided into two cultural subgroups of approximately equal size, is the exception. The unequal social status of the two groups magnifies the difficulties, as does the language barrier. It is evident that many of the problems in attempting to modernize the social and economic institutions of a developing country are intensified when a significant proportion of the population is not fully integrated into national life. The problem of cultural heterogeneity in

Central America pales, however, when compared to the more severe social and economic inequities that are so prevalent in the region.

2.2 POPULATION: SIZE, GROWTH, AND STRUCTURE

In recent decades Central America drew attention as the major world region with the highest rate of population growth (Table 2.2). The combined population of the Central American republics grew from approximately five million people in 1920 to slightly more than 17 million by 1970, and to an estimated 24 million by 1983—an increase of 380 percent over a little more than a half-century. At current rates of natural increase the population of the six republics will double within the next 20 to 30 years and reach some 40 million people by the end of this century. Such rapid growth contributes significantly to the intense social and economic problems facing the region.

As in other developing areas of the world, the population explosion in Central America since the end of World War II was induced by the importation of modern drugs and insecticides that cut death rates while birth rates stayed practically the same. Between 1950 and 1975 the population growth rate of the region peaked at 3.1 percent per year. Since then the growth rate has declined somewhat; it is now slightly below 3.0 percent. The decline in the regional population growth rate, however, was due primarily to only two nations, Costa Rica and Panama, although Salvadoran growth rates also declined somewhat. The growth rates in the other countries are still high and can go even higher, given expected further reductions in mortality rates.

Regional averages conceal significant differences in demographic behavior among the Central American countries. Costa Rica and Panama have progressed notably in their demographic transition. In these two countries life expectancy at birth is approaching levels in developed countries and fertility has declined considerably. The total fertility rate (TFR)[2] in Costa Rica in 1983 stood at about 3.7 children per woman while in Panama it was 3.9. In the other countries the TFR ranged from 5.7 in

Guatemala to a high of 6.5 in Honduras. In recent years, fertility decline seems to have slowed significantly in Costa Rica, whereas the decline has proceeded at a rapid pace in Panama and has been slow, if not uncertain, in the other countries of the region.

All of the Central American countries have embraced official family planning programs to reduce fertility both on demographic and humanitarian grounds. The success of these programs seems to be determined by the socioeconomic conditions in the countries in which they operate. Costa Rica and Panama, the countries with the more equitable living conditions and the highest levels of socioeconomic development, have been able to achieve lower fertility sooner than their neighbors. Recent data show that more than half the sexually active women in these two countries are practicing contraception; in El Salvador 34 percent are, and in Guatemala, Honduras, and Nicaragua, less than 20 percent. Thus it appears that the most significant fertility declines in some countries have resulted from considerable progress in socioeconomic conditions, coupled with organized family planning programs. The impact of these programs in countries with only minor progress in socioeconomic conditions seems to have been very limited.

Due to declining mortality and high fertility, Central American age structures have acquired the characteristic shape found in developing countries. These age pyramids have a very wide base, with 45 percent or more of the population under 15 years of age and only small percentages over age 64. As a consequence, dependency ratios tend to be high, with approximately one person of working age (15–64) for each individual above or below that age group. In developed countries, by comparison, there are approximately two persons of working age for every dependent individual. The effects of declining fertility on age pyramids are already evident in Costa Rica and Panama; by 1983 less than 40 percent of the total population in these two countries was under 15 years of age.

The present structure of the population pyramids of the Central American countries has great significance for the future growth of population and of the labor force. The potential for reducing the absolute numbers of births is lessened since each year a greater number of women reach childbearing age. Even if fertility rates were to decline drastically overnight, the size of the labor force would continue to increase for the next 15 years, since future workers have already been born. Thus, "correcting" the population problem is not an immediate panacea for the many social and economic problems of the region, but rather a long-term solution. Over the short to medium term, equal attention should be focused on other areas of concern if living conditions the people of Central America are to be improved.

2.3 POPULATION DISTRIBUTION AND MIGRATION

Population settlements in Central America, following pre-Columbian patterns, have concentrated in the more climatically congenial highlands away from the coastal areas, except in Panama. In more recent decades there have been significant population displacements toward the coastal lowlands, as well as from rural to urban areas, and occasional large migrations across international borders within the region and beyond. All the countries show marked imbalances in population distribution and most still have thinly settled areas. One exception is El Salvador, where even the least productive and most inaccessible areas are settled.

Between 1950 and 1980, urban growth in Central America, especially of the capital cities, has been substantial. These cities increased their populations by at least two and one-half times, with Tegucigalpa and Managua almost quintupling (Table 2.4). Yet by 1970 the percentage of the total population classified as urban had not exceeded 50 percent in any of the countries, although it did so by 1980 in Nicaragua and Panama (Tables 2.3 and 2.5). In general, the urban percentages in the Central American republics are low when compared to Latin America overall (63 percent) and the developed world (71 percent). Given the high rates of population growth in the region, the potential for future urban growth is significant and the population of the cities should continue to increase rapidly during the next few decades. The continuous urban population growth is certain to exacerbate the severe pressures felt as cities strive to provide services, jobs, and housing.

This urbanization process, while largely induced by population growth, has also been determined by uneven patterns of regional economic development and structural imbalances. A disproportionate share of public and private investment capital has gone to the cities, thus enhancing the differences in living conditions between urban and rural areas.

Marked differentials in access to land in rural areas and, more recently, agricultural modernization and increased land concentration have also contributed to the migratory process. One consequence is that the agrarian sector has not generated enough jobs to absorb the rapidly expanding rural labor force. High unemployment and underemployment forces many peasants to migrate to the cities in search of work. Others seek unoccupied lands within their own countries, migrate to expanding rural enclaves developed to produce agricultural commodities for the export markets, or look for land or employment opportunities in neighboring countries. Seasonal migrations of rural laborers are also heavy and often cross national borders.

In recent years, continuous civil disturbance has led to temporary displacement of tens if not hundreds of thousands of Central Americans as refugees. Political instability also intensifies emigration from the region to the United States and, according to recent reports, to Mexico as well.

For years, emigration—primarily to the United States—has been regarded by many as one of the few ways to achieve a better life. Poor employment prospects and, more recently, a deplorable political, social, and economic environment have helped to intensify emigration including ever-growing numbers of undocumented migrants. The evidence at hand suggests that a significant proportion of migrants to the United States have skills above the average in their home countries. As a result these countries are losing workers trained at their expense in skills much needed at home. Central America is an archetype of the "brain drain;" the higher the education level the higher the emigration propensities. For example, between 1959 and 1967, according to some estimates, 24.8 percent of graduates from universities and technical institutions in Honduras emigrated to the United States. The comparable figure for Nicaragua is 23.7 percent and for El Salvador an astonishing 40.7 percent. The long-term consequences of this drain of skilled manpower should not be underestimated.

One positive feature of emigration, aside from relieving unemployment pressures, is that the migrants send money back to relatives. In many countries in other parts of the world, the impact of such remittances as a source of family income is very substantial, though they do not seem to be an important source of capital investments that may help develop the home countries' economies. In Central America, there are no precise data on their significance, and it remains to be seen whether the positive effects of remittances outweigh the negative consequences of emigration.

2.4 EMPLOYMENT STRUCTURE OF THE WORKING ACTIVE POPULATION

Employment is one of the most serious problems confronting the Central American republics. While new jobs have been generated at a relatively slow rate, the working-age population has increased at rates of about three percent per year. Given the high fertility levels in the region and the resultant age structure, each year's entrants to the labor force outnumber the preceeding year's, thus adding to the pressures on the employment market.

These pressures are further aggravated by the nature of the regional economy. Most of the economically active population depends on the agricultural sector, where nearly half are directly employed (Table 2.6). Yet this is the sector in which job opportunities are expanding at a slower pace and the potential for future employment growth is more limited. In fact, employment opportunities may be shrinking due to agricultural modernization, increased land concentration, and the fact that some countries have little virgin land left under cultivation.[3] These points are supported by Table 2.7, which shows the estimated growth rates of the economically active population and the agricultural and non-agricultural sectors for each republic. In every country the non-agricultural growth rates exceed the agricultural, and in some—Costa Rica and Nicaragua, for example—by a factor of four or more. Some recent estimates indicate that in the rural sector of four countries, 20 percent or more of the economically active population is underutilized (including the unemployed, seasonally unemployed, and underemployed). In El Salvador nearly half the rural labor force is not productively employed.

The main reason for the higher growth rates of the non-agricultural labor force, aside from normal urban growth, is rural-to-urban migration. But in the cities, not enough new jobs are created to absorb the whole labor force. Thus, a considerable proportion of the urban population is unemployed or underemployed, just as in the agricultural sector.

In urban areas as in rural, development strategies have not given sufficient consideration to the employment question. Most new industries have not been large users of labor, but have depended rather on considerable capital investment. In Guatemala, for example, it has been estimated that every new modern-sector job has required a capital input of about $10,000 (US). These developments suggest that further industrial growth in the region should depend more heavily on the production factor most abundant in the region—labor— rather than on scarce and expensive capital investment. Thus, attention should be focused as much as possible on intermediate technologies, even though their products may not be competitive in international markets with those of more advanced technologies. Some measure of protectionism may be needed—high import tariffs, perhaps—despite the fact that this can lead in the long run to inefficient economies.

The burgeoning urban labor force, unable to find employment in the modern formal sector, often has been forced into marginally productive occupations in the faster-growing informal sector. Not all features of the informal sector are negative, however. Even in that sector, urban wages tend to be higher than in rural areas. Cities also offer services and amenities not available in the countryside. Thus, rural-to-urban migrants report improvements in their living conditions. And recent research has suggested that the entrepreneurial skills displayed by many workers in the informal sector, if properly channeled and assisted, could lead to the expansion of certain economic areas and to increased labor utilization. Actions might well be taken to enhance the vitality and economic efficiency of the informal sector.

Open unemployment rates are also high, exceeding (in 1973) ten percent of the economically active population in every country except Costa Rica and Panama (Table 2.8). As high as these rates are, PREALC (the International Labor Organization's regional employment program) considers that open unemployment is not as serious a problem as underemployment (which, admittedly, is hard to measure or even define) since those who can afford to remain unemployed do not face conditions as dire as those who are forced to take a job—any job— in the informal sector. Consequently, conditions for the very poor seem to be worsening. For example, the World Bank has estimated that, in Guatemala, the equivalent unemployment level reached 31 percent of the economically active population in 1973. The estimate takes into account those who, although partially employed, have incomes below the minimum wage levels. In urban areas the resultant unemployment rate was 12.2 percent; in rural areas it was 42 percent. In certain rural areas of Guatemala, between 52 and 57 percent of the annual income of *minifundistas*(proprietors of very small agricultural holdings) is earned through seasonal labor. Seasonal labor is highly unstable; wage rates are very low, and may barely keep the peasants and their families at or above subsistence level. The plight of the rural population is not as precarious in Costa Rica and Panama, but in Honduras, Nicaragua, and El Salvador it is probably comparable to that of Guatemala.

The employment situation may have further deteriorated under the impact of increased energy-import costs since 1973, a generally worsened economic climate, political instability, and social strife. In El Salvador, for example, unemployment rates increased from 7 percent in 1979 to approximately 17 percent in 1980. The underemployment rate has risen to 39 percent in the same period. A similar trend has been observed in Costa Rica, where the unemployment rate rose from 4.5 percent in July 1978 to 9.3 percent in April 1982. The increases have been more marked in urban than in rural areas. High levels of unemployment and underemployment have continued into 1984 as the political and economic crisis continues unabated.

The relative levels of development of the Central American republics are reflected in the sectoral distribution of the labor force (Table 2.6). In Costa Rica and Panama the percentages of the labor force in agriculture are significantly lower than in other countries, with higher percentages in other sectors of the economy. Likewise, the percentages of family workers tend to be lower in those two countries, suggesting a more modernized economic structure. Modern economies have high percentages of individuals working for salaries or wages. In Costa Rica almost three-fourths of the economically active population earns a livelihood as employees or wage earners, a much higher percentage than elsewhere in the region. The opposite is true for the other countries, including Panama; the percentage of employers and workers on their own account reaches about 40 percent in Guatemala and Honduras. Many of these are holders of small agricultural plots or urban workers in the informal sector. Levels of income and skills are usually low among these two groups.

2.5 LAND TENURE

Perhaps the main factor in the instability of some Central American nations is the regional land tenure pattern. These patterns are crucial, given the high regional dependency on agriculture, since this sector absorbs nearly 50 percent of the economically active population and generates approximately 25 percent of the regional Gross Domestic Product.

According to agricultural census data (primarily from the censuses of the 1960s), in Central America (excluding Panama) nearly 80 percent of the small family or subfamily farms accounted for only 10 percent of all farmland (Table 2.9). In contrast, less than half of one percent of large landowners held nearly 40 percent of all farmlands. Within Central America in the early 1960s, El Salvador and Honduras showed extreme cases of uneven land concentration, since almost 90 percent of all farms were too small to provide enough output for the sustenance of a rural family (these figures exclude the landless rural population). By about 1970 the most uneven land distribution patterns were found in El Salvador and Guatemala. In that year an estimated 87.4 percent of all farms in Guatemala and 90.4 percent in El Salvador had less than 7 hectares, the minimum farm size required to provide a family with adequate sustenance and productive employment. Comparable figures for Nicaragua, Honduras, and Costa Rica were 50.8 percent, 67.4 percent, and 68.0 percent, respectively.

When the landless rural labor force is included, over 80 percent of the rural labor force for the region as a whole (excluding Panama) falls into the land tenure classifications defined as incapable of generating enough income to support a family. This means that a majority of the rural population lives under precarious conditions. Rural out-migration and seasonal wage labor are commonly used by the peasant population to stay above a subsistence level.

The implications of highly skewed land tenure structures for the social and economic development of the region, and for patterns of income distribution, are considerable. The extent to which lands are utilized varies according to farm size. Land underutilization is often related to farm size; the smaller farms are more productive per unit of land simply because they are more intensively worked and less land is left idle. In the larger farms more extensive means of cultivation are used, a greater proportion of the land is left fallow, and large tracts are never used productively. Yet large farms tend to produce more per unit of cultivated land since they tend to use more modern and efficient agricultural techniques. Land productivity, however, when measured against the total size of the holding, declines as farm size increases.

Smaller farms tend to absorb more labor than larger farms, but productivity per worker is higher in the latter. In small farms, intensive agriculture leads to labor underutilization since more workers have to concentrate on small plots with generally primitive techniques. It follows that in Central America large farms tend to utilize less labor than they could, while smaller farms use an excess of labor at low levels of productivity. A more equal land tenancy system would lead to higher agricultural productivity and better use of labor. These are the standard conclusions of many agricultural studies which recommend extensive land reforms as one of the first priorities to facilitate the economic and social development of Central America.

There are clear signs that the Central American agrarian structures are changing and that the current situation is different from that observed in the 1960s (Table 2.10). The key question is how far Central American agrarian structures have changed. The evidence is uncertain; the results of various studies are hotly debated.

In recent years the number of peasant families with access to farmland appears to have increased in Costa Rica, Nicaragua, El Salvador, and Honduras, largely through land redistribution efforts. However, these efforts have followed a period in which the extent of landlessness rose considerably. Between 1950 and 1970, for example, the percent of landless peasants in Honduras increased from 26.1 percent to 31.2 percent. In El Salvador the percentage of peasants without land rose from 15.6 in 1950 to 19.8 in 1961, to 31.8 in 1971, and to a high of 41.1 percent in 1975. High rates of population growth, a tendency for increased land concentration, and other factors appear to be chiefly to blame.

The implementation of Phases I and III of the Salvadoran agrarian reform program, according to some of the more optimistic estimates, would benefit 38 percent of all peasant families—some 185,000 families (Table 2.11). A further 10 percent (50,000 families) would receive land if Phase II were carried out. However, even under the best of circumstances (that all three phases were implemented), 150,000 peasant families (31 percent of all farm families) would remain landless simply because there is no more productive land to be distributed; some estimates put the figure much higher. A shortage of farmland in El Salvador is a severe constraint for the success of any agrarian reform program there.

There is also some controversy concerning the rationale and eventual success of certain features of the agrarian reform program in El Salvador. Some doubts have been raised, for example, about the way in which lands are being assigned to the beneficiaries under the "Land to the Tiller" law (Phase III). Some observers claim that tying farmers to the plots they currently rent or sharecrop will keep many of them at a subsistence level, since many of these plots can maintain a limited level of productivity only if left fallow for a period of years. Other plots are too small or simply not suited to agriculture.

Still, it is obvious that the Salvadoran agrarian reform program is bringing about a significant transformation of the country's land tenancy pattern. Former landowners are to receive compensation for the farms they lose, according to fixed schedules of payment (part in cash, part in agrarian reform bonds). Some of the expropriated lands have been organized into cooperatives, while others have been granted to their new owners as individual plots. Providing extension services and credits is integral to land reform efforts; according to a 1983 evaluation, these are being reasonably provided despite the prevailing war conditions.

In Nicaragua the agrarian reform program of the Sandinistas was facilitated by the confiscation of farmlands held by the Somoza family and political associates. Nearly 23 percent of Nicaragua's farmland was confiscated and reorganized as state farms. Some rented lands were organized into production cooperatives. Small landholders have received help in organizing service and credit cooperatives. Under the July 1981 agrarian reform law, unused, underused, and rented lands on holdings above a certain size (depending on region) will be expropriated and distributed to the peasantry as both individual and collective property. When necessary, subsistence landholders benefiting from the program will receive workable plots in locations different from those they presently occupy. With the implementation of this stage of the Nicaraguan agrarian reform program, about half of the country's farmland will have been affected. Some, but not all, of the expropriated land owners will receive compensation in long-term agrarian reform bonds.

The land reform effort in Honduras has consisted primarily of the distribution of state-owned and *ejidatario* land, although it has also included purchases of private plots. Land has often been distributed or organized into cooperatives only after it had been illegally invaded by landless peasants. Purchases of private land have been paid for with long-term state-issued agrarian bonds; the land reform beneficiaries, as in El Salvador, are expected to pay the state for the land they receive. The Honduran government has promoted the formation of rural cooperatives and generally provides some support services, credits, and agricultural extension services. It is estimated, however, that by the late 1970s no more than 9.3 percent of the landless and *minifundista* rural population had benefited from the agrarian reform programs of nearly two decades.

Land reform programs in El Salvador face difficulties not found in Honduras and Nicaragua: agricultural lands are in much shorter supply in El Salvador. El Salvador has population densities much higher than its neighbors and has few virgin lands left. High rates of population growth will maintain pressures on the land, whether or not comprehensive agrarian reform programs are instituted.

The Costa Rican land reform program has been more comprehensive. Its far-reaching results can be at least partly explained by a national consensus emanating from the favorable political context in this country. Between 1962 and the early 1980s, under the Costa Rican agrarian reform program 5,000 families were settled and 25,000 other families received titles for the land they occupied. In total more than 160,000 hectares were affected. Some government policies have been aimed toward identifying pockets of extreme rural poverty, then correcting the situation by local land distribution or colonization projects. These projects owe much of their success to "Rural Development Regions" created to place within the peasants' reach the technical and financial support they need to become eventually self-supporting. State lands have been an important component of the Costa Rican agrarian reform program, but since the availability of these lands is limited, more recent phases of the program have concentrated on the expropriation of privately owned plots with compensation.

In brief, although under quite different political, social, and economic conditions, both Costa Rica and Honduras seem to be officially committed to, and are gradually achieving, a more equitable pattern of land tenancy. Similar developments are taking place in most other countries of the region. In Panama fairly progressive governments anticipated the long-term strife latent in a largely ignored peasantry and gave considerable attention to rural development, including more equitable access to land. The agrarian changes in El Salvador and Nicaragua, though responding to different conditions, should radically change the rural structures of these two countries as well. In Guatemala the situation remains explosive and the resistance to comprehensive agrarian reform programs among the powerful rural oligarchy seems strongest.

Over the short-to-medium term, land reform programs may have adverse effects on economic performance. Rural productivity may decline and private capital may flee the country. A nation's ability to earn foreign exchange may also be affected, since land reform beneficiaries tend to switch expropriated lands from export to subsistence crops. However, it appears certain that the social and political benefits far outweigh the economic costs that may have to be borne during the period of adjustment. The Costa Rican experience even suggests that economic gains may be fast in coming if necessary supporting services (marketing, extension services, etc.) are provided to the farmers.

Recent evidence from El Salvador shows that, despite some of these problems and despite even the civil war, "productivity in the land reform sector is about the same as in the rest of agriculture, both holding at about the average for the five years before land reform, 1975–79...and except where guerrilla activity has forced beneficiaries to abandon farms, employment is up somewhat over previous levels. If peace is restored, Salvadorans will soon increase exports, replace food now being imported from Guatemala, and develop food processing and other agricultural ventures" (Strasma, et al., 1983:10). In addition, some of the most significant direct costs of agrarian reform programs could be deferred by postponing or extending the payments for expropriated lands over several decades and by helping the beneficiaries become productive enough to pay for the land they receive. It seems likely, however, that considerable money from official and private sources is required during the early phases of agrarian reform projects.

2.6 INCOME DISTRIBUTION

The uneven pattern of rural landholdings and the precarious living conditions of a large percentage of the Central American urban population is reflected in income distribution. While no systematic and fully dependable set of figures is available for all countries, there is enough information for a general picture. In countries such as El Salvador and Honduras the average family income of large landholders exceeds the average family income of landless peasants and holders of sub-family farms by more than a hundredfold (Table 2.13). Income differentials among other farm-size groups are not as substantial, but are considerable between holders of family or larger farms and those working sub-family farms or less, particularly in El Salvador and Guatemala. Of all Central American countries, Costa Rica appears to have the most equitable pattern of rural income distribution, although it is still relatively skewed. It is likely that Nicaragua's income inequality has been sharply reduced since the 1979 revolution, although poverty levels can hardly have changed very significantly.

Estimates of income distribution show that in 1969, 38.0 percent of the Honduran population lived below a poverty line defined as a per-annum income of $75 (US). The percentages were much lower in El Salvador (18.4 percent) and Costa Rica (8.5 percent). Other sources indicate that the most uneven income distributions in Central America are those of Guatemala, Honduras, and El Salvador. Costa Rica and Panama generally have a more equitable income distribution. Still, by the late 1970s, 21 percent of the Panamanian population was estimated to be "extremely poor" and nearly 40 percent "poor." More recent attempts by ECLA to measure income distribution patterns show that, by 1978, half of the population in each country below the national income median received 21 percent or less of national income, while the highest 5 percent received a fourth or more (Tables 2.14 and 2.15). These estimates suggest that over the past few years income differentials have grown. ECLA has concluded that while the relative incidence of poverty may not have risen during the 1970s, the absolute number of poor families has. High rates of population growth, highly unstable political conditions, increasing rates of inflation, and stumbling economies all promote regressive income distribution.

One exception is Costa Rica. Evidence suggests that Costa Rica's income inequalities were reduced between the early 1960s and 1970s and that, just as importantly, "the proportion of families below an absolute poverty line...fell from about 20 percent to 10 percent" (Fields, 1980:189). In 1971, 25.3 percent of national income went to the three lowest quintiles of the population in Costa Rica. In Honduras, by contrast, the same population subgroup received only 15.3 percent of the total income. The

10 percent of the population with the highest income in Costa Rica received 39.5 percent of it; the corresponding figure in Honduras was 50 percent. The same income group in the United States received 26.6 percent of all income.

Fields attributes the improvements in the Costa Rican income distribution to various factors, one of which is the favorable performance of its free open economy. From the early 1960s to the early 1970s, "Costa Rica reversed its trade orientation, switching from emphasis on import substitution to greater reliance on export promotion. The main exports stimulated, both by encouraging expansion and by diversification, were agricultural products. This emphasis on agricultural exports helped spread the benefits of growth throughout the country. In addition, Costa Rica gave high priority to investments in economic infrastructure, including agricultural extension. Other factors of note in the 1960s were high and rising levels of education..., early family planning efforts, good public health conditions, and a land distribution that was relatively even by Latin American standards. In short, the policy orientation in Costa Rica...was one of decentralized development" (Fields, 1980: 185). Later agrarian reform efforts and a noted increase in employment in the state sector probably contributed to an even more balanced pattern of income distribution.

2.7 EDUCATION

Despite clear indications of progress, Central American education remains deficient. As with other social indicators, educational levels are superior in Costa Rica and Panama.

According to the latest national census, illiteracy rates for the population 15 years of age and over ranged from a low of 11.6 in Costa Rica to a high of 53.8 in Guatemala (Table 2.16). In every country the illiteracy rates were considerably lower than they had been in earlier decades; in other words, a progressively smaller percentage of the population could not read or write. However, the *absolute* number of illiterates has increased because the expansion of the educational system has not stayed abreast of population growth, due to a shortage of teachers and resources and their poor geographical distribution.

Consistent rural/urban differentials in illiteracy rates are found in all six countries. Illiteracy rates are more than twice as high in rural than in urban areas, indicating that educational facilities are distributed unevenly. A recent survey found that in Guatemala 44 percent of the urban school-age population and 76 percent of the rural were not attending school. Part of the large differential was attributed to the concentration of the Indian population in rural areas; as observed earlier, many of them are marginalized from the dominant national culture. Among the rural ladinos, enrollment levels were much lower than among the urban ladinos. A similar situation was reported for El Salvador, in which less than two-thirds of rural primary-school-age children attend classes as compared to the more than nine-tenths attending in urban areas. Attrition rates in El Salvador and elsewhere have also been found to be higher in rural schools.

Sex differentials in illiteracy rates are narrow in all Central American countries except El Salvador and Guatemala. In all cases, male illiteracy rates are lower than female. The great disparities in Guatemalan rates reflect the relative isolation of Indian women, perhaps due to cultural factors.

Enrollment figures show that between 1971 and 1977 the absolute number of children attending primary school rose by more than 20 percent in all countries except Costa Rica, where enrollment levels were already high (Table 2.17). These increases can be attributed partly to population growth. In every country, data on school enrollment and literacy by age indicate that the younger students are attaining progressively higher levels of education. In Panama 76 percent of the primary school population in 1974 was enrolled; this figure was even higher in Costa Rica.

Higher educational attainment among the younger groups and the expansion of educational facilities have resulted in a growth of enrollments at higher educational levels. In all countries (except Guatemala) with available data from 1971 to 1977, secondary and higher education enrollments soared and in some cases doubled, and this was particularly evident at the university level. A more precise indication of progress is provided by Panamanian data showing that, by 1974, 72 percent of the secondary school population was attending school, and 17 percent of the post-secondary-age population was going to some type of educational institution. One problem is that the scope and orientation of the system of higher education in some Central American countries is not adequate to satisfy the development needs of the region. Too much emphasis is placed on the humanities and not enough on technical fields that relate to the needs of these countries.

2.8 HEALTH CONDITIONS

A cursory examination of the most basic health indicators reveals marked differentials in health standards among the countries as well as within individual countries. Costa Rica, and to a lesser extent Panama, have attained high levels of life expectancy and significantly reduced infant mortality (Table 2.3). The structure of mortality by cause for these two countries is more like that of developed areas where the principal causes of death are degenerative in nature (Table 2.21). Most preventable deaths caused by infections or by a combination of infectious diseases and malnutrition have been eliminated in Costa Rica and Panama.

In other countries of the region, life expectancy levels are substantially lower; infant mortality rates in some exceed 100 per thousand live births. Though firm data are hard to get, it is apparent that the distribution of deaths is dominated by infectious causes (in Guatemala, Honduras, El Salvador, and Nicaragua, the principal cause of death is gastroenteritis, mainly afflicting young children) which at present can be easily controlled with adequate nutrition, basic health care, and essential sanitation.

Indicators of availability of health services show substantial differences from country to country (Tables 2.19, and 2.20). In Costa Rica and Panama the number of physicians, nurses, and other health personnel per 10,000 inhabitants is considerably higher than in the rest of the region. Access to sanitary facilities (e.g., potable water and modern sewage systems) is also better in Costa Rica and Panama.

Within a country, health differentials are also substantial—between rural and urban areas, for example, although they are probably narrower in the countries that have made more progress upgrading social services. Even in Costa Rica and Panama, with life expectancy levels approaching those found in developed countries, infant mortality levels are much higher in the rural areas where relatively fewer social and medical services can be found and nutritional and educational levels are lower. The situation is truly grim in the least developed countries. In some rural areas of Guatemala it has been estimated that half the children die before reaching age five.

Following standard Western practices, health care in Central America has depended on curative approaches that largely rely on highly trained physicians and hospital facilities. As in most other countries of the world, the distribution of hospitals and physicians is highly uneven; most concentrate in urban areas, particularly the capital cities. In some rural sections of Guatemala probably no more than 15 percent of the lowest income group receives even the most rudimentary health services. Some of the most glaring inequities in access to health care have been reduced as governments have tried to bring basic services to the rural population. Specially trained paramedics and primary-care rural health units are the backbone of these improved services. In short, mortality and health differentials in the region can be attributed to uneven access to health services, educational inequities, and differentials in housing and sanitary facilities.

2.9 NUTRITION

The health status of the population is also determined largely by nutritional standards. These, in turn, depend on factors such as income distribution, dietary habits, availability of nutritious foods, and the way food is distributed within households. All of these factors seem to influence the average levels of nutrition—generally poor—found in most Central American countries. In some countries, average nutritional levels are well below the international accepted minimums, especially among the most disadvantaged social groups.

Some estimates indicate that per capita calorie availability kept pace with population increases throughout the 1960s, but probably fell behind during the 1970s. Other estimates suggest that per capita food production may have increased throughout the mid-1970s, except in Honduras. Whether food production was able to grow at a faster rate than population is only one of the many factors to consider when evaluating the nutritional situation in the region. What is more critical is the way foodstuffs are distributed and how readily all sectors of the population can get them.

The emerging picture is disturbing. Nutritional surveys in 1967 and 1974–76 indicate that average nutritional levels among children under age five deteriorated between those years (Table 2.22). In this group, which suffers some of the highest mortality levels in malnourished populations, the number of malnourished children increased by 67 percent for the region as a whole. In absolute numbers this means that by 1974–76 there were more than one million children suffering from malnutrition in Central America. The only decrease was in Costa Rica, which reported a 13 percent decline. Costa Rica's success can be attributed to improvements in income distribution; efforts to minimize the impact of extreme poverty; a relatively good economic performance, especially of the agricultural sector; and smaller family sizes because of declining fertility. Opposite tendencies in other countries of the region account for the increases in malnutrition.

More recent data from El Salvador indicate a continuation of these negative trends. By 1980, 500,000 rural children and 175,000 urban children were malnourished.[4] Of the total, some 20 percent (approximately 135,000 children) were suffering from severe malnutrition. As these figures suggest, malnutrition is closely associated with poverty and social class. It is more prevalent among the landless and the rural small landholder. In Guatemala, nearly 35 percent of the rural population is malnourished: "about 20 percent of the total rural population was still fortunate enough to be able to consume about 80 percent of the recommended calorie intake; about 10 percent consume less than 70 percent of the minimum nutritional balance and the remaining 5 percent consume less than 60 percent of the recommended diet. The situation is even worse for the protein balance: the protein consumption of the poorer one-half of the population is only 56 percent of the requirements" (World Bank, 1978, p.18).

Malnutrition takes its greatest toll among young children, especially ages one through four; if not breast-fed, these children are more vulnerable to gastrointestinal attacks and certain infectious diseases, such as measles, that in combination with poor nutrition lead to high mortality. The long-term implications of poor nutrition are also severe, since malnutrition interferes with proper physical and intellectual development of the children and eventually with their capacity to lead a fully productive life.

2.10 HOUSING

All Central American countries are facing a difficult, if not critical, housing situation. A very high proportion of dwellings, both in urban and rural areas, are built with non-permanent materials and lack the most basic sanitary facilities (Table 2.18). Again the situation is better in Costa Rica and Panama. El Salvador, Guatemala, and Honduras have extremely primitive housing conditions. In these three countries, for example, less than 35 percent of dwellings had electricity at the time of the latest housing censuses, as compared to 66 percent in Costa Rica. Only in Costa Rica and Panama did more than half the dwellings have piped water. For every country conditions in rural areas are much worse than in urban areas, and even in cities they tend to be unsatisfactory.

"The 1971 census [in El Salvador] reported that 80 percent of the stock of rural housing and 51 percent of the urban stock were judged 'inadequate' to meet basic needs. Only 26 percent of the urban housing units are constructed of permanent materials" (AID, 1980b: p.6). The same source reports that "in 1975, a third of the households in the San Salvador metropolitan area were renting rooms in slum tenements. Another fifth of the households occupied illegal land subdivisions (*colonias ilegales*) and about a tenth were in squatter settlements (*tugurios*). In short, some two-thirds of the households in the San Salvador metropolitan areas live in informal settlements." As some researchers have suggested, the quality of these dwellings, and hence the quality of life of their inhabitants, can be improved by even a minimum of government support: basic sanitary services, paved roads, electricity, and some help in buying durable materials for improvements. The situation in rural areas was much worse. In one rural area only 5 percent of the dwelling units had walls built with permanent materials.

At the close of the 1970s the shortage of adequate housing in Guatemala was estimated at nearly 750,000 units. In Panama an estimated 473,000 new housing units will be needed between 1981 and 2000. Similar situations prevail in other countries and will continue to worsen as the existing housing stock deteriorates and the population rapidly expands.

2.11 RECOMMENDATIONS

This brief survey of social conditions puts in somber perspective the conditions under which a majority of the people of Central America live. In Costa Rica, and to a lesser extent Panama, the basic needs of most appear to be fulfilled, but most of the inhabitants of the other countries must constantly struggle to secure the most rudimentary necessities for survival. A majority of Central Americans are poorly educated; many are illiterate. They are poorly fed, unprotected from communicable diseases, and thus subject to the ravages of ill health. High mortality is common yet easily avoidable. Employment opportunities are few—in both the rural areas and the expanding cities—and most workers are unable to earn enough to maintain a decent living standard. In the countryside the concentration of land in the hands of a privileged few has perpetuated extreme social and economic inequalities that hinder progress. These inequalities foment the social eruption that in recent years has shattered the traditional fabric of Guatemala, El Salvador, and Nicaragua and now threatens to engulf the other nations of the region as well.

One recommendation eclipses—and in fact encapsulates—all others: those in authority must act now to help satisfy the basic needs of the downtrodden. This is not an easy process, politically or otherwise, since many of those who hold power are the same ones who are apt to lose the most. But political courage, favorable economic conditions, social and political stability, and a considerable infusion of foreign economic aid all appear crucial for the emergence of more just and equitable societies. Some of the recommendations below can be highly effective at low cost; others would require more resources and take years before they might bear fruit.

2.11.1 Education. Solving the myriad problems facing Central America can surely be helped by raising the educational levels of the people. The ability to read and write, a basic human right, is now beyond the reach of nearly four out of ten Central American adults. Universal literacy should be a key short-term priority. Medium-term objectives should include the upgrading of educational skills at all levels, including reforms to make formal training more relevant to the conditions of the region. A much-improved geographical distribution of educational facilities and a massive mobilization of existing resources—and especially of trained personnel—would be essential. Increasing the professionalism of the teaching career through status, tenure, and pay should be encouraged. Striking a proper balance between the resources assigned to higher education and those allocated to lower educational levels should be a key topic in the educational research agenda. A graduated scale of fees by level of family income, for example, could lead to more equitable opportunity; those with high family incomes could be required to pay more and those with very low income could receive a free university education. Thus, scarce resources could be better distributed, allowing for the expansion of primary and secondary enrollments, but not at the expense of higher education.

2.11.2 Public Health. Better health standards can be achieved, up to a point, through basic preventive health measures and a nutritious diet. Vaccines, dissemination of basic health information, and the use of paramedics trained in the diagnosis and treatment of common and relatively treatable diseases through simple methods— with the technical backup of more skilled personnel— can improve health standards dramatically and produce a drastic decline in needless mortality. Increased levels of education as well as efforts to decentralize the medical establishment would contribute to these goals. Mandatory service in rural areas by newly graduated physicians and other health personnel, in those countries not already doing so, would help; so would the training of selected rural inhabitants as paramedics and sanitation specialists. Efforts should be made to extend the network of maternal-child health care centers to reduce the very high infant morbidity and mortality rates. Proper sanitation, better infant care, more preventive medicine, the encouragement of breast-feeding, and other measures can best be handled by making more of these centers available. Changing culturally established habits of nutrition and other folk practices detrimental to health can best be approached through primary health care centers oriented to mothers and their children and through adequately trained paramedic personnel.

2.11.3 Population. The very high rates of population growth in the Central American countries—even in those that have already achieved some significant fertility declines—undoubtedly aggravate the social and economic problems of the region. There is no question that slowing down the pace of population growth would bring about an earlier and easier solution to some of these problems. However, that should not be an end in itself. What is really in the balance is the welfare of the population of Central America. Lowering the population growth rate should help by easing the mounting pressures on basic social services, alleviating the accelerating demand for jobs, etc. Rapid population growth is at least partly responsible for deteriorating nutritional levels and for absolute increases in the number of illiterates. This growth is also a factor in the extremely poor housing situation in Central America and in the high levels of unemployment and underemployment. Rapid population growth also adds to the pressures on the land that force many rural people to migrate to the cities.

The important question is how to reduce population growth rates. Improving health, at least over the short run, will have the opposite effect since mortality levels will decline further, thus leading to a rise in natural increase rates. The obvious alternative is to motivate potential parents to limit their childbearing and provide them with the modern means to do so. Effective family planning programs would be an essential component of this approach.

Some analysts say the demand already exists for family planning; such programs, in fact, have played an important role in the fertility declines of Costa Rica and Panama. Other analysts believe that family planning programs will only succeed under certain conditions. Most students of these matters would agree that, with improvements in social and economic conditions, potential parents will be motivated to practice modern contraception if properly informed, and if the means are at hand at reasonable monetary and psychic costs. The best way to reduce birth rates is through sound socio-economic development and the availability of contraceptives.

The emotional, moral, political, and religious sensitivities that family planning programs touch must be kept in mind. National family planning programs, already established in all Central American countries, must be expanded in harmony with conditions in each country and under the guidance of members of these societies who know the problems and cultural idiosyncrasies and would respect the dominant values. The Mexican experience with a national family planning program suggests that this is by far the most fruitful approach, since this program—legitimized by a national consensus, official and otherwise—has proven quite effective in a very short time. But the benefits of fertility reductions come only after a considerable time lag. In the interim, other social measures (to reduce unemployment, improve health, etc.) should be undertaken to improve the living conditions of those who now exist at substandard and impoverished levels.

2.11.4 Elimination of Basic Structural Inequalities. Central America has needed for decades, and still does, some drastic reforms of its agrarian structures. Costa Rica, Panama, and Honduras have already begun this process, largely through evolutionary means, yet in full awareness of the social conflicts agrarian reforms were intended to minimize. Nicaragua and El Salvador are in the process of carrying out far-reaching agrarian reforms. Guatemala, despite much discussion, seems to be resisting action. Colonization attempts may serve as temporary palliatives, but are probably incapable of providing enough land to the landless, even in those countries with the greatest amount of unsettled territory. The eventual solution for the land issue lies in the more equitable distribution of holdings now in *latifundios* (large land holdings). Questions that need to be answered involve compensation for expropriated land, at what price, and to what extent. Land redistribution alone will not suffice. Effective agrarian reforms must include technical support to the beneficiaries as well as the development of the infrastructure necessary for integrated rural development.

How agrarian reforms should be implemented obviously will depend on the social, political, and economic conditions facing each country (or even regions within countries) and on the available resources. Political and other pressures may speed up agrarian reforms in ways that could hardly be anticipated, as is now occurring in El Salvador.

Labor absorption tends to be higher in small to medium farms or in agricultural cooperatives farmed for the economic benefit of those who work them. So agrarian reforms should help ease unemployment pressures both directly and indirectly (by raising aggregate demand), although over the short-to-medium term the reform may have negative economic repercussions. Steps could be taken to counteract these negative effects. In urban areas, policies should aim at productively absorbing the burgeoning labor force. For the short term, assuming plentiful resources, they should include public works that reduce unemployment while laying the groundwork for future development. The combined impact of these measures, together with tax reforms, should contribute to more equitable income distributions.

2.11.5 Housing. Since the housing deficit is so severe and the rates of population growth so high, it would take many years to build dwellings to adequately house all the population of Central America even with nearly unlimited resources. Hence, the best practical recommendation is to allocate a significant proportion of whatever resources are available now towards the upgrading of the existing housing stock. This should include floors of concrete (or some such material), sanitary facilities, clean water supplies, and access to building materials at reduced costs, so that the dwellers themselves may gradually improve their abodes. The establishment of "sites and services" programs in urban areas, with the financial backing of the state, should alleviate the housing shortage, especially if accompanied by zoning changes that favor the poor. Programs similar to the one in Costa Rica to improve the dwellings of the rural population by providing materials and technical services could be begun or expanded in other countries. These measures will also help to raise health standards.

Considerable improvements in housing standards may be achieved in a relatively short time and at a relatively low cost. Long-term solutions will depend on the development of a native industry well endowed with credits, dynamic entrepreneurs, a competent labor force, and the vigorous participation of the state sector, all in a much-improved economic environment. The employment potential of the housing industry and its linkages with other sectors of the economy should not be overlooked in long-term development plans.

These are some simple and obvious suggestions to improve the living conditions of the population in Central America. The achievement of these goals will require decades and considerable resources, both human and physical. The most pressing question is how to satisfy the more basic needs of those who have little. Most of the measures above will require tremendous political will and/or outside pressures. But the only real alternatives are radical changes in the systems or the continued repression of those who clamor for a decent life. Even with the most optimistic forecasts of massive foreign assistance—whether from official sources or the private sector—solving these problems will not be easy. Trade-offs between social needs and economic realities will have to be carefully evaluated. Difficult years lie ahead, since as basic needs are met, new needs are likely to arise. The medium-term challenge facing the countries of Central America is to fulfill the basic needs of their people. Over a longer time horizon, these nations must develop a social and economic system capable of evolving in order to keep pace with the changing aspirations of their populations.

NOTES

1 See Chapter 1 for a brief summary of Spanish colonial rule in Central America.
2 The total fertility rate (TFR) indicates the average number of children that would be born to each woman in a population if each were to

live through her childbearing lifetime (usually considered ages 15–49), bearing children at the same rate as women of those ages actually did in a given year.

3 Recent land reform programs are counteracting the land concentration tendencies.

4 These figures may not be comparable with those previously referred to and may be affected by the disruptions of the national economy by civil war.

SELECTED REFERENCES

Adams, Richard N. *Crucifixion by Power: Essays on Guatemalan National Social Structure, 1944–1966*. Austin: University of Texas Press, 1970.

Anderson, John E., et al. "Determinants of Fertility in Guatemala." *Social Biology* 2, No. 1 (1980): 20–35.

Arias, Jorge. *La Poblacion de Guatemala*. Guatemala: CICRED, 1976.

Blutstein, Howard I., et al. *Area Handbook for Costa Rica*. Washington, DC: US Government Printing Office, 1970.

———. *Area Handbook for Honduras*. Washington, DC: US Government Printing Office, 1971a.

———. *Area Handbook for El Salvador*. Washington, DC: US Government Printing Office, 1971b.

Bonner, Raymond. "Gains from Salvador Land Distribution Disputed," New York *Times*, April 19, 1982, p. A14.

Buttari, Juan J., ed. *Employment and Labor Force in Latin America: A Review at National and Regional Levels*. Programa de Estudios Conjuntos sobre Integracion Economica Latinoamericana (ECIEL). 2 vols. Washington, DC: Organization of American States, 1979.

Capa, Cornell, and J. Mayone Stycos. *Al Margen de la Vida*. Programas Internacionales de Poblacion. Washington, DC: Population Reference Bureau, 1974.

"Centro Latinoamericano de Demografia." *Boletin Demografico* 14, No. 27, (January 1981).

Confederacion Superior Universitaria Centroamericana/Programa Centroamericano de Ciencias Sociales. *Estructura Agraria, Dinamica de Poblacion y Desarrollo Capitalista en Centroamerica*. San Jose, Costa Rica: EDUCA, 1978a.

———. *Estructura Demografica y Migraciones Internas en Centroamerica*. San Jose, Costa Rica: EDUCA, 1978b.

Deere, Carmen Diane. "Agrarian Reform in Central America and US Foreign Policy: El Salvador and Nicaragua," paper presented at the Latin American Studies Association, annual meeting, Washington, DC, March 3–6, 1982. 22 pp.

Dombrowski, John, et al. *Area Handbook for Guatemala*. Washington, DC: US Government Printing Office, 1970.

Durham, William H. *Scarcity and Survival in Central America*. Stanford, California: Stanford University Press, 1979.

ECLA, FAO, OIT, IICA, SIECA, OCT, and OEA. *Tenencia de la Tierra y Desarrollo Rural en Centroamerica.* San Jose, Costa Rica: EDUCA, 1976.

ECLA. "La Pobreza y la Satisfaccion de Necessidades Basicas en el Istmo Centroamericano (avances de una investigacion Regional)", CEPAL/MEX/SEM, 4/12, Mexico, March 31, 1981.

Fernandez, Mario, and Anabelle Schmidt. *La Poblacion de Costa Rica.* San Jose, Costa Rica: CICRED, 1976.

Fields, Gary S. *Poverty, Inequality, and Development.* Cambridge: Cambridge University Press, 1980.

Fox, Robert W., and Jerrold W. Guguet. *Tendencias Demograficas y de Urbanizacion en America Central y Panama.* Washington, DC: Banco Interamericano de Desarrollo, 1978.

Grupo Asesor de la FAO para la Integracion Economica Centroamericana (GAFICA). *Perspectivas para el Desarrollo y la Integracion de la Agricultura en Centroamerica.* Vol. 2. Guatemala, 1974.

International Labour Office. *Growth, Employment and Basic Needs in Latin America and the Caribbean.* Geneva, 1979.

———. *Labour Force 1950–2000, Estimates and Projections,* "Latin America." Volume 3. Geneva, 1977.

LeoGrande, William M. "A Splendid Little War: Drawing the Line in El Salvador." *International Security* 6, No. 1, (Summer 1981): 27–52.

Lizano Fait, Eduardo. "Towards a National Employment Policy: The Case of Costa Rica." *International Labour Review* 120, No. 3 (May-June 1981): 361–374.

Mayer, Enrique, and Elio Masferrer. "La Poblacion Indigena de America en 1978." *America Indigena* 39, No. 2 (April-June 1979).

Medica, Vilma N. *La Poblacion de Panama.* Panama: CICRED, 1976.

Monteforte Toledo, Mario, et al. *Centro America: Subdesarrollo y Dependencia.* 2 Vols. Mexico: Universidad Autonoma de Mexico, Instituto de Estudios Sociales, 1972.

Nicaragua, Republica de, Ministerio de Educacion. *La Education en el Primer Ano de la Revolucion Popular Sandinista.* Managua, Nicaragua, 1980.

Office of International Health, Public Health Service, US Department of Health, Education and Welfare. *Syncrisis: The Dynamics of Health,* "Panama." No. 1. Washington, DC, 1972a.

———. *Syncrisis: The Dynamics of Health,* "Honduras." No. 2. Washington, DC, 1972b.

———. *Syncrisis: The Dynamics of Health,* "El Salvador." No. 5. Washington, DC, 1972c.

———. *Syncrisis: The Dynamics of Health,* "Nicaragua." No. 11. Washington, DC, 1972d.

Organizacion de los Estados Americanos (OEA), Department de Asuntos Educativos. *Los Deficits Educativos en America Latina.* Washington, DC.

Pan American Health Organization (PAHO/OPS). *Health Conditions in the Americas, 1973–1976.* Washington, DC, 1978.

Pan American Health Organization (PAHO/OPS). *Salud para todos en el Ano 2000: Estrategias.* Washington, DC, 1980.

Pan American Health Organization (PAHO/OPS). *Health Conditions in the Americas, 1977–1980.* Washington, DC, 1982.

Parrlberg, Don, Peter M. Cody, and Ronald J. Ivey. *Agrarian Reform in El Salvador.* Washington, DC: Checchi and Company, 1981. Mimeo.

Posas, Mario. "Politica Estatal y Estructura Agraria en Honduras (1950–1978)." *Estudios Sociales Centroamericanos* No. 24 (Sept.-Dec. 1979): 37–116.

Programa Regional de Empleo para America Latina y el Caribe (PREALC). *El Problema de Empleo en America Latina: Situacion, Perspectivas y Politicas.* Santiago, Chile: Oficina Internacional del Trabajo, 1976.

Programa Regional de Empleo para America Latina y el Caribe (PREALC). *Mercado de Trabajo en Cifras, 1950–1980.* Santiago, Chile: Oficina Internacional de Trabajo, 1982.

Prosterman, Roy L., Jeffrey M. Riedinger, and Mary N. Temple. "Land Reform and the El Salvador Crisis." *International Security* 6, No. 5, (Summer 1981): 53–74.

Ruiz Granadino, Santiago. "Modernizacion Agricola en el Salvador." *Estudios Sociales Centroamericanos* No. 22 (Jan.-April, 1979): 71–100.

Ryan, John Morris, et al. *Area Handbook for Nicaragua.* Washington, DC: US Government Printing Office, 1970.

Salazar N., Jose M., Ennion Rodriguez C., and Jose M. Salazar X. "Costa Rica: Una Politica Agraria Innovadora." *Estudios Sociales Centroamericanos* No. 20 (May-August 1978): 47–110.

Seligson, Mitchell A. "Cooperative Participation Among Agrarian Reform Beneficiaries in Costa Rica," paper presented at the Latin American Studies Association annual meeting, Washington, DC, March 3–6, 1982. 49 pp.

———. "La Reforma Agraria en Costa Rica, 1942–1976: La Evolucion de un Programa." *Estudios Sociales Centroamericanos* No. 19 (Jan.-April 1978): 55–82.

Strasma, John, Peter Gore, Jeffrey Nash, and Refugio I. Rochin. *Agrarian Reform in El Salvador,* (Mimeo) Checchi and Company, Washington, D.C., 1983.

Teller, Charles, Mauricio Culagovski, and Jose Aranda-Pastor. *Inter-relacion Desnutricion, Poblacion y Desarrollo Social y Economico,* Instituto de Nutricion de Centro America y Panama (INCAP), Guatemala, 1980.

Teller, Charles, and Erwin Diaz. *Catalogo de Datos Demograficos para la Planificacion Alimentaria-Nutricional en Centro America y Panama,* Instituto de Nutricion de Centro America y Panama (INCAP), Guatemala, 1980.

Torrado, Susana. "El Exodo Intelectual Latinoamericano Hacia los EE. U.U. Durante El Periodo 1961–1975." *Migraciones Internacionales en las Americas* 1, No. 1 (1980): 19–39.

United Nations. *Patterns of Urban and Rural Population Growth*. Population Studies No. 68. New York, 1980.

US Agency for International Development. *Country Development Strategy Statement, Fiscal Years 82–86*. "Costa Rica." Washington, DC, January 1980a.

———. *Country Development Strategy Statement, Fiscal Year 82*. "El Salvador." Washington, DC, January 1980b.

———. *Country Development Strategy Statement Fiscal Year 82*. "Guatemala." Washington, DC, January 1980c.

———. *Country Development Strategy Statement Fiscal Year 83*. "Honduras." Washington, DC, January 1981.

———. *Country Development Strategy Statement Fiscal Year 83*. "Panama." Washington, DC, January 1981.

Weil, Thomas E., et al. *Area Handbook for Panama*. Washington, DC: US Government Printing Office, 1981.

World Bank. *Guatemala: Economic and Social Position and Prospects*. Washington, DC, 1978.

———. *El Salvador: Demographic Issues and Prospects*. A World Bank Country Study. Washington, DC, 1979.

TABLE 2.1
Indigenous Population of the Central American Countries According to Various Social Dimensions, 1978

	Indigenous Population (in thousands)	Percent of National Population	Percent of the Indigenous Population Integrated to Some Extent to National Economies	Percent of the Rural Population	Percent of the Urban Population
Costa Rica	10	0.6	100.0	0.9	0.4
El Salvador*	100	2.3	—	—	—
Guatemala	3,739	59.7	75.7	81.8	51.7
Honduras*	107	3.2	—	—	—
Nicaragua*	43	1.8	—	—	—
Panama	121	6.8	22.3	3.7	—

Source: Enrique Mayer and Elio Masferrer, "La Poblacion Indigena de America en 1978," America Indigena, Vol. 39, No. 2, April-June, 1979, Table 1, pp. 220-221.
*Data unreliable.

TABLE 2.2
Estimated and Projected Population (in thousands); Central American Republics, 1950 to 2000.

	1950	1960	1970	1975	1980	1985	1990	2000
Costa Rica	858	1236	1732	1965	2279	2600	2937	3596
El Salvador	1940	2574	3582	4143	4797	5552	6484	8708
Guatemala	2962	3966	5353	6243	7262	8403	9676	12739
Honduras	1401	1943	2639	3093	3691	4372	5105	6978
Nicaragua	1109	1472	1970	2318	2733	3218	3778	5154
Panama	832	1095	1480	1698	1953	2189	2439	2943
Total	9102	12286	16756	19460	22715	26334	30419	40118

Source: Centro Latinoamericano de Demográfica, Boletin Demográfico, Vol. 16, No. 31, Santiago, January 1983, Table 1, pp. 1-3.

TABLE 2.3
Basic Demographic, Social, and Economic Indicators: Central America and Selected Regions, 1983

	Population (millions)	Crude Birth Rate	Crude Death Rate	Rate of Natural Increase	Total Fertility Rate	Years to Double	Infant Mortality Rate	Population Under Age 15	Population 15-64	Population Over Age 64	Life Expectancy at Birth	Urban Population	Physical Quality of Life Index*	Per Capita Gross National Product
Costa Rica	2.4	29	4	2.5	3.7	27	19.1	37	59	4	70	44	85	1476
El Salvador	4.7	36	10	2.6	6.3	27	53**	45	52	3	64	41	64	636
Guatemala	7.9	42	10	3.2	5.7	22	66**	44	53	3	59	37	54	1159
Honduras	4.1	45	10	3.5	6.5	20	87	47	50	3	58	36	53	591
Nicaragua	2.8	47	11	3.6	6.4	19	89	48	50	2	56	53	55	874
Panama	2.1	29	6	2.3	3.9	31	34	39	57	4	70	51	79	1908
Latin America	390	31	8	2.3	4.3	30	65	39	57	4	64	65	71	2063
World	4677	2.9	11	1.8	3.9	39	84	34	60	6	62	41	65	2754
More Developed Countries	1158	15	10	0.6	1.9	118	19	23	66	11	73	70	92	8657
Less Developed Countries	3519	33	12	2.1	4.5	32	93	38	58	4	58	29	55	728

Source: Population Reference Bureau, 1981 and 1983, *World Population Data Sheet*, Washington, D.C. 1981 and 1983.

*"The Physical Quality of Life Index (PQLI) was developed by the Overseas Development Council, Washington, D.C., in response to the need for a non-income measure that summarizes the many aspects of human wellbeing. It combines three indicators—infant mortality, life expectancy at age one, and literacy—into a single composite index. The index runs from 0 to 100, 0 being the lowest level of wellbeing and 100 being the highest." PQLI data were obtained from the 1979 version of the World Population Data Sheet.

**There are strong reasons to believe that the infant mortality figures for El Salvador and Guatemala understate the true levels by a wide margin.

TABLE 2.4
Absolute Number of People Residing in the Capital Cities of the Central American Republics in 1950 and 1980 and Percent of the Total Population of the Countries They Represent:

	Absolute Size of the Population in the Capital Cities		Percent of the Total Population in the Capital Cities		Percent Increase in the Population Size of the Capital Cities between 1950 and 1980
	1950	1980	1950	1980	
San Jose, Costa Rica	146,000	508,000	18	22	248
San Salvador, El Salvador	213,000	858,000	11	18	303
Guatemala, Guatemala	337,000	1,143,000	11	21	324
Tegueigalpa, Honduras	72,000	406,000	5	11	464
Managua, Nicaragua	109,000	662,000	10	25	507
Panama, Panama	217,000	794,000	27	41	266

Source: Robert W. Fox and Jerrold W. Huguet, *Tendencias Demograficas y de Urbanizacion en America Central y Panama*, Banco Interamericano de Desarrollo, Washington, D.C. 1978, Cuadro 5, p. 8.

TABLE 2.5
Percentage Urban; Central American Republics, 1950-2000

	1950	1960	1970	1975	1980	1990	2000
Costa Rica	34	37	40	41	43	49	56
El Salvador	36	38	39	40	41	46	53
Guatemala	30	33	36	37	39	44	52
Honduras	18	23	29	32	36	43	51
Nicaragua	36	41	47	50	53	60	66
Panama	36	41	48	51	54	61	67

Source: United Nations, *Patterns of Urban and Rural Population Growth*, Population Studies No. 68, New York, 1980, Table 50, pp. 159-162.

TABLE 2.6
Industrial Structure of the Total Economically Active Population; Central American Republics, 1960 to 1980.

	Costa Rica 1960	Costa Rica 1970	Costa Rica 1980	El Salvador 1960	El Salvador 1970	El Salvador 1980	Guatemala 1960	Guatemala 1970	Guatemala 1980	Honduras 1960	Honduras 1970	Honduras 1980	Nicaragua 1960	Nicaragua 1970	Nicaragua 1980	Panama 1960	Panama 1970	Panama 1980
Agriculture	51.7	42.7	34.4	63.2	57.9	52.4	63.7	60.1	55.4	71.2	64.1	56.9	62.0	51.9	41.8	50.2	40.2	33.0
Mining	0.3	0.3	0.3	0.1	0.1	0.1	0.1	0.1	0.1	0.4	0.3	0.3	0.9	0.6	0.4	0.1	0.2	0.0
Industry	11.5	13.6	15.9	12.2	11.8	10.8	12.8	13.6	14.9	8.2	11.0	14.7	11.6	13.5	15.0	7.6	9.3	10.8
Construction	5.4	6.6	6.6	3.8	3.0	3.9	3.7	4.2	5.6	2.1	3.1	3.9	3.2	3.9	4.6	4.2	6.0	6.8
Electricity	1.0	1.1	1.4	0.2	0.3	0.4	0.2	0.3	0.4	0.2	0.3	0.7	0.2	0.7	0.7	0.5	1.1	1.4
Commerce	9.4	10.7	13.0	6.1	8.0	9.2	6.5	7.3	7.9	4.5	6.9	9.5	6.5	8.9	11.5	9.0	11.4	12.6
Transportation	3.7	4.2	5.2	2.0	2.2	2.3	2.2	2.5	2.5	1.5	2.3	3.6	2.3	3.2	4.3	2.9	3.6	4.4
Services	16.9	20.8	23.2	12.4	16.7	20.9	10.8	11.9	13.2	12.0	12.0	10.5	13.3	17.3	21.7	19.9	23.6	26.0
(Canal Zone)																(5.4)	(4.6)	(4.1)
Total	100.0	100.0	100.0	100.0	100.0	100.0	100.0	100.0	100.0	100.0	100.0	100.0	100.0	100.0	100.0	100.0	100.0	100.0

Source: Programa Regional del Empleo para América Latina y El Caribe, Mercado de Trabajo en Cifras, Santiago, Chile, 1980, Tables I-26, I-41, I-46, I-51, I-65, and I-70, pp. 46, 53, 56, 58, 65 and 68.

TABLE 2.7
Rates of Growth of the Economically Active Population by Sector: Central American Republics, 1960-1970.

	Total	Agricultural	Non-Agricultural
Costa Rica	3.9	1.0	6.1
El Salvador	3.5	2.5	4.7
Guatemala	2.8	2.2	4.0
Honduras	3.2	3.0	3.7
Nicaragua	2.7	1.1	4.3
Panama	4.1	1.9	5.2

Source: Programa Regional del Empleo para America Latina y El Caribe (PREALC), El Problema del Empleo en America Latina: Situacion Perspectivas y Politicas, Santiago, Chile, 1976, Cuadro 1, p. 5.

TABLE 2.8
Estimated Unemployment Rates for Central American Countries; Circa 1973.

Costa Rica (1973)	7.1
El Salvador (1974)	13.1
Guatemala* (1973)	13.0
Honduras (1973)	10-12
Nicaragua, Urban (1973)	18.7
Panama (1973)	6.5

Source: PREALC, El Problema del Empleo, Cuadro 4, p. 8 and * for Guatemala, The World Bank, Guatemala: Economic and Social Position and Prospects, Washington, D.C., 197 p. 14.

TABLE 2.9
Farm Distribution According to Size of Holding: Central American Countries (Excluding Panama), Latest Agricultural Census Years

	Central America	Costa Rica	El Salvador	Guatemala	Honduras	Nicaragua
Percent of Area	100.0	100.0	100.0	100.0	100.0	100.0
Micro-farms[a]	0.7	0.3	3.9	0.8	—	—
Sub-family[b]	9.1	2.9	18.0	13.5	12.4	3.5
Family[c]	16.2	14.2	20.6	13.5	27.4	11.2
Multi-family[d]						
Medium	35.6	41.2	19.8	31.4	32.7	44.1
Multi-family[e]						
Large	38.4	41.4	37.7	40.8	27.5	41.2
Percent of Farms	100.0	100.0	100.0	100.0	100.0	100.0
Micro-farms	24.1	43.7	47.2	21.3	—	2.2
Sub-family	54.8	24.3	44.2	67.1	67.5	48.6
Family	15.0	19.8	6.7	9.5	26.4	27.4
Multi-family						
Medium	5.6	11.3	1.5	2.0	5.7	20.3
Multi-family						
Large	0.5	0.9	0.4	0.1	0.4	1.5

Source: CEPAL, FAO, DIT, IICA, SIECA, OCT, OEA, *Tenencia de la Tierra y Desarrollo Rural en Centroamerica*, Editorial Universitaria Centroamericana, EDUCA, San Jose, Costa Rica, 1976, Table 6, p. 48.

[a] —Farms so small they can hardly be classified as such. Product is consumed entirely by the growers.
[b] —Farms large enough to provide employment for less than two people with the typical incomes, markets, and levels of technology and capital now prevailing in the region.
[c] —Farms large enough to provide employment for 2 to 3.9 people on the assumption that most of the farm work is being carried out by the members of the farm family.
[d] —Farms large enough to provide employment for 4 to 12 people.
[e] —Farms large enough to provide employment for more than 12 people.

TABLE 2.10
Percent Distribution of Rural Families by Land Tenure Status: Central American Countries Excluding Panama, 1979

	Landless	Farms with less than 35 Hectares	Farms with more than 35 Hectares
Nicaragua	32.6	50.1	17.3
Guatemala	26.5	70.9	2.6
El Salvador	26.0	71.3	2.7
Honduras	20.0	74.9	5.1
Costa Rica	5.6	73.1	21.3

Source: United States Agency for International Development, *Honduras: Country Development Strategy Statement, Fiscal Year 1983*, Washington, D.C., January 1981, Table III, p. 5.

TABLE 2.11
Distribution of Farm Families and of Farms by Size, El Salvador, circa 1981

	Number of Farm Families People	Number of Farm Families Percent	Number of Farm Hectares Hectares	Number of Farm Hectares Percent
Holdings over 500 hectares (Phase I)	34,658	7.2	224	12.1
Holdings of 100.1-500 hectares (Phase II)	50,000	10.4	343	18.5
Decree 207 lands	150,000	31.2	178	9.6
Holdings of less than 100 hectares not subject to Agrarian Reform	95,342	19.8	1,112	59.9
Landless Laborers	150,000	31.2	—	—
Total	480,000	100.0	1,855	100.0

Source: Don Parrlberg, Peter M. Cody and Ronald J. Ivey, *Agrarian Reform in El Salvador*, presented to the United States Agency for International Development, Checchi and Company, Washington, D.C., December 1981, Exhibit V-1, p. 96.

TABLE 2.12
Composition of the Rural Labor Force by Land Tenure Status: Central American Countries (Excluding Panama), 1960s Agricultural Censuses (Guatemala: Agricultural Census of 1950)*

	Central America	Costa Rica	El Salvador	Guatemala	Honduras	Nicaragua
Total	100.0	100.0	100.0	100.0	100.0	100.0
Landless	22.7	42.0	15.6	16.5	26.1	31.4
Micro-farms	15.7	—	39.9	17.8	—	1.4
Sub-family	44.1	25.0	37.3	56.0	49.9	33.4
Family	12.3	20.4	5.7	7.9	19.5	18.8
Multi-family Medium	4.8	11.6	1.2	1.7	4.2	14.0
Multi-family Large	0.4	0.9	0.4	0.1	0.3	1.0

Source: CEPAL, et al, *Tenencia de la Tierra y Desarrollo Rural en Centro America*, Cuadro 8, p. 70.
*For definitions, See Table 9.

TABLE 2.13
Average Family Income by Land Tenure Status: Selected Central American Countries (in Central American Pesos), 1960s Agricultural Census

	Nicaragua Average Income	Nicaragua Ratio to Average	El Salvador Average Income	El Salvador Ratio to Average	Guatemala Average Income	Guatemala Ratio to Average	Costa Rica Average Income	Costa Rica Ratio to Average
Multi-family* Large	18,226	20.2	25,748	44.3	40,000	88.3	20,473	17.1
Multi-family Medium	2,248	2.5	7,106	12.2	8,000	17.7	2,117	1.8
Family	717	.8	1,408	2.4	1,300	2.9	1,084	.9
Sub-family	445	.5	420	.7	220	.5	908	.8
Micro-farms	380	.4	302	.5	—	—	—	—
Landless	370	.4	229	.4	340	.8	727	.6
Average Income	902	—	581	—	453	—	1,199	—

Source: CEPAL, et al., *Tenencia de la Tierra y Desarrollo Rural en Centroamerica*, Cuadro 19, p. 72.
*For definitions, See Table 9.

TABLE 2.14
Central America: Estimated Income Distribution and Income Levels per Capita in 1970 United States Dollars; 1978.

	Costa Rica Percent	Costa Rica Income	El Salvador Percent	El Salvador Income	Guatemala Percent	Guatemala Income	Honduras Percent	Honduras Income	Nicaragua Percent	Nicaragua Income	Panama Percent	Panama Income
Lower 10 percent (poorest)	1.5	132.4	0.8	37.1	1.3	6.73	2.1	61.5	1.2	50.8	0.6	55.0
Lower 20 percent	4.0	176.7	2.0	46.5	3.5	90.5	5.5	80.7	3.0	61.9	2.7	120.0
30 Percent Under the Median	17.0	500.8	10.0	155.1	13.0	224.4	14.3	140.0	13.0	178.2	10.0	304.6
30 Percent Over the Median	30.0	883.8	22.0	341.2	25.5	440.1	26.0	254.6	26.0	356.2	27.0	822.6
Highest 20 Percent	49.0	2165.2	66.0	1535.5	58.0	151.6	54.2	796.3	58.0	1198.9	60.3	2710.1
Highest 5 Percent (Wealthiest)	25.0	4218.2	33.0	2467.8	30.0	3106.8	28.0	645.3	23.0	1866.2	30.0	5483.3

Source: Comision Economica para America Latina, *La Pobreza y la Satisfaccion de Necesidades Basicas en el Istmo Centroamericano*, (Avances de una investigacion Regional), CEPAL/MEX/SEM.4/12, Mexico, March 31, 1981, Cuadro 1, p. 12.

SOCIAL CONTEXT

TABLE 2.15
Percent of National Per Capita Income Received by Income Group; Central American Countries, 1978.

	Guatemala	El Salvador	Honduras	Nicaragua	Costa Rica	Panama
Lower 10 Percent	12.9	8.0	21.2	12.3	15.0	6.0
Lower 20 Percent	17.4	10.0	27.8	15.0	20.0	13.3
21 to 50 Percent	43.3	33.4	48.3	32.6	56.9	33.5
Lower 50 Percent	33.0	24.1	40.1	26.8	42.2	25.5
Higher 20 Percent	189.9	231.3	174.6	191.1	146.2	198.2
Higher 5 Percent	500.0	432.6	467.4	352.8	379.6	503.3

Source: Comision Economica para America Latina, *La Pobreza y la Satisfaccion de Necesidades Basicas en el Istmo Centroamericano* (Avances de una investigacion Regional), CEPAL/MEX/SEM.4/12, Mexico, March 31, 1981, Cuadro 4, p. 17.

TABLE 2.16
Central American Republics: Absolute Number of Illiterates Among the Population 15 Years of Age and Over and Illiteracy Rates for the Total Population, by Urban/Rural Residence and by Sex

Country	Census Year	Absolute Number of Illiterates 15 Years of Age and Over	Total	Urban	Rural	Male	Female
Costa Rica	1950	94,492	20.6				
	1963	109,460	15.6				
	1973	121,312	11.6	4.9	17.0	11.4	11.8
El Salvador	1950	644,514	59.0				
	1961	706,837	51.0				
	1971	816,716	42.9	21.8	59.0	39.2	46.4
Guatemala	1950	1,138,297	70.6				
	1964	1,450,826	62.0				
	1973	1,526,600	53.8	28.2	68.4	46.0	61.4
Honduras	1950	631,999	64.8				
	1961	642,022	52.7				
	1974	706,659	40.5	19.0	51.2	39.3	41.6
Nicaragua	1950	369,376	61.6				
	1963	399,585	52.7				
	1971	410,755	40.5	19.4	64.6	41.6	42.6
Panama	1950	132,978	30.1				
	1960	133,812	23.3				
	1970	175,383	21.7	6.3	38.1	21.1	22.6

Source: Organication de los Estados Americanos, (OEA), *America en Cifras 1977*, Washington, D.C. 1979, Tomo III, Cuadros 501-01 and 501-02, pp. 101-105.

TABLE 2.17
Central America: Absolute and Percent Increases in Educational Enrollments by Level of Education, 1971-1977.

		Primary Level		Secondary Level		Higher Education	
Country	Year	Absolute Change	Percent Change	Absolute Change	Percent Change	Absolute Change	Percent Change
Costa Rica	1971	356,147		85,459		18,581	
	1977	374,622	5.2	150,894	76.6	39,258	111.3
El Salvador	1971	535,113		88,635		13,400	
	1977	690,140	29.0	197,682	123.0	30,303	126.1
Guatemala	1971	531,122		—		—	
	1977	666,389	25.5	—	—	—	—
Honduras	1971	389,170		38,879		4,744	
	1977	498,582	28.1	70,725	81.9	16,368	245.0
Nicaragua	1971	309,913		54,690		9,381	
	1977	372,978	20.4	93,935	71.8	21,449	128.6
Panama	1971	287,565		86,795		13,456	
	1977	356,782	24.1	137,185	58.1	27,820	106.7

Source: OEA, *America en Cifras*, Tomo III, Cuadros 501-33, 501-57, and 501-74; pp. 114-117, 135-141 and 149-155.

TABLE 2.18
Percentage of the Population with Water Supply and Sewerage Services, by Urban and Rural Residence; Central American Countries, Around 1979.

	Water Supply							Sewerage Services		
	Total		Urban		Rural				
	House Connections	Easy Access	House Connections	Easy Access	House Connections	Easy Access	Total	Urban	Rural
Costa Rica (1979)	78	3	98	2	61	3	20	43	—
El Salvador (1979)	28	19	61	6	5	29	20	47	—
Guatemala (1979)	20	22	51	38	3	12	12	34	—
Honduras (1979)	27	28	50	41	15	20	15	43	—
Nicaragua (1979)	35	11	63	18	6	4	16	31	—
Panama (1977)	60	23	93	7	24	40	87	97	78

Source: Pan American Health Organization, *Health Conditions in the Americas, 1977-1980*, Washington, D.C. 1982, Tables VII-1 and VII-2, pp. 376-377. Data for all countries except Panama refer to 1979; water supply data for Panama refer to 1977 and for sewerage for 1976.

TABLE 2.19
Health Personnel per 10,000 Population; Central American Republics, Most Recent Data.*

	Physicians	Nurses	Nurses Auxiliaries
Costa Rica (1975)	6.6	5.5	21.9
El Salvador (1979)	2.9	3.8	7.7
Guatemala (1976)	1.2	1.1	5.6
Honduras (1979)	3.2	1.5	8.1
Nicaragua (1979)	3.6	3.7	15.7
Panama (1978)	8.5	11.0	18.2

*Dates in parentheses refer to physicians; all figures for nurses and nurses auxiliaries apply to 1980.
Source: Pan American Health Organization, *Health Conditions in the Americas, 1977-1980*, Washington, D.C., 1982, Table IV-15, p. 358.

TABLE 2.20
Hospital Beds per 1,000 Population, Total by Country and by Location; Central American Republics, Most Recent Information.

		Total		Capital City		Rest of the Country
Costa Rica	(1977)	3.5	(1972)	19.4		1.9
El Salvador	(1978)	1.8	(1972)	8.6		1.0
Guatemala	(1973)	2.0	(1972)	4.3		.6
Honduras	(1978)	1.3	(1976)	8.6		.8
Nicaragua	(1976)	2.2	(1977)	3.6		2.0
Panama	(1977)	3.9	(1977)	8.0		2.0

Sources: For Total Beds, Pan American Health Organization, *Health Conditions in the Americas, 1977-1980*, Washington, D.C., 1982, Table IV-2, p. 345; Data by Location from Organization of American States, *America en Cifras*, Vol. III, Cuadro 406-12, p. 50.

TABLE 2.21
Five Leading Causes of Death; Central American Republics

Costa Rica (1979)
1) Diseases of the Heart
2) Malignant Neoplasms
3) Accidents
4) Causes of Perinatal Mortality
5) Cerebrovascular Disease

El Salvador (1974)
1) Enteritis and Other Diarrheal Diseases
2) Accidents
3) Causes of Perinatal Mortality
4) Homicide, Legal Intervention and Operations of War
5) Influenza and Pneumonia

Guatemala (1978)
1) Enteritis and Other Diarrheal Diseases
2) Influenza and Pneumonia
3) Causes of Perinatal Mortality
4) Accidents
5) Diseases of the Heart

Honduras (1978)
1) Enteritis and Other Diarrheal Diseases
2) Diseases of the Heart
3) Homicide, Legal Intervention, and Operations of War
4) Influenza and Pneumonia
5) Causes of Perinatal Mortality

Nicaragua (1977)
1) Enteritis and Other Diarrheal Diseases
2) Diseases of the Heart
3) Accidents
4) Homicide, Legal Intervention, and Operations of War
5) Influenza and Pneumonia

Panama (1974)
1) Diseases of the Heart
2) Accidents
3) Malignant Neoplasms
4) Influenza and Pneumonia
5) Cerebrovascular Disease

Source: Pan American Health Organization, *Health Conditions in the Americas, 1977-1980*, Washington, D.C. 1982, Table II-a, pp. 270-276.

TABLE 2.22
Trends in the Prevalence of Malnutrition in National Samples of Children Under Five Years of Age and Estimates of the Absolute Number of Malnourished Children; Central American Countries, 1965-67 and 1974-76.

	Percent and Absolute Number of Malnourished Children in 1965-1967 %	n(000)	Percent and Absolute Number of Malnourished Children in 1974-1976 %	n(000)	Absolute and Percent Change From 1965-67 to 1974-76 %	n(000)
Guatemala	32.4	281	38.1	421	50.1	141
El Salvador	26.0	148	38.0	277	87.0	129
Honduras	29.5	124	38.0	224	79.9	99
Nicaragua	15.0	50	22.6	102	105.2	52
Costa Rica	13.7	38	12.3	33	−13.2	−5
Panama	11.9	27	21.5	57	116.2	31
Total	24.9	668	32.9	1,114	66.8	446

Source: Charles Teller, Mauricio Culagovski, Juan del Canto y Jose Aranda Pastor, "Desnutricion, Poblacion y Desarrollo Social y Economico: Hacia un Marco de Referencia," in Charles Teller, Mauricio Culagovski and Jose Aranda-Pastor, *Interrelacion Desnutricion, Poblacion y Desarrollo Social y Economico*, Instituto de Nutricion de Centro America y Panama (INCAP), Guatemala, 1980, p. 37.

CHAPTER 3
ECONOMIC CONTEXT

3.1 INTRODUCTION

An analysis of the economic structure and performance of the six Central American nations over the last two decades shows striking similarities and differences. All six countries are small; yet by Central American standards, Nicaragua is large, over six times the size of El Salvador. In population Guatemala outnumbers Panama by 3.6 to 1, and the population density of El Salvador is 12 times that of sparsely-populated Nicaragua. Using gross domestic product (GDP) as a measure of the size of an economy, Guatemala's economy is 3.4 times that of Honduras. Agriculture, the mainstay of all six countries, contributes about three times the percentage of the GDP for Honduras as for Panama. Guatemala is the most highly industrialized nation; Panama is the least. More than half the population of Nicaragua and Panama is urban, while in Guatemala and Honduras hardly more than a third of the population falls into this category. Natural resource endowment varies as well, with Guatemala being the only country so far to find petroleum deposits in commercial quantities.

In spite of these differences, there are similarities in the structural relationships and economic performance of the Central American countries. Many of the problems they face, together with their corresponding policy solutions, are common to all.

The economies of these nations are limited in size and very open to international trade. They have specialized over the years in only a few kinds of agricultural products, which are exported to traditional markets. These characteristics make them rather sensitive to external disturbances and changes in the terms of trade, but at the same time open up opportunities to exploit their foreign trade advantages. But these opportunities have not been fully exploited so far, because of the common economic strategy adopted in the 1960s.

This development strategy is closely linked to the establishment of the program for economic integration in the area. To overcome the limitations imposed by their small markets and by a balance of payments that depends on a few export products, the Central American nations, with the exception of Panama, decided to form a Central American Common Market (CACM) in 1958 and to embark on a policy of import substitution and protectionism for industries still in infancy. They eliminated customs duties among themselves, thus enlarging their markets, and levied very high tariffs selectively on the importation of finished goods from third countries. Raw and intermediate materials and capital goods were given duty-free status, and various other tax incentives and subsidies were granted to local industry.

Credit policies were directed toward financing industrial and agricultural production at subsidized interest rates, and the exchange rates were fixed for long periods of time, regardless of relative price changes at home and abroad, thus stimulating imports and discouraging the production of exportable goods. Prices and profit margins of many essential agricultural products were directly controlled by the governments, while the right to import or export such products freely was denied at times in order to ensure sufficient domestic production and consumption at prices different from those prevailing in world markets.

The formation of the Central American Common Market produced some positive economic effects in the early stages. The substitution of domestic for imported goods led to high rates of investment and growth and contributed to the development of a very active entrepreneurial group. The average growth rate in the 1960s was 6 percent. However, the limitations inherent in the import substitution and protectionist plans, together with other adverse developments, cost the CACM its dynamism in the 1970s and left it virtually stagnant in the 1980s.

Because of the unreasonably high tariffs on finished goods and the opportunity to import duty-free industrial materials and capital goods from abroad, most of the new investment generated in this period was directed toward import substitution activity. But instead of alleviating the chronic deficit in the balance of payments, the composition of imports simply changed: while 40 percent of total imports were finished goods and 60 percent raw materials and capital goods in 1960, the ratios in 1980 were 80 percent raw materials and capital goods and only 20 percent finished goods.

Studies have shown that industrial production for CACM markets was so profitable that investors did not risk time and effort in producing for third markets, where competition was more direct and aggressive. As a result, manufacturing was primarily concerned with the satisfaction of demand within the domestic market, and was very seldom oriented toward wider but more competitive markets such as the US, Japan, or the European Community.

Once the initial stage of easy substitution was completed, and the domestic market saturated, the CACM members found their export growth potential restricted. Additional sources of foreign exchange became limited, and so did their ability to finance imports of materials needed for industrial production. Then the long and unhappy history of external indebtedness began.

The misallocation of productive resources and the distortions of the relative prices of imports and exports contributed to the deterioration of other productive sectors. While finished industrial goods were granted full protection, agricultural products and other intermediate goods were not given protection at all. Instead, agricultural prices were often controlled; duties were levied on farm tools, fertilizers, and similar goods; and the exchange rates were kept artificially low. Thus imports of raw materials for industry became relatively inexpensive, while revenues from exports of agro-industrial products were penalized. The contribution of agriculture to the gross national product declined form 40 percent in 1960 to 20 percent in 1982.

The economic stagnation of both the industrial and agricultural sectors, the bias toward capital-intensive versus labor-intensive investments, and the imposition of high payroll taxes in Costa Rica and other countries aggravated the problem of employment and salaries in the private sector. The unemployment rate in Costa Rica grew from 5 percent in 1980 to 9 percent in 1983. As job opportunities became scarce, real wages stagnated, particularly in the rural areas, and were actually reduced during times of high inflation.

The employment and salary situations gave rise to many of the social problems discussed in Chapter 2 of this report. Popular dissatisfaction was reflected in part by the growing demands on the public sector to create new jobs and provide more social programs, such as education in Costa Rica and public health in Honduras. The reaction of the governments was to increase spending well beyond their capacity. The fiscal deficit of all the countries gradually worsened; in 1982 in Guatemala it reached 12.2 percent of GNP, in El Salvador 21.1 percent, in Honduras 21.8 percent, in Nicaragua 36.7 percent, in Costa Rica 15 percent, and in Panama 36.1 percent. Civil war, social unrest, and terrorism in various countries have contributed significantly to the burgeoning of fiscal deficits.

To meet the increasing public debt, the governments have turned more to external and internal financing, including the printing of money, thereby contributing to an expansion of aggregate demand, an increase in the volume of imports, and a deterioration in inflation and exchange rates, as was the case in Costa Rica from 1978 through 1982. But that exchange rate devaluation did not serve to stimulate exports, as industrial production was not able to compete successfully in markets other than the CACM.

The ideological inclination toward Marxist socialism of the Sandinista government in Nicaragua has moved the country away from the market-oriented economy toward a more centrally planned approach. Although there is still a considerable private sector, it is difficult to foresee its role in the future of the Nicaraguan economy.

In addition to the internal and external uncertainties caused by political unrest, excessive public expenditures, and the rigidities imposed by protectionism, economic development has also been retarded by the unrealistic credit and interest rate policies followed in most of the countries. As passive interest rates on savings and time deposits declined in real terms, the public did not find sufficient incentive to increase their holdings of domestic financial assets, preferring to convert actual savings into foreign exchange assets or to acquire land and other speculative, non-productive investments. The banking systems and other financial intermediaries were not able, therefore, to raise sufficient funds to satisfy the needs of economic development without increasing the money supply through re-discount at the Central Bank. In addition, the size of the public deficit has produced a crowding-out effect in the financial markets, reducing even more the capacity of the private sector to make its contribution to economic growth and the betterment of life for the population.

The economic scenario of the Central American nations is at present very complex. A more detailed discussion of the common trends and problems is offered in the following sections, and a number of policy recommendations which might contribute to finding solutions are advanced.

3.2 GLOBAL INDICATORS

In recent years the Central American nations have experienced economic growth rates considerably lower than in the 1960s. Real GDP per capita for the entire region has declined since 1980. It has declined in Nicaragua in 1978, 1979, and 1982; in El Salvador in 1979 through 1982; in Costa Rica and Honduras in 1980, 1981, and 1982; and in Guatemala and Panama in 1982. Preliminary data for 1983 suggest that real GDP may have decreased in all countries but Costa Rica, where it increased by 0.7 percent. The relative price stability of the 1960s gave way to near double-digit inflation in the first half of the 1970s, primarily as a result of inflationary pressures in the import sector and the expansion of government expenditures. More recently the record is mixed, with relative price stability returning to some countries while inflation accelerates in others. More importantly, the evidence quite clearly indicates that the creation of jobs in the Central American nations has continued to fall behind the expansion of the labor force, which intensifies an already serious unemployment/underemployment problem.[1]

3.2.1 GDP and Per-Capita GDP. During the 1960s the real GDP of the Central American economies grew at an average annual rate of 6 percent (Table 3.1). This growth performance compared favorably with that of Latin America as a whole, which expanded at a rate of 5.6 percent per year. The leaders in economic growth in Central America were Panama (8 percent per annum) and Nicaragua (6.9 percent). Honduras (4.8 percent) was the only Central American nation significantly below Latin American growth standards during the 1960s.

As mentioned before, one factor contributing to the relatively high levels of growth during the 1960s was the expansion of non-agricultural exports which followed the establishment of the Central American Common Market by Costa Rica, El Salvador, Guatemala, Honduras, and Nicaragua. Although two independent empirical analyses of the costs and benefits of the CACM have indicated that its formation had a sizable and positive impact on the area's growth, it has also been pointed out that the CACM has lost its dynamism in recent years. The rate of economic growth has declined, due in part to the political disturbances and terrorism in the area and in part to the limitations imposed by the import substitution policies and protectionism. One analyst has reported, however, that the creation of the CACM increased regional GDP growth rates by 0.6 percent per year; another has estimated that the CACM increased output by 3 to 4 percent of the region's GDP in 1972.

Because of fast-growing populations, the economic performance of the Central American nations in the 1960s is less impressive when analyzed in per capita terms (Table 3.2). In 1960, for instance, GDP per capita in 1980 US dollars for the six nations averaged $655 versus $822 for Latin America as a whole. The highest GDP per capita in the region was that of Costa Rica ($838), followed by Panama ($756), Guatemala ($728), Nicaragua ($695), El Salvador ($529), and finally Honduras ($469). By 1970, the region's GDP per capita had risen to approximately $890, a gain of 2.2 percent per year, while GDP per capita for Latin America as a whole grew by an identical 2.7 percent per annum to $1,110. Thus, despite faster-than-average growth performance during the 1960s, the GDP per capita gap between the Central American nations and the rest of Latin America did not close, due to the region's relatively rapid growth in population.[2]

Real economic growth during the first half of the 1970s declined to 5.2 percent per annum in Central America, while the total growth rate for Latin America was 6.5 percent. In addition to factors mentioned earlier, two natural disasters had an adverse impact on economic performance during this period: an earthquake destroyed 80 percent of Nicaragua's capital city of Managua in December 1972, and Hurricane Fifi lashed at Honduras' agricultural and industrial zones in September 1974. The highest growth performances were shown by Costa Rica (6 percent per annum) and Guatemala and Nicaragua (5.6 percent). Honduras' growth rate of 2.3 percent was the slowest in the region. On a per-capita basis, GDP expanded by an average of 2.2 percent per annum compared with 3.7 percent for Latin America as a whole. In Honduras GDP per capita actually declined by 0.8 percent per year, so that GDP per capita in 1975 ($541) was actually lower than in 1970 ($561).

During the second half of the 1970s the economic performance of the Central American nations was very uneven. The sharp recovery of coffee prices in 1976–78 boosted export earnings, but this positive development was counteracted by general political instability in the region. Again, special circumstances took a toll. Another hurricane struck Honduras in 1976; Panama was affected by uncertainty over the future of the canal; and an earthquake rocked Guatemala in 1976, causing 30,000 casualties and leaving a fifth of the population homeless. Yet despite its hurricane, Honduras recorded the strongest gain in real GDP (6.6 percent per year). At the other extreme, Nicaragua's GDP dropped by 1.8 percent per year. El Salvador achieved no significant change at all. Per-capita real GDP growth in the region fell to 1 percent per annum, with substantial decreases in real GDP per capita recorded for El Salvador and Nicaragua.

The economic performance of the countries of Central America has been deeply affected by the deterioration in the political and military situation since 1978, and by external economic factors as well. These factors include the second increase of oil prices in 1979 and the worst world recession in the postwar period, which severely reduced traditional exports, both in prices and in quantities, and generated the highest interest rate in the 20th century. As a result real GDP in Nicaragua shrank by 17.4 percent (19.4 percent on a per-capita basis) in 1979 and 1.2 percent in 1982 (3.7 percent on a per-capita basis). El Salvador showed a decline in real GDP of 9.5 percent

(12.1 percent in per-capita terms) in 1981 and 5.4 percent (8.1 percent in per-cpaita terms) in 1982. Official data on the national product for all countries for 1983 were not available at the time this report was prepared, but preliminary estimates suggest that real GDP stagnated in El Salvador and actually declined in all the other countries except Costa Rica. An equally pessimistic picture is forecast for the entire region in the next two to three years, unless some internal and external actions are taken in the short run.

3.2.2 Inflation. The price level in the Central American nations was quite stable during the 1960s. Inflation during this period as measured by either consumer price indices or wholesale price indices rose, on the average, less than 2 percent per year (Table 3.3). In El Salvador and Guatemala consumer prices rose only 0.7 and 0.8 percent per annum, respectively, while wholesale prices rose at an annual average rate of 1.1 percent. To a large extent, this price stability is attributable to the passive monetary and fiscal policies followed by the governments, although there is some evidence that the increased availability of goods and the reduction in transportation costs resulting from the formation of the CACM may have helped.

In the first half of the 1970s the price stability of the previous decade gave way to near double-digit inflation. Consumer prices in Costa Rica rose at a rate of 13.7 percent per year and in Nicaragua at 9.3 percent. The inflationary pressures were primarily in the import sector: in addition to the unprecedented price increases of crude oil, the price of industrial products imported from developed countries rose considerably. Expansive fiscal policies also helped to boost inflation, particularly in Costa Rica, where government spending has increased at an average rate of 35 percent in five years (1978–82). In the period 1975 to 1980, the record was mixed. Inflation in Panama fell to about 6.8 percent per year and in Honduras it hovered around 9.9 percent. However, Nicaragua, El Salvador, and Guatemala reached double-digit inflation rates of 19.4, 13.0, and 10.7 percent respectively. The situation was particularly acute in three countries: Costa Rica, where consumer prices in 1981 rose by 37.0 percent and in 1982 by 90.1 percent; Nicaragua, where consumer prices rose by 23.9 percent in 1981 and 24.8

percent in 1982; and El Salvador, where consumer prices rose by 14.8 percent in 1981 and 11.7 percent in 1982.

3.2.3 Structure of Domestic Product. Over the last two decades significant changes have occurred in the structure of production in the Central American countries (Tables 3.4, 3.5). The share of the primary sector (agriculture and mining) in the regional GDP, which approximated 29 percent in 1960–64, fell to about 23 percent in 1976–80. At the same time, the share of the secondary sector (manufacturing, construction, and such basic services as electricity, gas, water, transportation, and communications) rose from 25 to 33 percent, and that of the tertiary sector (services including commerce, finance, government, etc.) fell from 47 to 44 percent.

For the region as a whole, agriculture continues to be the most important economic activity, accounting for 23 percent of the region's GDP in 1979, reduced from 25 percent in 1970 and 29 percent in 1960. As discussed below, agricultural products generated most of the export earnings of the Central American nations.

The contribution of agriculture to each nation's GDP varied significantly in 1982, ranging from more than 29.9 percent in Honduras to 9.8 percent in Panama. In the other four countries, the contribution of the agricultural sector to GDP in 1982 was 20.7 percent for Costa Rica, 23.7 percent for Nicaragua, 25 percent for El Salvador, and 25.4 percent for Guatemala.[3] The most significant declines in the contribution of agriculture to GDP over the period 1960–82 occurred in Panama (from 18.5 to 9.8 percent) and El Salvador (from 30.8 to 25 percent); Honduras remained the most dependent on agriculture, recording the smallest decline (from 33.3 to 29.9 percent) during the same period.

While the region's agricultural output grew moderately during the 1960s, virtually no progress has been made since 1976 (Table 3.6). Between 1970 and 1980 agricultural output expanded 2.6 percent per year. In effect, per capita food production did not expand during the 1970s and declined after 1974. Between 1978 and 1980 the agricultural production of the region fell by 8.5 percent as a result of declines of 20.2 percent in El Salvador and 29.4 percent in Nicaragua. Between 1978 and 1980 the region's per capita food production fell by

11.1 percent, with Nicaragua's per capita food output declining by nearly 30.2 percent and El Salvador's by 16.2 percent.

In the decade of the 1960s, manufacturing output in Central America expanded rapidly, with the share of GDP generated by this sector rising from roughly 13.2 percent in 1960 to 17 percent in 1970 (Table 3.7). This expansion was particularly noticeable in Nicaragua where the manufacturing sector's share of GDP rose from 16 percent in 1960 to 21 percent in 1970. Gains in the manufacturing sector during this period can be attributed partly to the formation of the CACM, which eliminated intra-regional tariffs and erected high external tariffs, and to the adoption of import substitution policies. Industrialization schemes, developed by regional institutions and funded in part by the Alliance for Progress and other programs, were instrumental in the brisk expansion of the manufacturing sector.

Between 1970 and 1980 the share of GDP generated by manufacturing declined from 17 to 14 percent. The lack of dynamism in the manufacturing sector during the 1970s has been attributed to the end of the "easy" stage of import substitution, and to the difficulties the protected industries faced in competing successfully in third markets. Also significant in the decline of the share of manufacturing in GDP have been the sharp decreases in industrial output in war-torn El Salvador and Nicaragua, as well as reduced demand in these two countries for industrial products originating in the other countries.

3.2.4 Energy. The Central American nations depend on imported petroleum and petroleum products to meet the bulk of their commercial energy needs. They have no significant coal reserves and, with the exception of Guatemala, have not been successful in finding petroleum in commercial quantities.

Hydroelectric resources, estimated to be quite abundant, have been only partially developed. Yet, except in Nicaragua, sizable hydroelectric plants are expected to come on-line in the next few years. Preliminary analyses suggest that geothermal resources could make a significant contribution to the energy balance of the region, but so far they have been utilized very little. Conservation measures instituted since 1973 have curtailed the growth of energy consumption: for the region as a whole, per capita consumption of commercial energy stood roughly at the same level in 1979 as in 1975.

Between 1970 and 1980 the generation of electrical energy in the region doubled from 4,536 to 8,137 million kilowatt-hours. For the entire region 53 percent of the electric power generated in 1979 originated from thermoelectric plants (fueled with petroleum products), 43 percent from hydroelectric plants, and 4 percent from geothermal plants (all in El Salvador). Hydroelectricity is particularly significant in Costa Rica and El Salvador, where it accounted for 77 percent and 58 percent, respectively, of total electricity generated in 1979.

3.2.5 Employment/Unemployment. The statistical data related to employment/unemployment in Central America are very weak. Costa Rica and Panama are the only countries that carry out periodic employment/unemployment surveys. The fragmentary data available, either from official sources or from special studies, point out that failure of the economies to generate a sufficient number of job opportunities, especially in recent years, is one of the most critical problems plaguing the region.

In 1960 total employment in the five Central American Common Market (CACM) nations was the equivalent of 3.3 million man-years (Table 3.8). Between 1960 and 1971 employment in the CACM nations expanded by the equivalent of 1.1 million man-years, or at an average rate of 2.7 percent per year; particularly notable were gains in job opportunities of 3.4 and 2.9 percent per year in Honduras and El Salvador, respectively. These job-creation efforts were outpaced, however, by the expansion in the supply of labor, which was estimated to have increased during the same period by the equivalent of over 1.25 million man-years, or at the rate of 3 percent per year. By vigorous economic growth during the 1960s the CACM nations created the equivalent of 1.1 million man-years of new job opportunities—yet the equivalent of 250,000 man-years of new entrants into the labor force could not find employment and were added to the already large number of unemployed. For the period 1971–75, estimates suggest that the situation worsened. While the equivalent of 423,000 man-years of new jobs were created (a growth rate of 2.3 percent per year), the supply of labor grew at a faster rate—the equivalent of 506,000 man-years or 2.7 percent per year. Thus, from 1960 to 1975 not only did the CACM nations fail to reduce unemployment, but the unemployment gap increased by the equivalent of 223,000 man-years. As will be discussed below, the growing unemployment gap results largely from the lack of dynamism of productive investment. In addition, there is evidence to suggest that most of the new industrial investments in the region have been oriented toward capital-intensive production techniques, for which the cost per job created has been very high; consequently, relatively few job opportunities have been created. Recent studies have demonstrated that the contribution of industry to GNP in Costa Rica is much larger (22 percent) than its contribution to total employment (15 percent), and that it takes four times as much in financial investment to create a new job in industry than in the agricultural sector.

According to official data or special surveys, the open unemployment rate in Costa Rica in 1973 was 7.1 percent, while it was estimated to be 6.5 in Panama and 18.5 in the urban sector of Nicaragua (Table 3.9). For El Salvador, it has been estimated that the open unemployment rate in 1974 was 13.1 percent. There is no evidence to suggest that there have been any significant declines from these high unemployment rates; in fact, the open unemployment rate has been reported to have risen to 8.7 percent in Panama in mid-1979 and to 9.3 percent in Costa Rica in April 1982. The unemployment rate has decreased slightly in Costa Rica in 1983 due to the large absorption of labor by the public sector—10,800 new jobs from June 1982 to June 1983.

3.3 EXTERNAL SECTOR

The economies of the six Central American nations are characterized by a high degree of openness. In 1982, exports accounted for approximately 17 percent and imports comprised 24 percent of the area's GDP (Table 3.10). Rising prices for imported manufactured products, coupled with dramatic increases in world oil prices, have pushed up the import bill and led to a situation of chronic trade deficits. Exports tend to be concentrated in a few basic agricultural commodities; severe declines in world prices for these commodities throughout the late 1970s and early 1980s have had a deep impact on export earnings. To finance the rising import bill, the Central American nations have been forced to increase their external debt substantially.

3.3.1 Balance of Payments. The merchandise trade balance of the Central American nations deteriorated severely during the 1970s and early 1980s (Table 3.11). In 1970 the merchandise trade of the five CACM nations was roughly in balance (exports of $1,161 million versus imports of $1,130 million), while Panama's was in deficit by roughly $200 million. By 1975, the CACM countries ran a combined merchandise deficit of $350 million; when Panama is included, the deficit approximated $845 million for the entire region. In 1981, the last year for which detailed official balance-of-payments data are available for all six countries, the deficit for the region exceeded $2,049 million. Three Central American countries ran a merchandise trade surplus in 1981: Panama, Guatemala, and Nicaragua, where economic activity and imports declined severely as a result of the civil war.

The services account—which includes transactions in the category of freight and insurance on international shipments, transportation other than freight, travel, investment income, transactions in goods and services of central governments, etc.—underwent a similar though less abrupt pattern of deterioration for the CACM members. Though exports of services from these nations grew substantially, they were outpaced by growth in the income obtained by foreigners from their investments in the region; this resulted in massive net deficits in the services account. The picture for Panama is quite different, since the Panama Canal yielded substantial service income which exceeded debits in the services account. Thus, in 1981 Panama showed a surplus in the service account of more than $511 million. For the region as a whole, however, the services account recorded a deficit of $829 million in 1981. Net unrequited transfers, and payments without a quid pro quo—such as remittances by migrants to their families, contributions for missionary, educational, and charitable purposes, and official foreign aid grants—rose from $54 million in 1970 to approximately $375 million in 1979.

Spurred by these trends, the combined current account deficit of the six Central American nations reached $2,579 million in 1981, higher than the record deficit of $1,260 million in 1978 and a tenfold increase over the $240 million deficit reached in 1970. The 1979 current account deficit was particularly large in Costa Rica, where it amounted to more than 17 percent of that year's GDP. In 1980 it was 14.8 percent of GNP, but was reduced to 8.2 percent in 1982 by the vast devaluation that occurred in that and the previous year; it is expected to increase again to 12.6 percent in 1983.

In the 1970s, the Central American nations financed their burgeoning current account deficits by turning increasingly to capital from abroad. Net capital inflow into the region (private direct investment, private long-term capital flows, and government medium- and long-term capital transactions), which amounted to $295 million in 1970, rose to $1,490 million in 1978, dropped to $1,160 million in 1979, and rose again to $1,854 million in 1981, with long-term capital flows received by the official sector accounting for the bulk of the increases. Except in 1979 and recent years, these substantial long-term capital inflows have exceeded the current account deficit and produced a small positive basic balance for the entire region. International reserves of the Central American nations declined by $267 million in 1979.

3.3.2 Merchandise Trade. The composition of merchandise trade in Central America varies quite markedly, depending on whether it is inter- or intra-regional (Tables 3.12, 3.13). The main external markets for Central American exports in 1979 were the United States (35.4 percent) and the European Community (25.4 percent); intra-regional trade accounted for approximately one-fifth of exports. On the import side, the United States was the main source of extra-regional imports (33 percent), followed by other Latin American nations (14 percent) and the European Community (12.4 percent); approximately 16 percent of imports originated within the region. Trade with the Council for Mutual Economic Assistance (COMECON) members was insignificant, accounting for less than 1 percent of exports or imports.

In trade outside the region, primarily with the United States and the European Community, the predominantly agricultural Central American nations derive most of their export earnings from basic agricultural commodities: coffee, bananas, cotton, sugar, wood, and meat (Table 3.14). The importance of these commodities and the consequences of fluctuations in their world prices cannot be overstated. Coffee and banana exports accounted for almost 70 percent of Honduras' total export earnings in 1980. The key commodity exports of the Central American nations, and the percentage of 1980 export earnings accounted by each, were as follows:

	Coffee	Bananas	Sugar	Meat/ Frozen Meat	Cotton	Wood	Shrimp
Costa Rica	36.5%	16.9%	1.9%	7.1%			
El Salvador	53.8%				9.0%		
Guatemala	42.7%	4.3%	4.0%	1.0%	12.7%		
Honduras	51.3%	18.6%		6.4%		7.0%	
Nicaragua	36.8%			13.0%	6.7%		
Panama	15.0%	17.3%	7.9%				12.1%

Given the high concentration on a few basic export commodities, the Central American economies are vulnerable to fluctuations in export earnings caused by the volatility of commodity prices (Table 3.15). For example, between 1975 and 1977, the average world market price for the mild coffees typically exported by Central American nations rose from $0.65 to $2.35 per pound as a result of the adverse weather conditions that affected Brazilian production. Coffee export earnings of the Central American nations, particularly of El Salvador and Costa Rica, boomed. However, by 1980 coffee export prices had fallen to $1.54 per pound, and the consequent decline in export earnings deeply affected the economies.

In addition to dependence on the export of a few commodities for their earnings of foreign exchange, the Central American countries have discovered a new balance of payments constraint: they depend largely on imported materials for their industrial production. So, the reduction of foreign exchange earnings, loans, or bilateral aid limits the expansion of industrial production and growth. Central America's imports from outside the region are primarily manufactured goods (machinery and capital goods, transportation equipment, chemicals), foodstuffs from the United States and European Community, and crude oil from Venezuela and, lately, Mexico. Over the decade of the 1960s these import patterns were basically unchanged; however, the composition of imports during the 1970s changed substantially, reflecting the larger share accounted for by oil imports.

The burden of the so-called energy crisis on the Central American economies may be illustrated by the following: the combined oil import bill for Costa Rica, El Salvador, Guatemala, Honduras, and Nicaragua in 1970 amounted to $37.3 million, or 2.3 percent of total imports of these five countries (Table 3.16). For Panama alone, 1970 crude oil imports amounted to $59.7 million, or 16.7 percent of total imports. This very high oil import level, compared to other Central American nations, is largely attributable to the oil refining industry in Panama, and a significant portion is exported in the form of refined petroleum products. By 1975, the first year after the 1973–74 world oil price increases, the oil bill of five Central American nations (excluding Panama) had risen eightfold to $318 million or 8.3 percent of total imports; by 1979, it had climbed to $436 million or 12.2 percent of total imports. It should be stressed that the very large oil bill increase discussed above was primarily the result of price increases, since import volume remained almost constant or even declined during the 1970s.

In August 1980, the presidents of Mexico and Venezuela announced a joint oil supply financing facility which would make available "soft" loans to Caribbean and Central American nations to assist them in meeting their oil needs; all six Central American nations were designated as beneficiaries. The arrangement provides for Mexico and Venezuela to earmark up to 160,000 barrels of oil per day to meet the needs of the Caribbean nations. This oil would be sold at prevailing world prices. However, Mexico and Venezuela would extend five-year loans to cover 30 percent of the value of the oil at an interest rate of 4 percent per year. Should the loan receipts be used for high-priority development programs, particularly in the energy sector, the maturity of the loans could be increased to 20 years and the interest rate lowered to 2 percent. Specific contracts under the agreement have already been signed by all six Central American nations, and they have been continued in spite of the serious economic difficulties faced lately by both Mexico and Venezuela.

An important portion of the foreign trade of Central American nations takes place among the five members of the CACM: Costa Rica, El Salvador, Guatemala, Honduras, and Nicaragua. In 1979, 21 percent of the exports and 18 percent of the imports of these five countries occurred among themselves. Panama, not a member of the arrangement, has steadily increased its trade with the CACM nations; in 1979, 10 percent of Panama's exports went to the CACM while the five nations provided 5 percent of Panamanian imports. Because the commodity composition of intra-CACM trade differs substantially from the inter-regional trade of the Central American nations, it is useful to review the institutional framework, accomplishments, and problems of the CACM.

The CACM was formally created in December 1960 when representatives of five Central American nations signed the General Treaty on Central American Economic Cooperation. The treaty provided for the immediate elimination of tariffs on all intra-zonal trade (except those on a special list, less than 10 percent of the total, which would be the subject of further negotiations), and for the establishment of a rather high common external tariff. The treaty also contained provisions for the establishment of new "integration industries" in the region, following the principle of balanced development. Coordination of the CACM lies with the Permanent Secretariat of the General Treaty of Central American Economic Integration (SIECA). Other important regional organizations associated with the CACM include the Central American Bank for Economic Integration (CABEI), the main financial institution of the CACM plan; the Central American Clearing House, an institution administered by CABEI to facilitate inter-regional payments; the Joint Programming Mission, an instrument to introduce and promote regional development; the Central American Institute of Technological and Industrial Research (ICAITI) for providing technical support for industrial development; and the

Central American Institute of Public Administration (ICAP), an institution to train government officials in the administration of the integration program.

By June 1961, Guatemala, Nicaragua, and El Salvador had ratified the treaty, and it became operable for these three countries. Honduras ratified the treaty in April 1962 and Costa Rica in September 1963; with the latter ratification, the five-country Common Market became operative.

The CACM was quite effective during its first eight years of operation. As a result of the elimination of internal tariffs, intra-regional trade grew between 1960 and 1963 from 3.5 percent of the region's trade to more than 27 percent; exports of manufactured goods rose much more rapidly than exports of agricultural commodities, so that by 1968, two-thirds of intra-regional exports were manufactured commodities. Intra-industry specialization increased; instability in the export sector of some countries was reduced; and according to several studies, efficiency of resource use was enhanced in the region.

Despite this impressive performance, the overprotection granted to local industries and the policies on import substitution and subsidies created new economic difficulties for the entire region. Insufficient competition from third countries and the granting of generous tax benefits turned production toward the internal market, instead of expanding exports to larger markets. This led to a virtual stagnation of industrial production and increased unemployment problems. That, plus pressures building within the CACM, eventually led to disruption. The treaty establishing the CACM did not provide for preferential treatment for relatively less-developed countries within the region. By 1968, Honduras and Nicaragua had expressed dissatisfaction with the way in which the benefits of the CACM were being distributed; in their view, the remaining three countries, with more developed industrial sectors, were gaining the lion's share of the intra-regional industrial trade. The situation worsened in mid-1969 when open military confrontation between El Salvador and Honduras erupted. Shortly after, Honduras withdrew from the arrangement, and the CACM entered into a critical stage. Despite multilateral diplomatic efforts, Honduras has not returned to the fold of the CACM.

3.4 DEVELOPMENT FINANCING

Gross domestic investment as a percentage of GNP in Central America rose considerably during the 1960s and early 1970s, in some cases quite sharply. Despite these positive trends, the evidence is quite strong that investment would have had to expand considerably faster or undergo substantial changes in composition to have absorbed the new entrants into the labor force. In fact, the tax exemptions and subsidies granted to imported capital goods, coupled with the taxation of salaries to pay for social benefits and security, distorted the relative prices of capital and labor. Most new investments were channeled to capital-intensive industrial projects and relatively less to labor-intensive agricultural activity, thus augmenting the problems of underemployment and open unemployment.

Domestic savings, generally the primary source of development financing, also expanded during these two decades, but were insufficient to meet investment needs, so sizable external financing was required. The low national savings rates are symptomatic of the skewed income distribution and lack of integration of segments of the population into the national economy—a characteristic of several of the Central American nations—and policies by monetary and financial authorities which have not provided for positive real interest rates, nor adjusted them according to the conditions prevailing in the international financial markets in recent years. Financial policies in this respect have been rather conservative. The central banks have always been reluctant to stimulate domestic financial savings through adjustments of the interest rates paid to savings and time deposits. This attitude has prevented financial intermediaries from collecting from the public sufficient resources to finance the development projects internally, and has provoked a less efficient allocation of resources.

There was an attempt to liberalize the financial market in Costa Rica in 1978 which yielded some positive effects. Interest rates were adjusted to conform with inflation, and the banks were able to more than double their funds. However, the government was the beneficiary of the additional resources, which it used to finance its deficit. At present, interest rates in real terms are positive in Costa Rica, but the problem persists in the other Central American countries.

3.4.1 Investment/Savings. For the period 1960–64 gross domestic investment as a percentage of GNP in Central America averaged about 16 percent (Table 3.17). At one extreme, Panama and Costa Rica exhibited ratios of 18.6 and 18.4, respectively, while at the other, Guatemala's ratio was only 10.4 percent, the lowest in Latin America except for Haiti (7.9). For Latin America as a whole, the gross-investment-to-GNP ratio was 18 percent, with Brazil (22.2), Peru (24.2), and Venezuela (24.1) reaching significantly higher investment rates. During 1960–64 national savings in the Central American nations averaged 11.8 percent of GNP, enough to finance only 76 percent of investment needs (Tables 3.18, 3.19).

During the second half of the 1960s and the first half of the 1970s, the situation did not change drastically, although there was a general tendency for both the investment and savings ratios to rise. The savings coefficient as a percent of gross investment fell to 70 percent between 1965 and 1969 and to 68 percent between 1970 and 1974, suggesting the area's increased dependence on foreign capital. In more recent periods, the investment coefficient for the region rose to a high of 23.8 in 1977, declined to 23.1 in 1978, and fell to 19.3 in 1979. Investment rates in Nicaragua fell precipitously in both years. The investment coefficient also declined notably in Guatemala and El Salvador in 1979.

The national savings ratio fluctuated severely during the period 1975–79. Relatively high inflation rates; restrictions on the rate of return of financial instruments; and price controls on certain agricultural products, which led to negative real rates of return, dried up savings in the mid-1970s and reduced the incentives to invest. As inflation moderated, the savings ratio recovered to about 16 percent of GNP in 1976 and 18 percent in 1977. However, political and exchange-rate instability in the region and the attractiveness of virtually risk-free, high-yield savings instruments in the United States and other countries, which stimulated the flight abroad of savings, led to declines in the savings ratio to 15.4 percent of GDP in 1978 and 14.5 percent in 1979, and deepened the dependence on foreign capital for development.

3.4.2 Private Foreign Direct Investment. An important source of capital for the development of Central America has been private foreign direct investment. In 1960 net private foreign direct investment in the region amounted to $34.7 million, with almost all of it flowing into Guatemala and Panama. Foreign direct investment grew by 47 percent between 1960 and 1965 and doubled between 1965 and 1970 (Table 3.20). In the latter year, foreign investment was more evenly distributed among the countries, with the shares received by Panama and Guatemala falling to 31 and 21 percent, respectively. Costa Rica (24 percent), Nicaragua (14 percent), and Honduras (8 percent) showed significant increases.

The rising trend in private foreign direct investment continued through the first half of the 1970s; between 1970 and 1975, it increased by 71 percent to $187.6 million. In 1976, however, private foreign direct investment declined abruptly to $94.4 million, primarily as a result of disinvestments in Panama and reduced levels of investment in Guatemala. It recovered again in 1977 ($213.0 million), in 1978 ($218.1 million), and in 1979 (more than $216.1 million). Thus, between 1970 and 1979, private direct foreign investment roughly doubled, from $109 million per year to approximately $216 million per year.

In 1978 the value of US private direct investment in Central America amounted to $3,187 million (Table 3.21). Approximately $2,394 million, or 75 percent of the investments, was concentrated in Panama and the remaining $793 million in the other five Central American nations. US investments in Panama were primarily in finance and insurance (41 percent), trade (30 percent), and manufacturing (8 percent). For the other five countries, 36 percent of US investments were concentrated in manufacturing (primarily food manufacturing and production of chemicals and allied products), 12 percent in trade, and 8.3 percent in finance and insurance. US investors increased their position in Central America by $535 million in 1979 and $501 million in 1980 with the bulk of the new investment flowing into Panama. Nearly one fifth of the new investment went into the petroleum sector.

A portion of US private investments in Central America was insured against political risks by an institution of the US government, the Overseas Private Investment

Corporation (OPIC). OPIC insurance programs offer coverage in eligible developing countries against: a) the inability to convert into dollars the local currency received by the investor as profits, earnings, or return on the original investment; b) the loss of investment due to expropriation, nationalization, or confiscation by action of a foreign government; and c) loss due to war, revolution, or insurrection.

Between 1948 and September 30, 1980, OPIC and its predecessor agencies issued convertibility insurance to US investors in Central America for over $320 million, expropriation insurance for over $430 million, and war-risk insurance of approximately $345 million (Table 3.22). Insurance actually granted by OPIC has decreased in recent years due to the political instability in the area. The report of Kissinger's Commission (Appendix 1) suggested a review of OPIC policies to stimulate US private investment in Central America.

3.4.3 External Financing. In the 1960s and early 1970s, the Central American economies depended on external sources for a portion of their capital formation needs. The Central American nations generally were moderate borrowers, though there were substantial differences among countries. Multilateral institutions, official bilateral credits, and supplier credits were the most common sources of funds. Loan maturities differed substantially, but there was a large component of medium- and long-term loans (10–15 years or longer). Because external credits were generally used for developmental purposes, there was a close correlation between external debt and economic growth. However, beginning in 1974, these patterns changed abruptly; increasing portions of external financing provided by private commercial banks were used for consumption (primarily of oil) rather than productive investment.

Over one-half of the outstanding external public debt had maturity of more than 10 years in 1970 and 78.1 percent was held by multilateral institutions or by foreign governments. By 1975, after the unprecedented oil price increases, Central America's external debt had more than tripled to $3,776 million or 34.4 percent of GDP; by 1979, it had reached $8,401 million or 55.5 percent of the region's GDP (Table 3.23). The degree of indebtedness varied widely among the countries. Panama's debt in 1974 was equivalent to 92 percent of its GDP; the percentage was 79 percent for Nicaragua, 61 percent for El Salvador, 66 percent for Costa Rica, 61 percent for Honduras, and 12 percent for Guatemala. The debt had shorter maturity—only 43.7 percent had a maturity of over 10 years versus 51.5 percent in 1970 (Table 3.24)—and a larger share was held by private banks: 22.2 percent in 1979 versus 8.8 percent in 1970 (Table 3.25). The interest rate on the external debt held by private banks is not fixed but fluctuates according to conditions in the international financial markets.

The burden imposed on the Central American economies by the growing external debt and the increasing real interest rate in the international financial markets is illustrated by the following example. In 1970 the Central American nations met their debt servicing needs with the equivalent of 7.7 percent of their exported goods and services (Table 3.26). The ratio of external debt service to value of exports of goods and services in 1970 ranged from 12 for Nicaragua to 3.1 for Guatemala. By 1979, the debt-service-to-exports ratio for the region had climbed to 17.6 with the individual ratios ranging from 35.5 for Panama to 2.2 for Guatemala. Costa Rica now has one of the highest per capita external debts in the world (approximately $1,300). A large portion of these obligations were contracted, unfortunately, on short term and commercial conditions. This public debt has been restructured in what appears to be a favorable arrangement, providing for a three year period of grace and capitalization of overdue interest.

An important source of development financing for the Central American nations has been official developmental assistance either received bilaterally or channeled through multilateral institutions. By far the most significant sources of developmental assistance to the Central American nations have been the industrialized countries, members of the Development Assistance Committee (DAC) of the Organization for Economic Cooperation and Development (OECD). Up to 1979, assistance to Central America from the communist member-countries of the Council for Mutual Economic Assistance (COMECON) and from the OPEC nations was negligible.

Bilateral concessional assistance to the six Central

American nations from DAC members grew rapidly during the 1970s, from $82.8 million in 1970 to $218.7 million in 1979 (Table 3.27). Though concessional assistance trended toward expansion during the period, it fluctuated substantially as a result of spurts coinciding with relief for natural disasters. In the absence of these irregular fluctuations, actual assistance may have been markedly lower in view of the policies of some DAC members to target assistance to the least developed among the developing countries (mainly Asian and African countries).

Among the DAC countries, the United States was the principal source of economic assistance to the Central American nations. US economic assistance to the region, which amounted to $17.1 million from 1949–52, grew to $308.2 million from 1953–61 and reached $1,283 million from 1968–76 (Table 3.28). In 1977, US economic assistance amounted to $71 million, in 1978 to $85 million, and in 1979 to $123 million. Thus, US economic assistance from 1962–79 amounted to $1,578 million. This financial aid has been increased in recent years, and Kissinger's Commission recommended that the US increase aid to the region up to a total of $8 billion over the next five years.

Multilateral organizations such as the World Bank (officially named the International Bank for Reconstruction and Development, or IBRD) and its adjunct institutions, the International Finance Corporation (IFC) and the International Development Agency (IDA); the Inter-American Development Bank (IDB); the Organization of American States (OAS); the United Nations Development Program (UNDP); and other specialized United Nations agencies have provided development cooperation funds and technical assistance to the Central American nations. These organizations, which depend heavily on the DAC countries for funding, provided assistance to the Central American nations valued at $802 million during the period 1962–72 (Table 3.29). During 1973–79, the flow of assistance to Central America from these organizations rose to $2,647 million.

In recent years, the Central American nations have increasingly turned to the International Monetary Fund for assistance in financing their balance of payment deficits and foreign debt crises. In 1974 and 1975, Costa Rica, El Salvador, Honduras, Nicaragua, and Panama withdrew the equivalent of Special Drawing Rights (SDR)[4] 112.5 million from the IMF oil facility to finance balance of payments deficits arising from the escalation of world oil prices. The Central American nations also used the equivalent of SDR 85.1 million from the Compensatory Financing Facility, which enables members to draw on quotas when they experience difficulties produced by temporary shortfalls in export receipts attributable to circumstances largely beyond their control.

In 1980 Costa Rica, El Salvador, and Panama were granted stand-by arrangements by the IMF; in 1981, Costa Rica and the IMF discussed the feasibility of a stabilization agreement. Stand-by arrangements are typically short-term lines of credit opened by the IMF to guarantee the convertibility of a country's currency during periods of balance of payment deficit. As a requirement for the use of the Fund's resources, the recipient country generally agrees to certain conditions, usually referred to as "conditionality," aimed at redressing the payment imbalances. Costa Rica's one-year arrangement approved by the IMF for SDR 80 million in December 1982 was conditioned on systematic reductions in government expenditures, increases in taxes, and monetary and financial adjustments; Costa Rica has been successful in meeting specific adjustments to which it made commitments, achieving during the standby period an impressive reduction in inflation and a reasonable stability of the exchange rate. The generous foreign aid, particularly from the US, has contributed greatly to maintaining the exchange rate stability. Panama's arrangement for SDR 63.75 million over 20 months, concluded in April 1980, and El Salvador's one-year arrangement of June 1980 for SDR 10.75 million, were also conditioned on reductions in government expenditures and in central bank credits, respectively. Costa Rica has asked the IMF for another stand-by arrangement for 1984.

3.5 CONCLUSION AND RECOMMENDATIONS

In the 1960s and early 1970s the Central American nations made substantial economic gains. The confluence of political stability, relatively favorable prices for agricultural exports, increased intra-regional trade resulting from economic integration, and increased external cooperation in the region's development spurred by the Alliance for Progress created a favorable climate in which economic growth could occur. While real economic growth took place during this "golden" period, social development lagged behind, with the exception of Costa Rica and Panama. Social and economic structures which tended to perpetuate income and wealth differences did not evolve to provide the basis for an equitable distribution of economic gains. Excluding Costa Rica and Panama, government intervention in the economy to foster socio-economic development was minor.

As the decade of the 1970s began, the Central American nations were ill prepared to deal effectively with the rising economic challenges. The sluggish economic performance caused by the import substitution strategy and excessive protectionism; the breakdown of the CACM (which actually occurred in 1969 following the Honduras-El Salvador confrontation); the 1973 and 1974 oil crisis; the severe inflation; and the spotty growth record of the industrial countries, especially after 1979, generated enormous economic pressures which exacerbated economic and social inequities. Economic performance of the Central American nations during the 1970s and early 1980s has been very uneven and has lagged behind the rest of Latin America.

Considering that the area has one of the fastest growing populations in the world, economic gains on a per capita basis were hardly significant for the region as a whole, and actual declines in absolute terms were recorded in Nicaragua and Costa Rica. A significant portion of the economic growth achieved during the 1970s was financed through external loans, and the region's external debt rose substantially during that period, especially in Costa Rica, Nicaragua, and Panama. Some feeble attempts to integrate marginal segments of the population into the economic system and to redistribute land through agrarian reform were undertaken, but they appear to have been too little, too late.

In the 1980s and 1990s the Central American nations are sure to face unresolved social and economic challenges similar to those of the 1970s, along with some new ones. External financing has already begun to dry up, and the Central American nations may have to turn increasingly to the IMF for balance of payment relief in order to control their internal and external imbalances, and to secure enough public foreign aid to undertake the needed structural reforms without at the same time exposing the population to severe social costs. Foreign direct investment, which remained an important source of developmental financing during the early 1970s, may accelerate its flight unless political stability is achieved; the same concern applies to domestic capital. Servicing of the high external public debt, which already takes a considerable fraction of export earnings and public expenditures in some Central American countries, may retard economic relief from higher export prices. Chronic unemployment/underemployment problems are likely to deepen to risky levels as political instability discourages investment and reduces economic activity.

How will the Central American nations deal with these and other critical issues in the 1980s and 1990s? Will they seek quick-fix solutions or attempt the spadework necessary to get at deeply-rooted social ills? Is there still time to undertake social and economic reforms —or has time run out? These are complex questions which resist simple solutions. In the following paragraphs, some of these key issues will be identified and some policies recommended which might ease the stranglehold on economic development in Central America.

3.5.1 Reform Monetary and Fiscal Institutions to Increase Domestic Savings and Investment. The existing monetary and fiscal policies need to be reformed so that additional savings can be generated and channeled into the financial intermediation system, and sound investment projects can be assured adequate financing. Domestic savings generated in the region are insufficient to support an investment program which will make a significant contribution to the elimination of the unemployment/underemployment problem. In the long run, domestic savings can be increased by a more equitable distribution of income and wealth. In the short run, the monetary and fiscal authorities need to institute policies to make the real interest rate attractive to savers. These policies need to be applied in a flexible manner, taking into account domestic inflation, the rates prevailing in the main foreign financial markets, the expectations of changes in the exchange rates, and the supply and demand of financial resources, in order to maintain positive interest rates in real terms that are consistent with the real return on capital. Reportedly, substantial volumes of savings are flowing from Central American nations to US banks in Miami, driven by higher returns in US institutions and instability in the region. Aggressive policies to keep domestic savings at home are needed, as are those geared to encouraging domestic investment through more flexible price policies and better allocation of resources.

3.5.2 Target Investment Incentives to Maximize Employment Creation. A system of investment incentives giving highest priority to employment creation needs to be developed. Consideration might be given to activities such as food processing and canning and light industries for the domestic and export markets. Technical assistance from multilateral organizations (IDB, IBRD, etc.) could be utilized to evaluate the employment-creation contribution of projects, and resources from these and other institutions used to finance projects which will have high employment-creation potential. It will be necessary to eliminate or reduce substantially the bias in favor of capital-intensive investments, and to re-establish the true relative prices of capital and labor through a better functioning of the market system. A comprehensive legal and economic reform must be undertaken in most countries to improve the organization of production.

3.5.3 Establish National Export Development Strategies. Present and potential exports should be analyzed, and a comprehensive strategy to increase revenues from traditional and non-traditional exports developed. Elements which should be considered in such a strategy are: a) export promotion programs, b) export financing programs, c) flexible exchange rate policies, designed to maintain permanently the profitability of the exporting activity, d) temporary fiscal incentives for exporters, and e) a substantial reform of the tariff structures as suggested below. In targeting investments for export, it is necessary to be mindful of potential over-supply of some products in the world market, and of potential problems which might arise from protectionist actions by importing countries.

3.5.4 Implement Energy Policies to Reduce Dependence on Imported Petroleum. The Central American nations which possess vast hydric resources need to reduce their dependence on imported petroleum and their escalating oil import bills. Several initiatives may be studied in this area:

A. Exploration for potential oil resources should be stepped up. Funding for this purpose may be available from the IBRD and IDB. However, the Central American nations may find it more expedient to turn to the international oil companies, the technological leaders in this field. As long as the proper relationship of non-interference in domestic affairs is maintained, the oil companies may be able to provide services unavailable elsewhere without increasing the financial burden of the Central American nations.

B. Substantial untapped hydroelectric and geothermal energy resources should be harnessed using long-term financing available from the IBRD and the IDB, and concessionary loans from Mexico and Venezuela.

C. The possibility of using non-traditional energy sources, such as biomass, should be explored using these same funding institutions and technical assistance from other Latin American nations.

D. The price system should be used to promote the more efficient use of energy (gasoline and electricity), avoiding unnecessary subsidies and the misuse of the country's limited resources by the public enterprises in charge of the energy programs.

E. Household energy conservation should be promoted through educational programs.

3.5.5 Provide an Appropriate Climate for the Expansion of Foreign Investment. Despite the sensitive political problems it often raises, foreign investment brings important benefits to the recipient country and serves as an important mechanism for technological transfer. However, foreign investors often need to be reassured that they will be treated fairly and their investments will not be nationalized without appropriate compensation. Statements by each of the nations reaffirming their support of the principle of fair treatment for foreign investors would be useful to maintain and attract foreign investment.

An ancillary issue to such government statements is the actual insurance of US investments in the region. An important US program which insures investment by US citizens and corporations in developing countries against inconvertibility, expropriation, and war risks is operated by the Overseas Private Investment Corporation (OPIC). The US government should consider lifting or amending the present requirements to permit the full and more effective operation of OPIC in all six countries. Other countries should be encouraged to adopt similar programs.

3.5.6 Seek New Approaches to Deal with the Foreign Exchange Shortage Created by Chronic Balance of Payment Deficits. Chronic balance of payments deficits have led some Central American nations to resort to the imposition of protectionist measures, such as import surcharges and other limitations on each other's trade, which are bound to be counterproductive. These actions lead to retaliatory measures by other countries and, given the high level of trade interdependence among the Central American nations, are ineffective. The IMF stabilization programs, which are typically short-term in nature and assume the existence of normal conditions, are useful in controlling inflation and exchange rates instability in the short run, but impose severe performance criteria on the Central American nations which are difficult to implement at the same time that efforts are being made to improve the standard of living of their people. A concerted effort by the United States, the European Economic Community, and Japan to ease the liquidity problem of the Central American nations may be a complementary approach to deal with this problem as indicated in 3.5.9.

3.5.7 Reorganize the Public Sector and Revise Fiscal Policies and Taxation. As a result of the virtual stagnation of the private sector, and the political attitude favorable to the expansion of the role of government in economic development, the size of the public sector has grown beyond the economic capability of the Central American nations. The governments and their agencies have increased their share of GNP from 13.7 percent in 1970 to 23.8 percent in 1982, causing a transfer of resources from the more productive private sector to less productive government spending.

Due to the inability of private industry to absorb the

growing labor force, the government has become the employer of last resort. Yet the unemployment problem persists as the increased expenditures require more taxes on the private sector, which discourage investments and growth. If the government attempted to finance its deficit by borrowing in the internal or external markets, the result has been a crowding-out of the private firms from the financial market, or a burdensome increase in total foreign debt. In both cases, inflation, the exchange rate, and the cost of money tended to rise while production and growth stagnated.

To overcome these problems, the size of the public sector needs to be reduced, or limited at least, and the expansionary fiscal policies revised. There is little room for more expansion of employment in this sector. The excess labor force should be absorbed, therefore, by the revitalized private sector that should emerge after the introduction of the structural and financial reforms suggested in this chapter.

3.5.8 Restructure the Central American Common Market. Although the formation of the CACM in 1958 had a positive economic impact on the region during its first decade of operation, it became evident later on that the import substitution strategy and protectionist plans were responsible, together with other internal and external factors, for the stagnation of economic growth.

There is a need to reivse the tariff structure common to all Central American countries, the Central American Agreement on Tax Incentives, and the traditional policies for stimulating industrial investments. The objective should be to make industry more competitive so that it can export to third countries, and allow a more productive allocation of resources, particularly of those that are abundant, such as labor. The CACM needs to redefine its comparative advantages by taking into account the relative prices of capital, labor, and other resources, according to world prices. This will require a substantial change in the tax incentives and subsidies granted to capital; a reduction of payroll taxes, if possible; liberalization of exchange rates, interest, and monetary policy; and a profound revision of the generalized custom duties and tariffs. It would be necessary to undertake technical studies to modify this structure, taking into account that the level of the average effective protection is at present too high, that no protection whatsoever was afforded to locally produced intermediate goods, and that the tax benefits and protection for finished industrial products were given on a discriminatory basis. A substantial reduction of all tariffs, on a more even basis, with some temporary protection for the production of local raw materials and intermediate goods, would certainly make industry more efficient and competitive in third markets in the long run. The exchange rates should probably be adjusted upward, but the adjustments should help to stimulate exports, adjust the volume of imports, and balance the trade account.

All these changes should be announced as soon as possible, but implemented gradually to avoid or minimize the social and economic disruptions that will inevitably occur in such a comprehensive reform. Foreign aid and technical assistance should play a very important role in this transitional period.

3.5.9 The Role of Foreign Assistance. The structural changes suggested above call for the design of a new comprehensive economic strategy in which foreign assistance plays a very important role. The reduction of government expenditures, and the time needed for private production to adjust to the new economic model, will probably exacerbate unemployment. Foreign assistance would come in very handy to alleviate this transition problem. The financing of specific labor-intensive projects that yield returns on a short-term basis would be very productive.

As the tariff structure is modified and the level of duties reduced, there will be additional pressure on the balance of payments coming from increased imports of finished goods. The private sector will need some time before new exporting activities addressed to third countries are developed. Foreign assistance in the form of balance-of-payments support should be very useful, while the Caribbean Basin Initiative proposed by President Reagan in 1982 and adopted by the US Congress, and the more recent recommendations (January 1984) of Kissinger's Commission on Central America (see Appendix 1), will open up a unique opportunity for stimulating the productive sectors in Central America and facilitating the introduction of Central American products to the largest market in the world, as well as increasing foreign assistance to Central America.

The economic future of the Central American countries lies more in external growth than in internal production for the CACM. In order to implement this process, substantial amounts of foreign assistance will be needed. Fortunately, there are indications that friendly governments are prepared to provide such assistance in generous terms. A word of caution: foreign financial support should not be used to finance government spending nor to avoid the implementation of the structural changes that are necessary. If excess financing is provided with no requirements for internal changes, the governments will try to maintain the status quo. Linking the disbursement of soft loans and grants to the observance of IMF conditionality may prove useful but not sufficient. Central American officials need to be persuaded of the economic benefits associated with a prompt structural change, lest the social conditions and democratic institutions deteriorate to a point of no return.

NOTES

1 For a more detailed account of the unemployment/underemployment problem, see Chapter 2, "Social Context."

2 For a detailed account of Central America's population growth, see Chapter 2, section 2.3 "Population Size, Growth, and Structure."

3 It should be noted that in Nicaragua, the share of GDP originating from the agricultural sector declined from 23 percent in 1970 to 21.9 percent in the mid-1970s. The increase in the share of GDP accounted for by agriculture in 1979 can be attributed to the war conditions in the country affecting economic activity in general and the output of the industrial sector in particular.

4 SDRs are Special Drawing Rights, an artificial unit of account created by the International Monetary Fund to supplement traditional international reserves in the role of making payments between countries. The value of the SDR is set on a basket of currencies; the US dollar value of the SDR is calculated daily. For example, in 1974 and 1975, the average US dollar value of the SDR was $1.20264 and $1.21415, respectively. In 1980, the US dollar value of the SDR rose to $1.30153.

TABLE 3.1
Gross Domestic Product and Average Annual Growth Rates, 1980-1982 (in millions of US $ at 1980 prices)

	1960	1970	1975	1980	1981	1982	1960-1970	1970-1975	1975-1980	1981	1982
Costa Rica	1106.3	1970.1	2641.4	3410.3	3254.8	3053.0	5.9	6.0	5.1	-4.6	-6.2
El Salvador	1409.3	2439.7	3183.0	3342.1	3024.5	2861.9	5.6	5.5	0.6	-9.5	-5.4
Guatemala	2855.2	4878.5	6402.4	8454.6	8529.7	8231.2	5.5	5.6	5.7	0.9	-3.5
Honduras	933.3	1518.8	1709.6	2420.4	2432.1	2404.0	4.8	2.3	6.6	0.5	-1.2
Nicaragua	1044.4	2036.3	2668.6	2219.4	2408.0	2374.3	6.9	5.6	-1.8	8.5	-1.4
Panama	922.4	1980.5	2517.9	3325.5	3452.4	3493.9	8.0	4.9	3.4	3.8	1.2
Central America	8270.9	14823.9	19122.9	23172.3	23101.5	22418.3	6.0	5.2	3.7	-0.3	-3.0
Latin America	172457.9	298961.3	410465.4	536943.1	544319.0	538019.4	5.6	6.5	5.2	1.4	-1.2

Growth rates (percent per year)

Source: Inter-American Development Bank: *Economic and Social Progress in Latin America*, 1983 report, p. 363.

TABLE 3.2
Per Capita Gross Domestic Product and Average Annual Growth Rates, 1960-1982 (in US $ at 1980 prices)

	1960	1970	1975	1980	1981	1982	1960-1970	1970-1975	1975-1980	1981	1982
									Growth rates (percent per year)		
Costa Rica	838.1	1150.1	1353.2	1537.6	1433.0	1310.3	2.6	3.4	2.5	−6.8	−8.6
El Salvador	529.4	681.7	766.8	694.4	610.4	560.4	2.1	2.3	−2.3	−12.1	−8.1
Guatemala	728.2	927.6	1051.3	1208.0	1183.8	1110.7	2.2	2.6	2.7	−2.0	−6.2
Honduras	469.5	560.6	540.7	653.6	636.6	609.9	1.2	−0.8	3.4	−2.6	−4.2
Nicaragua	694.9	1067.3	1241.3	916.3	971.3	934.8	4.2	2.1	−4.1	6.0	−3.7
Panama	756.1	1323.0	1427.4	1754.9	1779.5	1759.2	4.8	1.7	1.3	1.4	−1.1
Central America	655.9	889.8	999.6	1038.5	1005.7	945.9	3.1	2.2	1.0	−3.2	−6.0
Latin America	821.8	1110.0	1334.5	1556.4	1540.8	1503.2	2.7	3.7	2.5	−1.0	−3.4

Source: Inter-American Development Bank. *Economic and Social Progress in Latin America*, 1983 report, pages 130 and 363.

TABLE 3.3
Central America: Consumer and Wholesale Price Indexes, 1960-1982 (1975 = 100)

	1960	1970	1975	1980	1981	1982	1960-1970	1970-1975	1975-1980	1981	1982
Consumer Prices											
Costa Rica (San José)	41.9	52.7	100.0	147.4	202.0	384.1	2.3	13.7	8.1	37.0	90.1
El Salvador (San Salvador)	62.0	66.2	100.0	184.3	211.6	236.5	0.7	8.6	13.0	14.8	11.7
Guatemala (Guatemala City)	61.4	66.6	100.0	166.0	185.1	185.4	0.8	8.4	10.7	11.5	0.2
Honduras (Tegucigalpa)	59.2	73.6	100.0	159.7	174.7	191.1	2.2	6.3	9.9	9.4	9.4
Nicaragua (Managua)	53.9	64.1	100.0	240.2	297.6	371.4	1.7	9.3	19.4	23.9	24.8
Panama (Panama City)	62.3	70.7	100.0	139.2	149.4	155.8	1.3	7.2	6.8	7.3	4.3
Wholesale Prices											
Costa Rica	35.3	45.1	100.0	184.2	292.4	608.8	2.5	17.3	13.0	58.7	108.2
El Salvador	57.8	64.7	100.0	185.0	195.7	211.2	1.1	9.1	13.1	5.8	7.9
Guatemala	56.1	62.6	100.0	165.6	185.0	173.9	1.1	9.8	10.6	11.8	−6.0
Panama	na	53.3	100.0	160.2	176.2	195.6	na	13.4	9.9	10.0	11.0

Source: World Tables (1982) Boletin Estadistico de la OEA and International Financial Statistics.

TABLE 3.4
Structure and Growth of Central American Gross Domestic Product[1], 1960-1980 (in percent)

	Agriculture and Mining				Manufacturing, Construction, and Basic Services[2]				Services (Trade, Finance, Government, and Others)			
	Average Share of GDP		Average Annual Variations		Average Share of GDP		Average Annual Variations		Average Share of GDP		Average Annual Variations	
	1960-1964	1976-1980	1976-1980	1980	1960-1964	1975-1979	1976-1980	1980	1960-1964	1976-1980	1976-1980	1980
Costa Rica	25.3	18.9	1.8	−0.9	24.9	36.4	7.4	2.5	49.8	44.7	5.4	1.0
El Salvador	31.4	23.0	0.3	−5.9	24.1	31.4	0.6	−14.9	44.5	45.6	1.8	−7.9
Guatemala	30.2	26.2	3.5	2.4	21.2	27.6	8.7	5.5	48.7	46.3	5.3	2.9
Honduras	35.9	31.3	4.9	−2.4	24.5	30.5	6.8	3.8	39.6	38.2	5.4	3.1
Nicaragua	26.6	25.1	−1.6	−9.0	26.5	36.0	−0.8	−17.7	46.8	38.9	−0.8	18.7
Panama	22.2	15.9	1.0	10.5	27.4	34.0	5.6	12.3	50.4	50.1	2.8	2.3
Central America	28.6	23.4	—	—	24.8	32.7	—	—	46.6	44.0	—	—
Latin America	20.7	15.1	—	—	35.9	43.9	—	—	43.4	41.0	—	—

Source: Inter-American Development Bank, *Annual Report 1981*, p. 109.
[1] At constant market prices converted to U.S. dollars of 1980 purchasing power.
[2] Basic services include electricity, gas and water, and transportation and communications.

TABLE 3.5
Central America: GDP by Sector of Origin, 1960-1982 (in millions of US $ at 1980 prices)

	1960	1970	1975	1980	1981	1982	1960-70	1970-75	1975-80	1981	1982
Costa Rica											
Agriculture	287.7	474.9	560.5	613.7	621.0	631.7	5.14	3.37	1.37	1.19	1.72
Manufacturing and Mining	157.1	366.3	561.0	749.2	721.2	674.4	8.84	8.90	6.03	−3.74	−6.49
Electricity, Gas, and Water	13.3	37.6	55.2	79.5	86.1	87.7	11.00	7.99	8.62	8.30	1.86
Construction	47.6	81.0	136.0	213.0	188.3	113.1	5.45	10.92	6.53	−11.60	−39.94
Wholesale and Retail Trade	232.3	392.2	455.3	615.3	501.5	412.2	5.38	3.03	6.74	−18.50	−17.81
Transportation and Communication	45.4	87.6	152.8	239.1	240.5	240.8	6.79	11.76	8.65	0.59	0.12
Financial Services	163.7	234.6	326.7	411.8	407.5	405.5	3.66	6.85	4.98	−1.04	−0.49
Government	99.6	194.1	272.1	341.7	346.8	349.6	5.48	3.67	4.96	1.49	0.81
Other Services	59.7	101.8	121.3	146.9	141.7	138.1	6.91	6.99	4.34	−3.54	−2.54
Total GDP (at market prices)	1,106.3	1,970.1	2,641.4	3,410.3	3,254.8	3,053.0	5.94	6.04	5.05	−4.56	−6.20
El Salvador											
Agriculture	434.4	639.3	802.5	860.3	773.2	716.0	3.94	4.66	1.53	−10.12	−7.40
Mining	2.8	3.7	4.6	4.0	3.9	3.9	3.03	4.70	−4.38	−2.50	0.00
Manufacturing	204.4	446.7	589.1	568.6	479.0	450.8	8.13	5.69	−1.37	−15.76	−5.89
Electricity, Gas, and Water	15.9	45.9	71.9	103.7	100.3	96.3	11.13	9.40	7.16	−3.28	−3.99
Construction	41.3	65.0	130.5	94.4	93.2	88.4	4.65	14.95	−3.67	−1.27	−5.15
Wholesale and Retail Trade	341.0	576.5	722.8	704.2	606.1	577.8	5.39	4.63	−1.11	−13.93	−4.67
Transportation and Communication	64.1	130.4	176.2	197.4	174.1	162.8	7.36	6.21	3.15	−11.80	−6.49
Financial Services	89.2	144.1	191.7	231.4	230.2	94.5	4.91	5.88	3.45	−0.52	−58.95
Government	114.0	186.4	248.6	338.4	346.4	337.7	7.02	3.97	0.19	2.36	53.17
Other Services	102.3	201.7	245.0	239.7	218.0	333.9	5.05	5.93	6.06	−9.05	−2.51
Total GDP (at market prices)	1,409.3	2,439.7	3,183.0	3,342.1	3,024.5	2,861.9	5.64	5.46	0.84	−9.50	−5.38

TABLE 3.5 (Continued)

	1960	1970	1975	1980	1981	1982	1960-70	1970-75	1975-80	1981	1982
Guatemala											
Agriculture	865.7	1,332.6	1,795.8	2,100.9	2,103.8	2090.2	4.41	6.15	3.53	1.42	−1.91
Mining	5.2	4.6	5.7	40.3	25.6	28.8	−1.20	4.24	42.68	−36.48	12.50
Manufacturing	368.7	769.9	969.6	1,407.7	1,373.2	1,304.6	7.64	4.72	7.84	−2.45	−5.00
Electricity, Gas, and Water	19.9	58.8	89.3	114.8	144.5	135.0	11.46	8.72	9.97	−0.21	−6.57
Construction	56.3	77.3	119.5	266.4	309.4	253.9	3.21	9.10	16.62	16.14	−17.94
Wholesale and Retail Trade	747.0	1,409.4	1,765.3	2,283.5	2,294.9	2,226.9	6.55	4.61	5.89	0.50	−2.96
Transportation and Communication	136.9	267.2	410.4	587.3	584.8	567.4	6.92	8.96	7.69	−0.43	−2.98
Financial Services	307.8	454.7	544.3	666.2	680.3	660.2	3.98	3.66	4.59	2.12	−2.96
Government	173.3	236.5	321.7	443.6	469.2	455.3	3.15	6.34	5.77	5.77	−2.96
Other Services	174.4	267.5	381.0	514.1	517.1	508.9	4.37	7.33	6.08	0.58	−1.59
Total GDP (at market prices)	2,855.2	4,878.5	6,402.4	8,454.6	8,529.7	8,231.2	5.50	5.59	5.94	0.89	−3.50
Honduras											
Agriculture	310.7	527.4	491.4	709.4	712.1	718.2	5.41	−1.37	7.11	0.38	0.86
Mining	15.6	33.7	42.9	52.6	53.7	52.2	8.05	4.85	6.09	2.09	−2.79
Manufacturing	111.8	220.3	253.5	397.5	411.0	406.1	7.05	2.79	10.26	3.40	−1.19
Electricity, Gas, and Water	6.5	18.1	23.6	44.7	44.5	45.7	9.94	5.43	17.00	−0.45	2.70
Construction	40.3	54.4	76.6	101.3	92.9	88.8	5.71	7.02	4.52	−8.29	−4.41
Wholesale and Retail Trade	120.9	181.4	208.5	298.8	295.8	287.3	5.18	2.82	5.58	−1.00	−2.87
Transportation and Communication	72.8	105.0	131.4	161.9	161.0	156.7	2.54	4.58	14.32	−0.56	−2.67
Financial Services	88.4	154.2	202.7	281.7	280.1	276.8	4.43	5.62	13.31	−0.57	−1.18
Government	39.0	51.8	66.2	113.2	117.8	114.9	1.86	5.02	18.55	4.06	−2.46
Other Services	127.4	172.4	203.1	259.3	263.1	257.2	1.87	3.33	12.52	1.46	−2.24
Total GDP (at market prices)	933.3	1,518.8	1,697.9	2,420.4	2,432.1	2,404.0	4.85	2.25	9.05	0.48	−1.16

Nicaragua

Agriculture	257.2	490.1	652.2	501.5	552.3	562.8	6.18	5.83	−2.04	10.13	1.90
Mining	12.4	72.3	58.0	27.0	27.7	22.5	1.32	−4.32	3.11	2.59	−18.77
Manufacturing	163.3	425.0	566.2	556.8	572.6	572.9	11.09	5.90	−1.61	2.84	0.05
Electricity, Gas, and Water	13.8	31.9	41.9	53.3	57.7	57.3	11.25	5.62	3.35	8.26	−0.69
Construction	22.8	73.2	140.5	53.0	76.6	57.1	11.72	13.93	9.98	44.53	−25.46
Wholesale and Retail	234.1	435.1	555.1	443.1	491.2	463.1	6.52	5.48	−5.75	10.86	−5.72
Transportation and Communication	59.5	110.6	144.3	134.7	149.4	143.4	6.53	5.47	−2.64	10.91	−4.02
Financial Services	125.7	153.1	163.1	155.2	165.8	155.2	4.40	1.27	−6.62	6.83	−6.39
Government	68.7	103.3	140.3	178.2	185.4	200.6	2.08	0.32	4.53	4.04	8.20
Other Services	87.1	137.8	158.4	116.7	129.3	139.4	4.82	4.48	−11.98	10.80	8.04
Total GDP (at market prices)	1,044.4	2,036.3	2,668.7	2,219.4	2,408.0	2,374.3	6.90	5.56	−3.46	8.50	−1.40

Panama

Agriculture	170.3	289.2	329.6	344.4	354.5	343.5	5.34	2.65	0.31	2.93	−3.10
Mining	1.7	3.7	5.3	6.0	7.0	7.4	7.83	7.44	2.33	16.67	5.71
Manufacturing	88.6	246.9	281.2	347.2	337.7	349.4	10.92	2.63	−0.46	−2.74	2.87
Electricity, Gas, and Water	13.6	42.3	71.7	103.8	109.8	119.7	11.97	11.15	6.47	5.78	9.02
Construction	55.7	132.3	162.9	245.3	273.8	268.6	8.96	4.25	1.50	11.62	−1.90
Wholesale and Retail Trade	142.0	312.2	379.0	494.9	495.7	475.9	8.14	3.95	0.98	0.16	−4.00
Transportation and Communication	38.2	118.7	188.2	340.2	360.9	347.4	11.95	9.96	13.11	6.08	−3.80
Financial Services	101.2	216.2	349.0	349.1	350.8	364.0	7.80	10.05	6.17	0.49	3.76
Government	110.5	228.5	331.3	390.2	419.3	431.9	7.47	7.13	3.41	7.46	3.01
Other Services	200.5	390.6	466.3	704.4	742.8	788.4	6.82	3.60	11.56	5.45	6.14
Total GDP (at market prices)	922.4	1,980.5	2,591.3	3,325.5	3,452.4	3,493.9	7.82	4.92	4.77	3.82	1.20

129

ECONOMIC CONTEXT

TABLE 3.6
Indices of Agrcultural and Food Production, 1970-80.
(1961-1985 = 100)

	1970	1972	1974	1976	1978	1980
Total Agricultural Production						
Costa Rica	148	158	161	173	189	187
El Salvador	117	118.	153	144	163	130
Guatemala	121	143	152	183	194	187
Honduras	127	138	137	142	166	180
Nicaragua	118	130	146	151	163	115
Panama	147	143	141	148	163	155
Central America	127	138	149	159	175	160
Per Capita Agricultural Production						
Costa Rica	118	119	116	119	126	120
El Salvador	92	87	105	93	99	74
Guatamala	99	111	111	126	127	115
Honduras	100	102	94	91	100	101
Nicaragua	97	100	107	105	107	71
Panama	119	110	102	102	106	97
Central America	103	105	107	107	112	97
Total Food Production						
Costa Rica	160	171	171	192	205	187
El Salvador	136	132	152	164	192	170
Guatemala	141	156	169	199	205	204
Honduras	127	133	129	131	154	163
Nicaragua	132	134	151	156	177	132
Panama	149	146	144	149	164	156
Central America	141	146	153	166	183	171
Per Capital Food Production						
Costa Rica	128	129	123	132	136	119
El Salvador	107	97	105	106	117	98
Guatemala	116	121	124	138	134	124
Honduras	100	98	88	84	92	92
Nicaragua	108	104	111	108	116	81
Panama	121	112	105	103	107	97
Central America	114	111	110	112	117	104

Source: U.S. Department of Agriculture, *Indices of Agricultural Production for the Western Hemisphere, 1970 through 1979* and updates.

TABLE 3.7
Structure of Manufacturing Value Added in Central America, 1960, 1970, 1980, 1982

	\multicolumn{4}{c	}{Percent of total value added in region}	\multicolumn{4}{c}{Share of manufacturing in GDP}
	1960	1970	1980	1982	1960	1970	1980	1982
Costa Rica	14.4	14.8	18.6	18.0	14.2	18.6	22.0	22.1
El Salvador	18.7	18.0	14.1	12.0	14.5	18.3	17.0	15.8
Guatemala	33.7	31.1	35.0	34.7	12.9	15.8	16.7	15.8
Honduras	10.2	8.9	9.9	10.8	12.0	14.5	16.4	16.9
Nicaragua	14.9	17.2	13.8	15.3	15.6	20.9	25.1	24.1
Panama	8.1	10.0	8.6	9.2	9.6	12.5	10.4	9.9

Source: Inter-American Development Bank, *Economic and Social Progress in Latin America*, 1983 report.

TABLE 3.8
Central American Common Market: Growth in Labor Demand and Supply

	Actual Employment 1960	\multicolumn{4}{c	}{Growth in Labor Demand}	\multicolumn{4}{c}{Growth in Labor Supply}
		\multicolumn{2}{c	}{(Thousand man-years)}	\multicolumn{2}{c	}{(Percent)}	\multicolumn{2}{c	}{(Thousand man-years)}	\multicolumn{2}{c}{(Percent)}
		1960-1971[a]	1971-1975[b]	1960-1971	1971-1975	1960-1971[b]	1971-1975[b]	1960-1971	1971-1975
Guatemala	1,254	339	167	2.2	2.5	362	151	2.3	2.3
El Salvador	741	284	121	2.9	2.8	318	151	3.3	3.4
Honduras	567	259	55	3.4	1.6	257	58	3.5	1.7
Nicaragua	367	113	30	2.4	1.5	131	59	2.8	2.8
Costa Rica	338	114	50	2.6	2.7	181	87	4.0	4.0
Central America	3,268	1,109	423	2.7	2.3	1,249	506	3.0	2.7

Source: Derived from data in Clark W. Reynolds and Gustavo A. Leiva, "Employment Problems of Export Economies in a Common Market: The Case of Central America," in *Economic Integration in Central America*, William R. Cline and Enrique Delgado, editors (Washington: Brookings Institution, 1978), tables 6, 10, and 12.
[a]Observed
[b]Estimated

TABLE 3.9
Economically Active Population and Unemployment Rates in Central America

	Economically Active Population (thousands)	Unemployment Rate (%)	Numbers Unemployed (thousands)
Costa Rica (1973)	578	7.1	41
El Salvador (1974)	1,464	13.1	192
Guatemala ( )	na	13.0	na
Honduras (1973)	847	10-12	93
Nicaragua (1973)[a]	na	18.7	na
Panama (1973)	552	6.5	36

Sources: OIT/PREALC, El Problema del Empleo en América Latina (Santiago de Chile, April 1976), pp. 8-10; for Guatemala-World Bank, Guatemala: Economic and Social Position and Prospects (Washington: The World Bank, 1978), p. 14.
[a] urban

TABLE 3.10
The External Sector in the Central American Economies, 1982 (in millions of US $)

	G.D.P.	Exports Value	Exports As a % of G.D.P.	Imports Value	Imports As a % of G.D.P.
Costa Rica	2,428.1	870.8	35.9	866.8	35.7
El Salvador	3,662.8	700.4	19.1	883.0	24.1
Guatemala	8,859.7	1,199.6	13.5	1,388.0	15.7
Honduras	2,801.5	684.2	24.4	711.7	25.4
Nicaragua	2,901.9	407.7	14.0	775.5	26.7
Panama	4,317.5	345.0	8.0	1,459.3	33.8
Central America	24,971.5	4,207.7	16.9	6,084.3	24.4

TABLE 3.11
Central American Nations: Balance of Payments, 1965-1981 (in millions of US $)

	1965	1970	1975	1980	1981	1965-70	1970-75	1975-80	1980	1981
Costa Rica										
Merchandise Exports, FOB	111.7	231.0	433.1	1,000.9	1,029.7	15.64	16.38	15.38	6.24	2.88
Merchandise Imports, FOB	−160.9	−286.8	−627.2	−1,375.2	−1,092.2	12.25	16.94	17.01	9.39	−20.58
Other Goods, Services and Income										
Credits	25.6	50.1	112.1	217.7	216.6	13.78	18.04	12.75	28.66	−0.51
Debits	−52.6	−74.1	−205.2	−521.8	−553.9	6.62	23.05	20.40	22.92	6.15
Unrequited Transfers (net)										
Private	4.9	3.4	9.5	19.8	26.5	−7.05	22.81	11.54	20.00	33.84
Official	3.5	2.5	0.1	−5.3	−0.1	−6.51	−47.47	47.58	23.26	−98.11
Current Account Balance	−67.8	−74.1	−217.6	−663.9	−373.4	1.79	24.04	24.59	18.94	−43.76
Long Term Capital Transactions	—	43.8	238.0	402.4	160.8	5.83	40.29	8.09	14.09	−60.04
Direct Investment	0.1	26.4	69.0	48.1	45.7	205.01	21.19	−29.29	13.44	−4.99
Portfolio Investment	—	−0.4	0.0	124.2	0.9	—	—	—	—	−99.28
Other Long-Term Capital Transactions	—	17.8	169.0	230.1	114.2	−9.97	56.85	6.34	−25.85	−50.37
Short-Term Capital Transactions	13.4	24.2	−59.9	39.3	−454.8	11.35	—	—	−5.76	—
Errors and Omissions (net)	15.5	−9.5	33.0	−69.4	81.8	—	—	—	—	—
Allocation of SDR's	0.0	4.2	0.0	5.6	5.3	—	—	0.49	1.82	−5.36
Monetization of Gold	0.0	0.0	0.0	0.0	−27.6	—	—	—	—	—
Changes in Valuation of Reserves	—	—	—	−64.5	0.6	—	41.88	94.79	—	—
Liabilities Held as Reserves by Foreign Authorities	0.0	−0.1	4.0	100.7	−5.6	—	175.95	—	—	—
Changes in Reserves	5.9	11.5	2.5	−33.2	70.3	21.40	7.43	—	—	—

TABLE 3.11 (Continued)

El Salvador	1965	1970	1975	1980	1981	1965-70	1970-75	1975-80	1980	1981
Merchandise Exports, FOB	190.0	276.1	533.0	968.6	794.1	4.44	17.69	12.69	−20.88	—
Merchandise Imports, FOB	−185.7	−194.7	−550.7	−906.6	899.5	0.95	23.11	10.48	−3.40	—
Other Goods, Services and Income										
Credits	24.4	24.4	67.0	195.4	172.2	0.00	22.39	23.87	−12.53	—
Debits	−54.6	−71.4	−169.6	−392.1	−382.6	5.51	18.89	18.25	−9.03	—
Unrequited Transfers (net)										
Private	9.7	12.4	25.1	17.4	45.2	5.03	15.15	−7.07	−61.25	—
Official	3.6	1.9	2.3	31.6	15.2	−12.00	3.9	68.89	386.15	—
Current Account Balance	−12.6	8.7	−92.9	−85.7	−250.4	—	—	−1.60	—	—
Long-Term Capital Transactions	—	−1.4	69.7	111.9	190.5	—	—	9.93	92.27	—
Direct Investment	7.2	3.7	13.1	5.9	−5.8	−12.47	18.17	−14.75	—	—
Portfolio Investment	—	0.0	0.0	−1.0	—	—	—	—	−82.46	—
Other Long-Term Capital Transactions	—	−5.1	56.8	107.0	—	—	—	13.58	44.79	—
Short-Term Transactions	−3.7	11.9	18.2	−73.7	—	—	—	—	−31.38	—
Errors and Omissions (net)	−3.1	−17.0	9.6	−209.4	—	33.20	—	—	−2.24	—
Allocation of SDR's	0.0	4.2	0.0	5.9	5.6	—	—	—	1.72	—
Monetization of Gold	0.0	0.0	0.0	0.0	—	—	—	—	—	—
Changes in Valuation of Reserves	2.4	0.0	0.0	0.7	—	—	—	0.00	75.00	—
Liabilities Held as Reserves by Foreign Authorities	0.1	0.0	0.0	0.0	—	—	—	—	—	−5.08
Changes in Reserves	−5.2	−6.4	−30.4	69.0	—	4.24	36.56	—	−45.92	—

Guatemala	1965	1970	1975	1978	1979	1980	1981
Merchandise Exports, FOB	192.1	297.1	640.9	1,092.4	1,221.4	1,519.4	1,299.0
Merchandise Imports, FOB	−206.1	−266.6	−672.4	−1,283.8	−1,401.7	−1,472.6	−1,540.0

Other Goods, Services and Income						
Credits	36.7	56.6	156.5	256.7	330.6	314.2	234.6
Debits	−64.8	−112.5	−268.6	−451.4	−482.5	−634.5	−649.5
Unrequited Transfers (net)						
Private	3.5	17.4	78.3	115.0	123.2	108.6	89.4
Official	4.0	0.1	−0.5	0.6	3.4	1.2	1.4
Current Account Balance	−34.6	−7.9	−65.8	−270.5	−205.6	−163.3	−565.1
Long-Term Capital Transactions		52.0	168.7	267.8	257.5	246.5	415.7
Direct Investment	14.1	29.4	80.0	127.2	117.0	110.7	127.1
Portfolio Investment		−1.5	−2.4	11.7	5.3	3.9	0.3
Other Long-Term Capital Transactions		24.1	91.1	128.9	135.2	131.9	288.3
Short-Term Capital Transactions	25.0	−27.2	11.8	131.1	−44.3	−316.0	−143.7
Errors and Omissions (net)	−20.9	−0.8	−10.7	−58.6	−44.3	−18.1	−11.3
Allocation of SDR's	0.0	4.2	0.0	0.0	6.9	7.0	6.6
Monetization of Gold	0.0	0.0	0.0	0.0	0.0	0.0	0.0
Changes in Valuation of Reserves		−3.6	−1.2	2.1	0.5	−1.6	−6.2
Liabilities Held as Reserves by Foreign Authorities	0.0	0.0	0.0	0.0	0.0	0.0	0.0
Changes in Reserves	−8.8	−16.7	−102.9	−71.9	29.3	245.5	303.9
Honduras						
Merchandise Exports, FOB	128.2	178.2	309.7	626.2	750.1	850.3	738.8
Merchandise Imports, FOB	−113.2	−203.4	−372.4	−654.5	−783.5	−954.1	−898.6
Other Goods, Services and Income						
Credits	11.9	20.6	41.0	80.4	102.7	117.2	119.4
Debits	−37.6	−65.8	−108.4	−226.5	−288.3	−351.7	−334.8
Unrequited Transfers (net)						
Private	0.4	2.9	4.9	4.5	6.9	7.5	8.9
Official	3.3	3.7	12.6	12.9	13.6	14.0	18.6
Current Account Balance	−7.0	−63.8	−112.6	−157.0	−198.5	−316.8	−302.7
Long-Term Capital Transactions		35.1	94.2	175.6	156.9	239.2	207.4

135

ECONOMIC CONTEXT

TABLE 3.11 (Continued)

	1965	1970	1975	1978	1979	1980	1981
Direct Investment	6.3	8.4	7.0	13.2	9.9	5.8	−3.6
Portfolio Investment	—	0.0	0.0	−0.6	−0.1	−0.1	−0.3
Other Long-Term Capital Transactions	—	26.7	87.2	163.0	147.1	233.5	211.3
Short-Term Capital Transactions	6.1	10.5	35.1	−21.4	68.3	11.9	25.3
Errors and Omissions (net)	−3.9	5.8	66.0	12.7	16.5	−40.5	11.1
Allocation of SDR's	0.0	3.2	0.0	0.0	4.6	4.7	4.4
Monetization of Gold	0.0	0.0	0.0	0.0	0.0	0.0	0.0
Changes in Valuation of Reserves	—	−0.1	−53.1	0.2	0.3	0.2	−17.5
Liabilities Held as Reserves by Foreign Authorities	0.2	−0.5	−0.6	0.0	−0.0	0.0	2.9
Changes in Reserves	−6.2	9.8	−54.2	−9.9	−25.0	73.0	69.0
Nicaragua							
Merchandise Exports, FOB	149.2	178.6	374.9	646.0	615.9	450.4	499.8
Merchandise Imports, FOB	−133.9	−178.6	−482.1	−553.3	−388.9	−802.9	−922.4
Other Goods, Services and Income							
Credits	—	39.2	82.9	85.9	67.2	63.6	73.4
Debits	—	−84.8	−117.4	−213.0	−205.7	−214.1	−235.4
Unrequited Transfers (net)							
Private	2.5	2.5	4.1	0.1	1.4	1.6	13.2
Official	—	3.6	12.5	9.4	90.2	122.3	57.1
Current Account Balance	—	−39.5	−185.1	−24.9	180.2	379.1	−514.3
Long-Term Capital Transactions	—	45.9	152.3	79.9	38.9	343.3	596.4
Direct Investment	—	15.0	10.9	7.0	2.8	—	—
Portfolio Investment	—	0.0	0.0	0.0	0.0	—	—
Other Long-Term Capital Transactions	—	30.9	141.4	72.9	36.1	—	—
Short-Term Capital Transactions	—	1.8	46.3	−173.1	−263.1	—	—

Error and Omissions (net)	−6.9	−0.6	−1.3	−10.0	−29.1	—
Allocation of SDR's	0.0	3.2	0.0	0.0	4.6	4.7	4.4
Monetization of Gold	—	0.1	0.0	0.0	0.0	—	—
Changes in Valuation of Reserves	—	—	—	1.1	−1.6	—	—
Liabilities Held as Reserves by Foreign Authorities	—	−0.5	−1.3	−10.9	5.3	—	—
Changes in Reserves	−18.2	−10.3	−36.7	82.8	−8.5	—	—
Panama							
Merchandise Exports, FOB	92.5	130.3	330.9	301.9	334.0	373.4	374.6
Merchandise Imports, FOB	−192.4	−331.0	−823.1	−862.1	−1,104.9	−1,333.7	−1,458.9
Other Goods, Services and Income							
Credits	—	264.2	891.8	1,439.5	1,773.5	3,302.2	3,959.6
Debits	—	−131.7	−563.4	−1,086.1	−1,322.1	−2,602.3	−3,448.6
Unrequited Transfers (net)	−5.8	10.9	−25.6	−33.5	−37.2	53.6	49.0
Private		14.9	20.8	31.4	54.3	41.2	48.9
Official		−64.2	−168.6	−208.9	−302.4	−272.8	−573.4
Current Account Balance	—	119.8	185.4	452.9	301.3	295.3	283.3
Long-Term Capital Transactions	—	33.4	7.6	−0.7	40.3	45.2	45.4
Direct Investment	—	−1.1	1.1	70.1	204.1	16.2	25.4
Portfolio Investment	—	87.5	176.7	383.5	56.9	233.9	212.5
Other Long-Term Capital Transactions	—	15.4	77.8	−155.9	410.3	−429.1	−151.4
Short-Term Capital Transactions	3.9	−71.7	−117.3	−1.9	−436.3	417.9	370.0
Errors and Omissions (net)	0.0	4.7	0.0	0.0	6.0	6.2	5.8
Allocation of SDR's	—	0.0	0.0	0.0	0.0	0.0	0.0
Monetization of Gold	—	0.0	5.8	−8.0	0.5	−0.4	0.6
Changes in Valuation of Reserves							
Liabilities Held as Reserves by Foreign Authorities	—	0.0	0.0	0.0	0.0	0.0	0.0
Changes in Reserves	−0.6	−4.0	16.4	−78.2	20.6	−17.0	66.3

TABLE 3.12
Central America—Exports and Imports by Area or Country, 1974-1978 (in thousands of US $, Exports f.o.v, Imports c.i.f.)

	1974 Value	%	1975 Value	%	1976 Value	%	1977 Value	%	1978 Value	%	1979 Value	%
Costa Rica												
Exports	440.344	100.0	494.100	100.0	600.417	100.0	839.523	100.0	919.396	100.0	934.314	100.0
U.S.	142.104	32.3	207.257	41.9	237.125	39.5	262.383	31.3	341.803	37.2	346.847	37.1
C.A.C.M.	104.266	23.7	107.226	21.7	132.681	22.1	176.580	21.0	182.404	19.8	175.354	18.8
L.A.F.T.A.	4.468	1.0	18.228	3.7	21.277	3.5	27.335	3.3	9.235	1.0	15.068	1.6
E.C.	112.113	25.5	98.042	19.8	113.336	18.0	220.545	26.3	247.136	26.9	240.966	25.8
Mexico	1.800	0.5	9.536	1.9	10.490	1.7	4.193	0.5	847	0.1	378	0.1
Panama	18.263	4.1	17.544	3.6	21.700	3.6	23.590	2.8	28.650	3.1	35.457	3.8
Imports	719.663	100.0	693.969	100.0	800.253	100.0	1,059.276	100.0	1,211.663	100.0	1,446.126	100.0
U.S.	248.315	34.5	239.092	34.5	289.785	36.2	373.210	35.2	412.696	34.1	459.975	31.8
C.A.C.M.	114.021	15.8	114.720	16.5	136.043	17.0	168.582	15.9	203.349	16.8	213.748	14.8
L.A.F.T.A.	95.886	13.3	99.079	14.3	82.433	10.3	89.623	8.5	115.479	9.5	142.997	9.9
E.C.	101.020	14.0	100.588	14.5	96.430	12.0	129.290	12.2	145.951	12.0	179.857	12.4
Mexico	19.088	2.7	26.573	3.8	21.079	2.6	24.438	2.3	40.298	3.3	45.511	3.1
Panama	18.341	2.5	15.859	2.3	21.541	2.7	17.126	1.6	19.212	1.6	23.261	1.6
El Salvador												
Exports	462.415	100.0	513.378	100.0	720.727	100.0	972.262	100.0	630.958	100.0	1,031.720	100.0
U.S.	121.014	26.2	139.096	27.1	235.198	32.6	317.929	32.7	124.242	19.7	298.065	28.9
C.A.C.M.	149.819	32.4	141.759	27.6	176.052	24.4	211.635	21.8	233.565	37.0	266.617	25.8
L.A.F.T.A.	2.024	0.4	6.668	1.3	18.298	2.5	2.869	0.3	839	0.1	6.004	0.1
E.C.	112.461	24.3	124.749	24.3	181.455	25.2	318.939	32.8	154.197	24.4	336.755	32.6
Mexico	121	0.0	6.056	1.2	10.222	1.4	2.181	0.2	2	0.0	70	0.0
Panama	—	—	5.555	1.1	4.517	0.6	5.285	0.5	6.786	1.1	6.390	0.6
Imports	563.419	100.0	598.037	100.0	717.864	100.0	942.452	100.0	1,023.915	100.0	1,011.972	100.0
U.S.	173.779	30.8	188.177	31.5	205.081	28.6	276.989	29.4	317.276	31.0	294.951	29.1
C.A.C.M.	117.268	20.8	136.857	22.9	170.448	23.7	210.836	22.4	239.943	23.4	256.958	25.4

ECONOMIC CONTEXT

L.A.F.T.A.	73.913	13.1	70.853	11.8	75.717	10.5	120.394	12.8	116.922	11.4	138.917	13.7
E.C.	106.504	18.9	108.943	18.2	113.204	15.8	140.947	15.0	139.070	13.6	151.826	15.0
Mexico	13.862	2.5	13.237	2.2	13.167	1.8	18.320	1.9	25.575	2.5	27.202	2.7
Panama	3.051	0.5	3.274	0.6	4.191	0.6	8.060	0.9	7.184	0.7	8.224	0.8
Guatemala												
Exports	572.128	100.0	623.432	100.0	760.333	100.0	1,160.218	100.0	1,111.602	100.0	1,195.174	100.0
U.S.	188.270	32.9	143.724	23.1	267.159	35.1	383.608	33.1	339.038	30.5	322.328	27.0
C.A.C.M.	163.220	28.5	168.039	27.0	189.037	24.9	222.465	19.2	254.971	22.9	311.001	26.0
L.A.F.T.A.	6.947	1.2	5.064	0.8	6.946	0.9	9.275	0.8	8.691	0.8	10.668	0.9
E.C.	115.362	20.2	190.526	30.6	139.106	18.3	290.302	25.0	292.940	26.4	259.718	21.7
Mexico	4.475	0.8	3.636	0.6	4.592	0.6	5.910	0.5	5.297	0.5	9.312	0.8
Panama	4.155	0.7	5.096	0.8	6.729	0.9	8.863	0.8	707	0.1	1.795	0.2
Imports	700.457	100.0	732.591	100.0	838.430	100.0	1,052.507	100.0	1,260.661	100.0	1,361.756	100.0
U.S.	222.869	31.8	252.349	34.4	305.613	36.5	366.948	34.9	380.655	30.2	473.428	34.8
C.A.C.M.	122.063	17.4	103.137	14.1	106.406	12.7	105.405	10.0	207.582	16.5	207.556	15.2
L.A.F.T.A.	116.639	16.7	119.910	16.4	103.690	12.4	146.520	13.9	162.861	12.9	101.842	7.5
E.C.	124.418	17.8	128.798	17.6	129.660	15.5	172.042	16.3	211.335	16.8	218.072	16.0
Mexico	22.263	3.2	24.159	3.6	27.968	3.3	41.082	3.9	52.701	4.2	56.259	4.1
Panama	765	0.1	848	0.1	1.189	0.1	3.652	0.4	34	0.0	26	0.0
Honduras												
Exports	253.306	100.0	293.263	100.0	391.831	100.0	510.680	100.0	601.769	100.0		
U.S.	121.351	47.9	152.174	51.9	222.209	56.7	251.004	49.2	346.131	57.5		
C.A.C.M.	23.662	9.3	26.952	9.1	35.725	9.1	43.449	8.5	49.199	8.2		
L.A.F.T.A.	4.342	1.7	7.016	2.4	7.616	1.9	8.220	1.6	9.622	1.6		
E.C.	44.858	17.7	56.506	19.3	78.739	20.1	140.934	27.6	142.900	23.7		
Mexico	254	0.1	739	0.3	1.774	0.5	161	0.0	231	0.0		
Panama	4.430	1.7	4.844	1.7	1.516	0.4	858	—	1.030	0.2		
Imports	380.125	100.0	404.284	100.0	453.082	100.0	579.409	100.0	699.215	100.0		
U.S.	153.874	40.5	170.881	42.3	198.171	43.7	248.690	42.9	293.117	41.9		
C.A.C.M.	41.991	11.0	51.713	12.8	58.441	12.9	71.195	12.3	91.561	13.1		
L.A.F.T.A.	64.072	16.9	81.898	20.3	33.482	7.4	60.363	10.4	85.179	12.2		

TABLE 3.12 (Continued)

	1974 Value	%	1975 Value	%	1976 Value	%	1977 Value	%	1978 Value	%	1979 Value	%
E.C.	56.174	14.8	45.770	11.3	54.430	12.0	59.015	10.2	77.716	11.1		
Mexico	7.359	1.9	8.225	2.0	9.813	2.2	14.182	2.4	17.451	2.5		
Panama	1.401	0.4	1.732	0.4	2.588	0.6	6.176	1.1	6.879	1.0		
Nicaragua												
Exports	379.987	100.0	371.471	100.0	538.540	100.0	632.989	100.0	639.775	100.0	560.775	100.0
U.S.	72.166	19.1	103.828	28.0	167.057	31.0	149.254	23.6	156.675	24.5	186.899	33.3
C.A.C.M.	91.519	24.3	92.574	24.9	117.815	21.9	133.986	21.2	146.302	22.9	90.065	16.1
L.A.F.T.A.	6.204	1.6	1.786	0.5	7.872	1.5	16.507	2.6	2.951	0.5	3.407	0.6
E.C.	100.135	26.6	81.528	21.9	106.912	19.9	180.637	28.5	180.095	28.1	148.988	26.6
Mexico	772	0.2	410	0.1	4.501	0.8	7.506	1.2	437	0.0	532	0.1
Panama	2.162	0.6	1.017	0.3	1.955	0.4	2.212	0.3	2.979	0.5	959	0.2
Imports	559.005	100.0	516.864	100.0	532.137	100.0	761.927	100.0	593.930	100.0	359.996	100.0
U.S.	177.937	31.8	167.727	32.5	164.630	30.9	219.729	28.8	186.249	31.4	90.799	25.2
C.A.C.M.	130.671	23.4	112.678	21.8	140.342	26.4	164.456	21.7	138.924	23.4	111.161	30.9
L.A.F.T.A.	71.775	12.8	81.247	15.7	77.339	14.5	112.287	14.7	87.924	14.8	76.602	21.3
E.C.	93.842	16.8	74.068	14.3	69.267	13.0	95.856	12.6	68.350	11.5	34.799	9.7
Mexico	13.346	2.4	9.897	1.9	12.993	2.4	15.331	2.0	6.017	1.0	18.819	5.2
Panama	5.969	1.1	5.508	1.1	5.671	1.1	8.024	1.0	9.699	1.6	6.192	1.7
Panama												
Exports	210.511	100.0	286.445	100.0	236.666	100.0	249.497	100.0	244.252	100.0	291.576	100.0
U.S.	107.234	50.9	167.934	58.6	112.687	47.6	113.456	45.5	108.212	44.2	135.399	46.4
C.A.C.M.	14.256	6.8	14.771	5.2	16.732	7.1	26.705	10.7	26.580	10.9	29.625	10.2
L.A.F.T.A.	3.941	1.9	4.997	1.7	6.831	2.9	9.408	3.8	7.178	2.9	12.130	4.2
E.C.	37.035	17.6	39.706	13.9	48.296	20.4	41.505	16.6	46.559	19.1	43.883	15.1
Mexico	—	—	149	0.1	193	0.1	30	0.0	72	0.0	3.387	1.2
Imports	822.437	100.0	892.059	100.0	848.322	100.0	858.904	100.0	942.360	100.0	1,199.825	100.0
U.S.	234.135	28.5	248.865	27.9	272.706	32.1	262.707	30.6	307.826	32.7	395.028	32.9

C.A.C.M.	30.307	3.7	35.996	4.0	34.444	4.1	39.069	4.5	47.702	5.1	61.766	5.1
L.A.F.T.A.	253.890	30.9	234.191	26.3	244.045	28.8	231.117	26.9	238.762	25.3	275.266	22.9
E.C.	69.144	8.4	65.189	7.3	64.984	7.7	64.572	7.5	85.268	9.0	91.029	7.6
Mexico	n.a.	n.a.	9.679	1.1	9.400	1.1	10.907	1.3	12.477	1.3	14.198	1.2

Source: United Nations. 1980 Yearbook of International Trade statistics.

TABLE 3.13
Central America: Exports and Imports by Area or Country, 1979 (in millions of US)

	Costa Rica $	%	El Salvador $	%	Guatemala $	%	Honduras* $	%	Nicaragua $	%	Panama $	%	Total Except Panama $	%	Total $	%
Exports From:																
To:																
U.S.	346.8	37.1	298.1	28.9	322.3	27.0	346.2	57.6	186.9	33.3	135.4	46.4	1,500.3	34.7	1,635.7	35.4
C.A.C.M.	175.4	18.8	266.6	25.8	311.0	26.0	49.2	8.2	90.1	16.1	29.6	10.2	892.3	20.6	921.9	20.0
Panama	35.4	3.8	6.4	0.6	1.8	0.2	1.0	0.2	1.0	0.2	—	—	45.6	1.1	45.6	1.0
L.A.F.T.A.	15.1	1.6	6.0	0.1	10.7	0.9	9.6	1.6	3.4	0.6	12.1	4.2	44.8	1.0	56.9	1.2
E.C.	241.0	25.8	336.8	32.6	259.7	21.7	142.9	23.7	149.0	26.6	43.9	15.1	1,129.4	26.1	1,173.3	25.4
Mexico	0.4	0.1	0.0	0.0	9.3	0.8	0.1	0.0	0.5	0.1	3.4	1.2	10.3	0.2	13.7	0.3
Total	934.3	—	1,031.7	—	1,195.2	—	601.9	—	560.8	—	291.6	—	4,323.9	—	4,615.5	—
Imports of:																
From:																
U.S.	460.0	31.8	295.0	29.1	473.4	34.8	293.1	41.9	90.8	25.2	395.0	32.9	1,612.3	33.0	2,007.3	33.0
C.A.C.M.	213.7	14.8	257.0	25.4	207.6	15.2	91.6	13.1	111.2	30.9	61.8	5.1	881.1	18.1	942.9	15.5
Panama	23.3	1.6	8.2	0.8	0.0	0.0	4.7	0.7	6.2	1.7	—	—	42.4	0.9	42.4	0.7
L.A.F.T.A.	143.0	9.9	138.9	13.7	101.8	7.5	85.2	12.2	76.6	21.3	275.3	22.9	545.5	11.2	820.8	13.5
E.C.	179.9	12.4	151.8	15.0	218.1	16.0	77.7	11.1	34.8	9.7	91.0	7.6	662.3	13.6	753.3	12.4
Mexico	45.5	3.1	27.2	2.7	56.3	4.1	17.4	2.5	18.8	5.2	14.2	1.2	165.2	3.4	179.4	3.0
Total	1,446.1	—	1,012.0	—	1,361.8	—	699.2	—	360.0	—	1,199.8	—	4,879.1	—	6,078.9	—

Source: United Nations, 1980 Yearbook of International Trade Statistics.
*Data for 1978 has been used.

TABLE 3.14
Principal Commodity Exports of Central American Countries (in millions of US $)

	1960 $	1960 %	1970 $	1970 %	1975 $	1975 %	1978 $	1978 %	1979 $	1979 %	1980(P) $	1980(P) %
Costa Rica												
Total exports	77.3	100.0	230.8	100.0	493.3	100.0	843.8	100.0	924.5	100.0	1,005.1	100.0
Coffee	39.9	51.6	73.0	31.6	96.9	19.6	307.9	36.5	312.6	33.8	246.5	24.5
Bananas	19.0	24.6	66.7	28.9	144.1	29.2	143.0	16.9	169.4	18.3	191.8	19.1
Sugar	na	na	na	na	42.3	8.6	15.9	1.9	17.1	1.8	na	na
Meat	na	na	na	na	32.6	6.6	60.3	7.1	81.6	8.8	70.7	7.0
El Salvador												
Total exports	116.8	100.0	236.2	100.0	531.4	100.0	848.2	100.0	1,128.2	100.0	na	na
Coffee	76.7	65.7	120.8	51.1	190.8	35.9	440.5	51.9	624.6	60.7	na	na
Cotton	15.8	13.5	23.2	9.8	76.4	14.4	100.5	11.8	87.0	7.7	na	na
Guatemala												
Total exports	116.5	100.0	298.2	100.0	640.9	100.0	1,113.4	100.0	1,270.3	100.0	na	na
Coffee	82.6	70.9	102.6	34.4	166.0	25.9	475.9	42.7	433.0	34.1	464.2	na
Sugar	0.1	0.1	9.2	3.1	115.6	18.0	44.2	4.0	53.5	4.2	68.5	na
Cotton	5.8	5.0	27.2	9.1	75.9	11.8	141.7	12.7	192.4	15.1	166.6	na
Bananas	17.3	14.8	21.6	7.2	34.5	5.4	48.0	4.3	48.0	3.8	na	na
Meat	na	na	12.7	4.3	16.9	2.6	10.7	1.0	41.1	3.3	10.6	na
Honduras												
Total exports	63.1	100.0	172.1	100.0	295.0	100.0	607.6	100.0	732.5	100.0	na	na
Bananas	28.2	44.7	75.4	43.8	61.5	20.8	142.1	23.4	199.9	27.3	na	na
Coffee	11.9	18.9	25.9	15.0	56.9	19.3	211.0	34.7	196.9	26.9	na	na

Wood	8.2	13.0	16.2	9.4	38.5	13.1	42.3	7.0	42.1	5.7	na	na
Frozen meat	na	na	na	na	18.3	6.2	38.9	6.4	60.8	8.3	na	na
Nicaragua												
Total exports	62.6	100.0	178.0	100.0	375.1	100.0	646.0	100.0	na	na	na	na
Cotton	14.6	23.3	34.1	19.2	95.6	25.5	148.0	22.9	na	na	na	na
Meat	3.1	5.0	26.5	14.9	27.0	7.2	67.7	10.5	na	na	na	na
Coffee	19.2	30.7	32.0	18.0	48.1	12.8	199.6	30.9	na	na	na	na
Sugar	3.4	5.4	9.8	5.5	42.6	11.4	19.6	2.9	na	na	na	na
Panama												
Total exports	27.8	100.0	110.5	100.0	286.5	100.0	245.6	100.0	287.9	100.0	na	na
Bananas	18.1	65.1	61.8	55.9	59.5	20.8	71.4	29.1	65.4	22.7	61.6	na
Oil derivatives	na	na	21.5	19.5	128.3	44.8	60.1	24.5	72.1	25.0	82.6	na
Shrimp	5.0	18.0	10.2	9.2	19.0	3.5	29.6	12.0	44.0	15.3	43.0	na
Sugar	na	na	na	na	49.4	17.2	19.5	7.9	23.7	8.2	na	na

Sources: *Boletín Estadístico de la OEA* (July-September 1980) and *International Financial Statistics*, various issues.

TABLE 3.15
Prices of Principal Agricultural Exports from Central America, Quotation[1] and Index (1975 = 100)

	Bananas		Coffee		Cotton		Sugar		Meat	
	US$/MT	Index	US Cents/lb.	Index	US Cents/lb.	Index	US Cents/lb.	Index	US Cents/lb.	Index
1971	140.6	57.0	45.0	68.8	35.8	65.0	4.5	22.1	61.0	101.5
1972	161.5	65.5	50.3	76.8	37.5	68.1	7.4	36.3	67.2	111.8
1973	164.8	66.8	62.3	95.3	54.0	97.9	9.6	46.8	92.0	153.1
1974	184.1	74.6	65.9	100.7	66.4	120.6	30.0	146.4	71.7	119.3
1975	246.7	100	65.4	100	55.1	100	20.5	100	60.1	100
1976	258.6	104.8	142.7	218.2	79.6	144.6	11.7	57.2	71.6	119.2
1977	276.0	111.9	234.7	358.8	72.1	130.9	8.1	39.5	68.4	113.8
1978	287.3	116.4	162.8	248.8	72.9	132.4	8.1	39.6	96.8	161.0
1979	323.5	131.1	173.5	265.2	77.4	140.6	12.6	61.3	131.1	218.1
1980	370.8	150.3	154.2	235.7	94.2	171.0	21.0	102.6	125.9	209.5

Source: OAS, *Boletín de Precios Internacionales de Productos Básicos*, various issues.
[1] Quotations: Bananas: U.S. importers' wholesale price at U.S. ports.
  Coffee: Mild coffees, average of El Salvador Central Standard, Guatemala prime washed, and Mexico prime washed, ex-dock New York.
  Cotton: Mexico S.M., 1-1/16″.
  Sugar: World market, Contract No. 11 (Caribbean bulk sugar, f.o.b. stowed Caribbean ports).
  Meat: U.S. import price for beef, 90 percent visible lean, frozen and deboned, f.o.b. U.S. ports.

TABLE 3.16
Central America: Total Imports and Imports of Crude Petroleum (millions of US $, c.i.f.)

	1970	1975	1978	1979	1980
Costa Rica					
Total imports	316.7	694.0	1,211.7	1,408.6	1,457.2
Crude petroleum	5.1	60.0	101.2	168.4	163.4
Crude petroleum %	1.6	8.7	8.4	12.0	11.2
El Salvador					
Total imports	213.0	598.0	1,023.9	1,021.5	na
Crude petroleum	2.6	62.1	76.4	114.4	na
Crude petroleum %	1.2	10.4	7.5	11.2	na
Guatemala					
Total imports	284.3	732.6	1,285.6	1,503.9	na
Crude petroleum	10.9	69.3	87.3	na	na
Crude petroleum %	3.8	9.5	6.8	na	na
Honduras					
Total imports	221.0	404.3	699.2	832.0	1,018.4
Crude petroleum	10.9	63.1	76.3	112.8	na
Crude petroleum %	4.9	15.6	10.9	13.6	na
Nicaragua					
Total imports	199.0	516.9	780.0	331.7	na
Crude petroleum	7.8	63.4	57.8	40.4	na
Crude petroleum %	3.9	12.3	7.4	12.2	na
Panama					
Total imports	357.0	892.1	953.7	1,185.3	na
Crude petroleum	59.7	323.0	208.2	301.6	385.5
Crude petroleum %	16.7	36.2	21.8	25.4	na
Central America (excl. Panama)					
Total imports	1,591.0	3,837.9	5,000.4	3,593.8[a]	na
Crude petroleum	37.3	317.9	399.0	436.0[a]	na
Crude petroleum %	2.3	8.3	8.0	12.2[a]	na

Sources: *Boletín Estadístico de la OEA* and *International Financial Statistics*.
[a] Does not include Guatemala.

TABLE 3.17
Central America: Gross Domestic Investment, 1960-1979 (percentage of GDP at current prices)

	Average 1960-1964	Average 1965-1969	Average 1970-1974	1975	1978	1979
Costa Rica	18.4	19.6	24.1	22.4	23.5	24.5
El Salvador	14.2	14.3	17.0	22.5	23.7	18.6
Guatemala	10.4	13.0	14.6	16.4	21.6	18.8
Honduras	14.4	18.1	20.1	19.5	27.7	28.4
Nicaragua	17.0	20.9	21.8	22.3	13.1	−1.3
Panama	18.6	21.8	29.2	31.8	28.9	26.6
Central America*	15.5	18.0	21.1	22.5	23.1	19.3

Source: Inter-American Development Bank, *Economic and Social Progress in Latin America—1980-81 Report*, p. 65.
*Unweighted average

TABLE 3.18
Central America: Gross National Savings, 1960-1979 (Percentage of GDP at current prices)

	Average 1960-1964	Average 1965-1969	Average 1970-1974	1975	1978	1979
Costa Rica	12.7	10.7	12.7	10.4	12.7	9.6
El Salvador	11.7	10.5	13.7	15.6	14.3	20.6
Guatemala	7.3	9.5	12.0	12.6	15.4	14.0
Honduras	12.3	14.1	13.1	6.4	18.2	18.6
Nicaragua	14.0	12.8	13.1	9.1	10.2	8.8
Panama	13.0	18.0	21.1	23.4	21.3	15.4
Central America*	11.8	12.6	14.3	12.9	15.4	14.5

Source: Inter-American Development Bank, *Economic and Social Progress in Latin America—1980-81 Report*, p. 66.
*Unweighted average

TABLE 3.19
Central America: Relationship Between Savings and Investment, 1961-1979 (Gross national savings as a percentage of gross domestic investment)

	1961-70	1971-75	1978	1979
Costa Rica	61.0	50.6	54.1	39.4
El Salvador	31.2	77.1	60.5	110.8
Guatemala	73.8	80.3	71.2	74.3
Honduras	77.6	64.2	65.7	65.4
Nicaragua	71.2	61.2	77.7	na
Panama	78.6	71.1	73.7	57.9
Central America*	73.9	67.4	67.2	69.6**

Source: Inter-American Development Bank, Economic and Social Progress in Latin America—1980-81 Report, p. 66.
*Unweighted average
**Excludes Nicaragua

TABLE 3.20
Central America: Private Foreign Direct Investment (in millions of US $)

	1960	1965	1970	1975	1978	1979
Costa Rica	1.6	0.1	26.4	69.0	47.0	46.0
El Salvador	4.9	7.2	3.7	13.1	23.3	na
Guatemala	16.8	14.1	22.5	80.0	127.3	117.1
Honduras	−7.6	6.3	8.4	7.0	13.1	9.9
Nicaragua	1.7	8.2	15.0	10.9	7.0	2.8
Panama	17.3	15.2	33.4	7.6	−0.8	40.3
Central America	34.7	51.1	109.4	187.6	216.9	216.1*

Sources: Inter-American Development Bank, Economic and Social Progress in Latin America, various issues, and World Bank, World Tables 1980.
*Excludes El Salvador

TABLE 3.21
U.S. Direct Investment Position in Central America, Yearend 1978, 1979, 1980 (in millions of US $)

	Total 1978	Total 1979	Total 1980	Central America (excluding Panama) 1978	1979	1980	Panama 1978	1979	1980
All Industries	3,187	3,722	4,223	793	848	1,033	2,394	2,874	3,190
Mining and smelting	26	44	39	26	39	39	—	5	0
Petroleum	147	502	720	48	113	154	99	389	566
Manufacturing	469	574	657	285	360	417	184	214	240
Food products	106	w	w	90	w	w	16	w	w
Chemicals and allied products	220	225	279	92	116	128	128	109	151
Primary and fabricated metals	18	w	w	17	w	w	1	0	0
Machinery	w	1	35	w	30	34	9	1	1
Transportation equipment	3	4	4	−1	4	4	4	0	0
Other manufacturing	w	w	w	w	w	w	27	w	w
Transportation, communications, and public utilities	98	105	na	73	75	na	25	30	na
Trade	812	634	666	95	92	85	717	542	581
Banking	na	w	w	na	w	w	na	41	w
Finance and Insurance	1,040	1,454	1,392	66	13	17	974	1,441	1,375
Other Industries	594	w	w	201	w	w	393	242	w

Sources: Obie G. Whichard, "U.S. Direct Investment Abroad in 1979," *Survey of Current Business*, 60:8 (August 1980), pp. 26-27, and Whichard, "U.S. Direct Investment Abroad in 1980," *Survey of Current Business*, 61:8 (August 1981), pp. 31-32.

w—Suppressed in source to avoid disclosure of individual companies, but included in totals.

TABLE 3.22
Cumulative Political Risk Insurance Issued by OPIC in Central America (in thousands of US $) From Inception in 1948 to September 30, 1980

	Original Maximum Convertibility	Original Maximum Expropriation	Original Maximum War Risk
Costa Rica	88,817.6	141,728.0	117,720.2
Active	29,239.4	26,340.5	8,806.9
Terminated	59,578.2	115,387.5	108,913.3
El Salvador	21,468.4	31,157.0	16,090.6
Active	16,065.5	24,860.2	15,690.6
Terminated	5,402.9	6,296.8	400.0
Guatemala	4,091.7	6,416.7	—
Active	3,044.7	3,044.7	—
Terminated	1,047.0	3,372.0	—
Honduras	58,910.4	82,797.5	49,304.0
Active	45,402.2	48,074.6	39,711.9
Terminated	13,508.2	34.722.9	9,592.1
Nicaragua	17,844.5	24,819.6	20,264.8
Active	7,132.9	11,908.3	5,091.8
Terminated	10,751.6	12,911.3	14,363.0
Panama	129,374.3	143,276.5	140,979.9
Active	128,037.5	130,814.1	124.529.3
Terminated	1,336.8	12,462.4	16,450.6
Central America	320,506.9	430,195.3	344,359.5
Active	228,922.2	245,042.4	193,830.5
Terminated	91,624.7	185,152.9	149,719.0

Source: Calculated from official OPIC data.

TABLE 3.23
Central America: Outstanding External Debt (in millions of US $ and percent of GDP)

	1966 Value	%	1970 Value	%	1975 Value	%	1977 Value	%	1978 Value	%	1979 Value	%
Costa Rica	141	22.3	227	23.0	730	40.2	1,300	56.0	1,616	61.6	1,869	65.8
El Salvador	82	9.2	126	10.2	383	17.3	450	16.4	667	21.7	726	23.7
Guatemala	97	6.0	176	7.3	282	6.4	662	11.4	790	12.0	836	12.0
Honduras	77	14.4	144	19.4	451	38.7	812	54.8	918	53.6	1,186	60.9
Nicaragua	129	19.9	220	24.6	802	48.9	1,146	56.8	1,144	56.8	1,213	78.5
Panama	108	14.9	290	25.1	1,128	54.6	1,850	80.7	2,424	94.6	2,571	91.8
Central America	634	14.5	1,183	18.3	3,776	34.4	6,220	46.0	7,559	50.1	8,401	55.5
Latin America	13,231	13.3	21,133	13.9	55,727	19.2	87,327	24.7	109,797	27.7	146,157	34.1

Sources: Jorge Espinosa Carranza, "La Deuda Externa y el Desarrollo Económico Latinoamericano," *Boletín Estadístico de la OEA*, 2:1-2 (January-June 1980), pp. 10, 16; and Inter-American Development Bank, *Annual Report 1980*, p. 106.

TABLE 3.24
Structure of External Public Debt[1] by Maturities, 1966-80 (in Percent, Based on Total Outstanding at Year End)

	Up to 5 years			More than 5 and up to 10 years			More than 10 and up to 15 years			More than 15 years		
	1966	1970	1980	1966	1970	1980	1966	1970	1980	1966	1970	1980
Costa Rica	47.7	27.9	42.7	14.5	18.8	29.3	11.9	20.3	13.1	25.9	33.0	14.9
El Salvador	26.1	31.1	20.3	20.3	17.7	20.6	15.6	17.6	20.6	38.0	33.6	38.5
Guatemala	63.0	40.5	23.4	19.2	14.6	25.1	10.2	12.0	21.6	7.6	32.9	29.0
Honduras	15.2	15.8	19.5	18.7	18.0	23.8	16.0	18.0	18.4	50.1	48.2	38.3
Nicaragua	32.5	40.2	22.1	16.4	16.1	36.3	14.8	15.2	19.0	36.3	28.5	22.6
Panama	22.2	38.4	44.8	25.4	12.0	33.5	13.8	12.0	11.9	38.6	37.6	9.8
Central America	34.5	32.3	28.8	19.1	16.2	28.1	13.7	15.9	17.4	32.8	35.6	25.5
Latin America	48.2	45.0	50.0	23.2	23.0	35.8	13.2	13.4	9.1	15.4	18.6	5.1

Source: Inter-American Development Bank, *Annual Report 1981*, p. 118.
[1] Debt repayable in foreign currency at more than one-year terms, contracted directly by public agencies or by private entities with government guarantee.

TABLE 3.25
Central America: Structure of the External Public Debt[1] by Type of Creditors, 1960-80 (In Percent, Based on Total Outstanding at Year End)

	Official Multilateral 1960	1970	1980	Official Bilateral 1960	1970	1980	Suppliers 1960	1970	1980	Private Banks[2] 1960	1970	1980	Other Credits[3] 1960	1970	1980
Costa Rica	12.7	46.7	38.9	36.4	35.7	16.5	9.1	4.4	2.4	21.8	8.8	37.7	20.0	4.4	4.5
El Salvador	93.9	51.6	64.4	—	34.9	32.2	—	—	—	—	11.1	2.4	6.1	2.4	—
Guatemala	31.4	30.7	70.0	47.0	34.1	30.0	—	1.7	—	21.6	25.6	—	—	7.9	—
Honduras	78.3	70.8	63.3	13.1	26.4	24.7	4.3	2.8	1.3	4.3	—	10.7	—	—	—
Nicaragua	65.8	40.5	32.3	29.3	33.6	31.2	—	4.5	1.0	4.9	21.4	35.5	—	—	—
Panama	11.8	32.4	23.5	44.1	31.0	11.9	—	24.5	1.3	—	2.1	50.4	44.1	10.0	12.9
Central America	49.0	45.5	48.7	28.3	32.6	24.6	2.2	6.3	1.0	8.8	11.5	22.8	11.7	4.1	2.9
Latin America	12.9	23.9	17.3	37.5	32.2	12.9	23.9	19.2	6.4	16.4	16.4	56.1	9.3	8.3	7.3

Source: Inter-American Development Bank, *Annual Report 1981*, p. 117.
[1] Debt repayable in foreign currency at more than one year terms, contracted directly by public agencies or by private entities with government guarantee. Includes the undisbursed balance.
[2] Includes also financial institutions other than banks.
[3] Includes nationalization and bond issues.
— Zero or not significant.

TABLE 3.26
Central America: Ratio of External Public Debt Service[1] to Value of Exports of Goods and Services[2], 1960-1980 (In Percent)

	Average 1960-1961	Average 1970-1971	1974	1975	1978	1979	1980
Costa Rica	4.8	10.1	9.6	10.6	23.2	23.4	16.7
El Salvador	2.4	4.8	4.7	9.1	2.6	2.5	3.5
Guatemala	2.3	7.7	3.8	1.7	1.8	2.2	3.6
Honduras	3.3	3.1	3.6	4.9	8.7	13.1	10.2
Nicaragua	4.9	12.0	10.8	12.5	13.5	8.3	14.6
Panama	1.5	8.6	18.2	8.5	60.6	35.1	33.5
Central America*	3.2	7.7	8.5	7.9	18.4	14.1	13.7
Latin America	14.4	13.7	11.1	14.8	27.3	28.5	24.0

Source: Inter-American Development Bank, *Annual Report 1981*, p. 119, and earlier issues.
*Unweighted average
[1] Total interest and principal payments
[2] Excludes payments on investment income

TABLE 3.27
Net Disbursements of Concessional Assistance by DAC[1] Countries to Central American Nations, 1970-1980 (in millions of US $)

	1970	1972	1974	1976	1978	1979	1980
Costa Rica	11.2	14.7	14.0	11.7	34.1	25.5	22.7
El Salvador	11.7	10.0	7.7	12.8	26.3	26.6	49.5
Guatemala	13.5	18.0	20.3	43.7	26.2	33.4	33.4
Honduras	10.5	10.3	14.5	23.0	33.9	41.7	47.6
Nicaragua	21.6	9.6	23.8	18.6	26.5	73.8	116.6
Panama	14.3	10.5	13.9	27.4	18.7	17.7	18.2
Central America	82.8	73.1	94.2	137.2	165.7	218.7	288.0

Sources: OECD, *Geographical Distribution of Financial Flows to Developing Countries, 1971-1977* and *Development Co-Operation—1931 Review* and earlier issues.
[1] Development Assistance Committee of the OECD.

TABLE 3.28
Total U.S. Economic Assistance to Central America, Fiscal Years 1946-1979 (in millions of US $)

	1949-1952	1953-1961	1968-1976	1977	1978	1979	1962-1979
Costa Rica	3.4	52.2	159.7	11.6	9.1	17.9	198.9
El Salvador	1.3	11.1	155.1	6.8	10.9	11.4	185.6
Guatemala	6.4	121.3	233.4	20.8	10.6	24.7	293.9
Honduras	1.3	35.1	187.9	12.2	17.1	29.2	248.7
Nicaragua	2.3	33.6	232.9	3.3	14.0	18.5	269.9
Panama	2.4	54.9	314.1	16.3	23.1	21.2	381.4
Central America	17.1	308.2	1,283.1	71.0	84.8	122.9	1,578.4

Source: Agency for International Development, U.S. Overseas Loans and Grants

TABLLE 3.29
Multilateral Assistance to Central America (in millions of US $)

	1949-1952	1953-1961	1962-1972	1974	1976	1977	1978	1979	Total
Costa Rica									
Total	—	18.8	173.1	39.9	81.6	84.2	131.4	36.4	695.7
IBRD	—	17.3	100.6	23.5	39.0	18.0	42.1	34.0	322.2
IFC	—	—	0.6	—	—	—	2.5	2.1	5.2
IDA	—	—	4.6	—	0.1	—	—	—	4.6
IDB	—	—	59.4	16.0	42.1	66.1	86.1	0.1	350.6
UNDP	—	1.1	5.7	0.4	0.1	0.1	0.7	0.2	10.1
Other UN	—	0.4	2.2	—	0.3	—	—	—	3.0
El Salvador									
Total	12.6	24.7	88.7	60.0	1.3	23.6	101.9	60.0	521.1
IBRD	12.5	22.2	32.6	17.0	—	6.7	32.2	23.5	214.3
IFC	—	0.1	0.8	—	—	—	—	—	1.0
IDA	—	—	13.6	—	—	6.0	—	—	25.6
IDB	—	0.2	30.5	41.4	—	10.1	69.6	29.5	250.6
UNDP	0.1	1.8	7.8	1.2	0.9	0.8	0.1	5.6	20.0
Other UN	—	0.4	3.4	0.4	0.4	—	—	1.4	6.0
Guatemala									
Total	—	21.6	123.7	48.0	151.4	84.3	108.7	2.2	616.5
IBRD	—	18.2	48.3	—	14.5	55.0	72.0	—	260.5
IFC	—	0.2	—	15.0	—	3.0	—	—	16.2
IDB	—	0.1	63.1	31.8	135.6	25.0	35.7	0.3	310.2
UNDP	—	2.3	7.8	1.2	0.2	1.3	0.8	1.9	17.0
Other UN	—	0.8	4.5	—	1.1	—	0.2	—	7.6
Honduras									
Total	—	32.5	142.6	21.1	31.6	155.0	33.8	177.0	712.2
IBRD	—	19.9	50.4	3.0	3.1	47.0	10.5	65.0	252.7
IFC	—	—	0.4	—	—	—	10.0	—	10.4
IDA	—	8.4	15.6	9.6	—	5.0	5.0	—	57.6
IDB	—	2.2	66.6	8.4	26.2	103.0	6.1	106.3	366.7
UNDP	—	1.7	6.7	0.1	2.3	—	1.9	4.2	19.1
Other UN	—	0.3	2.9	—	—	—	0.3	1.5	5.7
Nicaragua									
Total	5.2	33.7	133.7	20.3	40.1	55.2	66.6	39.0	481.6
IBRD	5.2	30.2	55.2	8.5	16.2	22.0	13.1	—	161.4
IFC	—	—	2.1	—	7.4	—	—	—	9.5
IDA	—	—	3.0	—	—	—	—	—	28.0
IDB	—	2.0	62.6	9.8	16.5	33.2	50.5	36.8	268.4
UNDP	—	1.0	7.9	2.6	—	—	—	1.7	14.6
Other UN	—	0.5	2.9	—	—	—	—	0.5	4.7
Panama									
Total	—	15.4	140.0	51.6	54.4	177.0	22.5	68.2	586.6
IBRD	—	14.0	69.4	30.0	12.1	57.5	12.0	34.0	257.6
IFC	—	—	1.5	21.5	—	—	3.8	3.0	8.0
IDP	—	—	53.0	21.5	42.2	119.0	5.4	29.0	294.7
UNDP	—	1.0	13.0	0.1	0.1	0.5	1.3	1.7	21.7
Other UN	—	3.4	0.1	—	—	—	—	0.5	4.3

Source: U.S. International Development and U.S. Overseas Land and Grants.
*Less than $50,000.
10—Transitional Quarter

CHAPTER 4
POLITICAL CONFLICT AND VIOLENCE

4.1 INTRODUCTION

Political conflict and violence have become an intrinsic element in the historical development of most Central American nations. In societies characterized by economic backwardness, social inequalities, inflexibility, political polarization, and lack of institutional legitimacy, conflicts over ideas, perspectives, or interests have commonly been settled by violence. And it is the combination of social and economic problems and arbitrary use of political power that has created conditions for ferment and revolution in Central America. During the 1930s and 1940s, the frustrations and aspirations of some sectors of the population were channeled either through violent mass movements, such as the 1932 rebellion in El Salvador, or through labor unions and political parties able to find a place in the political system, such as occurred in Costa Rica.

But the appearance of new parties and movements in the political arena of Central America became more evident during the second half of the 20th century, at a time when the military was becoming better trained and organized and, therefore, more self-assured. Among the new movements tailored to various ideologies, there were Social Democrats, Christian Democrats, and Marxist-Leninists. The latter are of special concern to US national security interests, due to their loyalty to Soviet and Cuban interests. It is precisely the increasing interest and involvement of the Soviet Union and Cuba in the region, mainly through indigenous groups, that has distorted popular aspirations and threatened to transform oligarchic societies into totalitarian regimes, without the opportunity of a due political process.

4.2 COMMUNIST INVOLVEMENT AND TACTICS

The Cuban revolution and its economic and military ties with the Soviet Union brought the Cold War and East-West conflict to the Western Hemisphere with a searing immediacy in the 1960s. This does not mean that the communist international movement or the Soviet Union had neglected Central America; the abortive Indians' and peasants' insurrection of 1932 in El Salvador was the first effort to transform a Central American mass movement with deep roots in local conditions into a Soviet-led revolution. During the 1940s, communists gained influence in the Costa Rican government, and even more in Guatemala during Jacobo Arbenz's regime. But despite these precedents, it was the rise of the Castro regime in Cuba that made communism the clear and lasting threat that it is today.

The Bay of Pigs fiasco in 1961 and the missile crisis of 1962 are reminders of US efforts at preventing the spread of Soviet influence in the hemisphere. However, the Castro regime still poses a threat both to democracy and to US interests in Central America by its support of Marxist-controlled revolutionary movements in the region, as well as in Latin America and the Third world countries.

In January 1966, the Tri-Continental Conference brought revolutionaries from Asia, Africa, and Latin America to Havana under the sponsorship of the Cuban government. The avowed purpose of the Conference was to develop a network of assistance to support struggling revolutionary movements in the Third World. A study by a specially appointed committee of the Organization of American States[1] concluded that:

> The first Afro-Asian-Latin American Peoples' Solidarity Conference held in Havana from January 3–15, 1966...was inspired, organized and directed at the initiative and with the active support of the governments of the Soviet Union, Communist China and Cuba, together with other communist governments....
>
> The Tri-Continental Conference marks a new stage in communist world strategy, with the creation in Havana of an international organization, aimed primarily at providing support to armed subversive movements, in order to bring about the overthrow of existing governments and establish communist governments dependent upon extra-continental communist powers....The aid provided by the Soviet

Union...and other communist countries to these subversive movements is, of course, nothing new, nor is the fact that Cuba is serving as the principal agent based in this hemisphere. What is new is the declaration of this interventionist policy, so openly expressed; the identification of major targets and final objectives, so clearly stated; and even more important, the creation of an organization to give this effort an aspect of tri-continental support.

As a follow-up of the Tri-Continental Conference, the Latin American Solidarity Organization (OLAS) was established in 1967, with the aim of coordinating and supporting the actions of Marxist revolutionary movements in Latin America.

The decade of the 1960s witnessed a proliferation of radical revolutionary movements in Latin America, culminating in the ill-fated Bolivian attempt of Ernesto "Che" Guevara to unleash a continental revolution against the United States. Guevara's failure, Cuba's internal economic problems, and the rapprochement between the US and the USSR prompted Castro to cool off his military adventurism for awhile. By the mid-1970s, however, Cuban involvement in Africa became evident and renewed efforts in Latin America were underway. The chronic instability and growing unrest in Central America must have seemed tempting indeed.

The Department of the Americas of the Communist Party is now in charge of Cuban operations in the area, and its tactics differ from those of the 1960s. At that time, revolutionary actions were concentrated in small groups of fanatics—called "focus" groups—which were usually opposed by the orthodox communist parties of Latin American countries. By the end of the 1970s, however, the emphasis had changed to "strategic unity", not only among different revolutionary groups but also between these groups and non-Marxist groups opposed to the status quo.

One definition of this strategy was provided by Jesús Montané, a member of the Political Bureau of the Secretariat of the Communist Party of Cuba and Chief of the party's General Department of Foreign Relations. In a paper he read on April 3, 1982 before an international conference on Marxist theory related to Latin America and the Caribbean, he praised the outcome of the "tactical unity between Marxist-Leninists and Christians." He said that in Latin America and the Caribbean "this intelligent policy of strategic and temporal unity should embrace all patriotic sectors that may exist in the army, intellectuals with different ideologies, middle sectors of the population and even some of the bourgeoisie."[2]

The first testing ground for the new strategy was Central America, and first of all Nicaragua. The unification pact of the three factions of the Sandinista Movement announced in March 1979, and the establishment of a nine-man directorate, were the first steps toward "strategic unity" with democratic groups opposing Somoza's dictatorship. It is almost impossible to imagine how the Sandinistas could have gained power in Nicaragua without this Cuban-influenced strategy, which led to the creation of the five-member junta in June 1979.

The unification of guerrilla groups was accomplished later, through Cuban mediation or pressures, in El Salvador, Guatemala, and Honduras. But by this time the second step of the strategy was already clear, so the movement became less effective in reaching "unity" with non-Marxist groups in those countries. Besides providing strategies and tactics, Cuba has been the main source of supplies, military advice, and political and diplomatic support to guerrilla groups in Central America, and through its guidance they have coordinated actions aimed at supporting each other. The result has been a regionalization of conflict in the area. This fact, combined with the local revolutionary ferment in most Central American countries, has made the problem a very difficult one to face.

4.3 MULTILATERAL EFFORTS

Deterioration of the political environment, internal violence, foreign intervention, and the danger of war in the area have led to a variety of multilateral efforts aimed at developing democratic institutions, opening channels for negotiations, promoting economic and social development, avoiding the danger of armed confrontation, or neutralizing the role of foreign powers in Central America. Besides the Central American countries themselves, several other countries such as Colombia, Venezuela, Mexico, the United States, Jamaica, and the Dominican Republic have been involved in these multilateral efforts, which in many instances have shown different (and at times conflicting) objectives.

The first important collective initiative was taken in January 1982 by the governments of Costa Rica, Honduras, and El Salvador. At a meeting in San Jose, their foreign ministers established the Central American Democratic Community (CACD), with objectives such as the development of democratic institutions, respect for human rights, condemnation of all forms of foreign intervention and military build-up, rejection of subversive actions, and promotion of economic and social development. They also invited all Central American and Caribbean nations that shared these objectives to become members of the Community.

Almost immediately Nicaragua rejected the idea, and later on the initial efforts to incorporate Guatemala failed. Between January and May the governments of Costa Rica, Honduras, and El Salvador changed and the CACD lost even the weak momentum it had achieved.

In October of the same year the idea of a regional approach to the conflict in Central America led to the establishment, again by Costa Rica, El Salvador, and Honduras, of the Forum for Peace and Democracy, during a meeting in San Jose, also attended by representatives from the United States, Colombia, the Dominican Republic, Jamaica, and Belize. Having a democratic government became a prerequisite for affiliation with the Forum, whose principal objectives were to promote democracy and dialogue among states and to examine all peace proposals regarding Central America, as part of a regional solution.

Nicaragua's reaction was very hostile; the presence of the United States at the meeting, it claimed, defined the Forum as part of a conspiracy against its regime. Venezuela and Mexico, which had previously proposed a formula for peace in Central America, reacted coolly; Guatemala, suffering from internal political problems, showed no interest; and the non-Central American members of the group became more observers than supporters. So, by January 1983, when the presidents of Panama, Mexico, Colombia, and Venezuela met on the Panamanian island of Contadora—constituting what is now called the Contadora Group—the Forum had become a feeble has-been. It did succeed, however, in establishing in San Jose a regional institution for giving advice and support to electoral processes in Central America, and it also opened the way for a greater coordination among Costa Rica, El Salvador, Honduras, and Guatemala vis-a-vis Nicaragua in the Contadora Group.

Since its inception, the Contadora Group became the best known and most legitimate multilateral instrument for dealing with the Central American crisis. However, its achievements have been almost nil, despite several meetings of its members with representatives from the Central American countries. So far, the most visible outcome of the Contadora Group has been a "Statement of Principles," consisting of 21 points, which Costa Rica, Nicaragua, Honduras, El Salvador, and Guatemala agreed to sign (see Appendix 3 for details of the political plan of the Contadora Group). The statement calls for observance of the territorial integrity of states, an end to illegal arms trade and subversion in the area, and support for political pluralism. But the statement has not changed the critical situation in the area, mainly because its language is too vague and because the sources of tensions remain alive. On January 8, 1984, the foreign ministers of Guatemala, El Salvador, Honduras, Nicaragua, and Costa Rica, at the end of a meeting with the Contadora Group, agreed to a set of specifications for carrying out the 21 points of the statement. They established three commissions: for security matters, for policy matters, and for economic and social matters. The commissions soon established their calendars and working programs.

Since it started, the Contadora Group has had to face conflicting priorities and objectives, with Costa Rica, Honduras, El Salvador, and Guatemala on one side and Nicaragua on the other. Conflicts have also surfaced among Colombia, Venezuela, Panama, and Mexico. Nicaragua has called for bilateral negotiations, refused to discuss its internal political situation, and regarded the promotion of democracy as an intervention in its internal affairs. But the other four Central American countries have put emphasis on multilateral negotiations and the promotion of democratic institutions as requisites for easing the tensions in the area. Mexico seems to lean towards the Nicaraguan position and Colombia and Venezuela toward the opposite view, while Panama has sent out contradictory signals. Also, Nicaragua has tried to go beyond the group and discuss the Central American crisis in the United Nations, while the other four Central American countries prefer the forum of the Organization of American States (OAS). Given this situation, it appears unlikely that the Contadora Group can go beyond appeasement and reduction of tensions and come to grips with their cause.

But despite its shortcomings, the Contadora effort has gained a lot of international support and has added some momentum to the drive for negotiations. The United States has not been aloof to these efforts. Besides indicating support for the Contadora Group, the Reagan Administration on April 28, 1983 appointed former Democratic Senator Richard Stone as its special envoy to Central America, with the main task of exploring avenues for peaceful resolutions of conflicts. The Caribbean Basin Initiative (CBI) announced by President Reagan on February 24, 1982 was a first effort to help resolve the economic problems of the area. One of its components, consisting of $350 million for direct help to beneficiary countries, was approved by Congress in the summer of 1982. But another element, the lifting of customs barriers for a wide variety of products from Central America and the Caribbean, had to wait for congressional approval until July 1983 (see Appendix 2 for details of the CBI). On July 19, 1983, President Reagan took another important step by naming former Secretary of State Henry Kissinger chairman of a "National Bipartisan Commission" on Central America, whose main task was advising the President on medium- and long-term US policies and actions for facing the problems of the area.

All three of President Reagan's initiatives are at different stages of development and accomplishment. Although Ambassador Stone has been in contact with most of the principals in the conflict in Central America and has achieved some degree of flexibility, especially on the part of both the government and guerrillas in El Salvador, contacts between the two groups have not produced any basis for a political solution. In Nicaragua, the Sandinista regime has not even been convinced of the importance of talking to political adversaries, and is closed to negotiations, in spite of its promise for elections in 1984. The CBI has begun its direct assistance to the area, but its trade measures are still in a process of adjustment. According to the US government, the amount of bilateral aid to Central America (Nicaragua excluded) during 1983, outside the CBI, has been $516.0 million for economic assistance and $196.5 for military support.[3] Kissinger's Bipartisan Commission on Central America delivered its report on January 10, 1984, but the US Congress has yet to act on the recommendations and allocate the funds required.

The fate of the Central American Democratic Community, the Forum for Peace and Democracy, the Contadora Group, and Ambassador Stone's efforts demonstrate how difficult it is to reach any kind of peaceful or negotiated solution in Central America if there is no change in the internal situation of its countries or the attitudes of adversary groups. This explains, to a great extent, why military options have an increasing appeal, even while such peaceful efforts have been under way. The Nicaraguan regime has built up the most powerful army in the area and, with the help of Cuba, is the main source of support to Salvadoran guerrillas. It has also helped guerrillas and terrorist groups in Honduras and Guatemala, and has been involved in terrorist actions in Costa Rica. The United States, on its part, has opened a training center in Honduras for Salvadoran troops, conducted extensive military exercises with Honduran troops, provided help and support to Nicaraguan rebels, and sent warships to the area. Also, at a meeting in Guatemala on October 1, 1983, the Defense Ministers of Guatemala, Honduras, and El Salvador—with the commander-in-chief of the Panamanian National Guard and the commander-in-chief of the US Southern Command as observers—reactivated the Central American Defense Council, which had been inactive since the 1969 war between Honduras and El Salvador.

So, by the end of 1983, while political efforts were underway, the military option remained the most tangible one, both at regional and national levels. The following sections examine briefly the situation in each country.

4.4 NICARAGUA

In Nicaragua the Somoza dynasty's corruption and political oppression could not subdue the opposition indefinitely. A turning point in the fate of Anastasio Somoza was the 1972 earthquake that killed 10,000 people in Managua. He turned the national disaster into personal profit as he channeled the international emergency assistance into his own bank accounts and those of his cronies. Further, his elite National Guard was allowed to sell relief materials, adding to their own personal advantage. Demands for a new marketplace were not met, and the promised reconstruction of the city never materialized. The dictatorship came under intense popular criticism, and lost much of its support from the middle class and even from most of the economic elite who had traditionally been a key power base for the dynasty, along with the National Guard. In the ensuing months, many joined the ranks of the Sandinista Front of National Liberation (FSLN), and many among the business sector began helping it financially. Groups in Costa Rica, Panama, Venezuela, and Mexico also started providing assistance to the FSLN. Its principal source of military support remained the government of Fidel Castro.

In December 1974, FSLN's members assaulted the home of a former Somoza cabinet member, killing him and some of his bodyguards and holding many hostages. The commandos demanded and got the release of 14 political prisoners, a ransom payment, and publication of a statement. The commandos were then allowed to flee to Cuba with the released prisoners.

Somoza reacted by suspending constitutional rights and announcing that the National Guard would destroy the "terrorists." The Guard seems to have gone beyond its avowed objectives as its soldiers raped, tortured, and executed hundreds of peasants. These events were denounced by the Catholic Church and discussed in the US House of Representatives Subcommittee on Interamerican Affairs of the House International Relations Committee. In 1977 a group of intellectuals and businessmen known as "the Group of Twelve" joined the opposition.

Pedro Joaquín Chamorro's newspaper *La Prensa* intensified its attacks on the government whenever press censorship was lifted. President Carter, departing from the traditional support that the United States had provided to Somoza, urged political changes and an improvement of the regime's stance on human rights. Also during this period, several democratic opposition groups spoke of dialogue with Somoza as a way of avoiding violence, but the dictator refused to make concessions; not even a mediation effort by the Organization of American States (OAS), which Nicaragua accepted, could make any headway.

The assassination of Chamorro on January 10, 1978 consolidated the opposition, emboldened their armed attacks, led to popular uprisings, and prompted President Carter to ask for an OAS peace-keeping force in Nicaragua, which never materialized. Faced with the FSLN final offensive in June 1979, the US public opinion reaction to the killing of an American reporter, and the OAS resolution of June 23 calling for Somoza's resignation, the dictator departed the country on July 17 of that year, leaving behind a power vacuum.

While the international news media were following the events in Nicaragua with increasing attention, the political profile of its future government was being formed at less spectacular levels and attracted very little attention. Armando Ulises Estrada, from the American Department of the Cuban Communist Party, had been making trips abroad to assemble a network for supplying weapons and logistical support to the Sandinistas. One of his responsibilities was to achieve cohesion among the three Sandinista factions. In fact, in March 1979 those factions (Prolonged Popular Struggle, Proletarian Tendency, and *Terceristas* or Third Force) announced unity and named a nine-man directorate, which so far remains unchanged. A secret operations center had been set up in San Jose, Costa Rica, and the northwest region of this country near the border with Nicaragua became both the landing place for planes coming with weapons from Cuba, Panama, and Venezuela, and the stronghold of the "southern front" of the war. Estrada's main efforts regarding Nicaragua stretched from 1977 through 1979. When the final offensive was launched in June 1979, Cuban military advisers maintained radio communications with Havana and were instrumental in training, arming, and transporting the international brigades that joined the Sandinistas.

In the last stages of the political, diplomatic, military, and journalistic campaigns that finally overthrew Somoza, the Carter Administration put emphasis on assuring ideological pluralism in the composition of the future Nicaraguan government. The so-called shuttle diplomacy now and then seemed to be making progress. American ambassadors and emissaries traveled back and forth to San Jose, Panama, and Managua, trying to reach a compromise between exiled Sandinistas and the Nicaraguan regime that would end the bloody contest while permitting participation of moderate sectors in the composition of a new government in Managua. On June 16, 1979 the rebel leaders met in San Jose, Costa Rica and named as a provisional government of Nicaragua a five-member junta composed of two FSLN members, one from the Group of Twelve, and two centrist representatives. Two days later the junta issued a program for government which promised political pluralism, freedom of the press, non-alignment, religious freedom, social reform, and the organization of a "national army" composed not only of FSLN's fighters but also of former members of the National Guard with a clean record.[4] The Sandinistas and their Cuban advisers, however, paid little heed to the concessions that supposedly had been secured from them. The Cuban Communist Party was in a position to decide who would or would not form part of the future Nicaraguan government, since they had almost full control of how and when insurgent military units would be formed and supplied, and since a hard core of international brigades trained in Cuba had been a part of the Nicaraguan insurgency. For those who controlled events from behind the scenes, the apparent coalition with democratic forces was nothing but a concession for the sake of appearances.

International pressure, especially from Venezuela, Costa Rica, Panama, Mexico, and even the United States, was decisive in Somoza's downfall. The June 23 resolution approved by the OAS, with support from the US government, urged the immediate and total replacement of the Somozist regime, the establishment of a democratic government with pluralistic composition, guarantees for the integrity of all Nicaraguans, and free elections as quickly as possible. At that moment, the US stopped all military aid to Somoza. When the dictator resigned the presidency and left the country on July 17, he was replaced by Dr. Francisco Urcuyo, president of the National Congress. On the morning after the resignation, President Urcuyo was told by General Somoza, calling from Miami, that Warren Christopher, number two man in the State Department, had warned him that if Dr. Urcuyo did not turn over power to the Sandinistas, the United States would turn

Somoza over to the insurgent forces. At 8 p.m. of the same day, Urcuyo fled to Guatemala with his closest associates, thus opening the way for the takeover by the revolutionary Sandinista forces.[5]

Faced with a war-torn country, the governing junta enacted immediate measures to consolidate power and secure foreign aid to rebuild Nicaragua. On July 20, one day after taking power, it decreed a "Fundamental Statute" abolishing the 1974 Constitution and laying the groundwork for what looked like a pluralistic reformist government. However, at the same time that the visible government, the junta, was taking actions apparently aimed at fulfilling the promises made during the insurrection, the real source of power, the National Directorate of the FSLN and its proxies, took immediate actions to create a parallel structure of control. The promise to create a "national army" was violated. Instead, the new army, later named the Popular Sandinist Army (*Ejército Popular Sandinista*, or EPS), was entirely composed of former guerrilla fighters. A separate police, a state security force, and a "popular militia" were set up, and the Sandinista Defense Committees (CDS) became the source of control in each neighborhood. The CDS are developed along lines similar to the Cuban model. They function through neighborhood political units involved in civil projects and vigilance against "counterrevolutionaries" at the local level, but in practice exert political control over all civilians. East Germans and Cubans have played an important role in setting up the state security apparatus under the Interior Minister, Commander Tomás Borge. The Nicaraguan government opted initially for 200 Cuban advisers, but today it is estimated that around 8,000 Cubans, including 2,000 military advisers, are stationed in Nicaragua. There are also acting advisors from North Vietnam, North Korea, the Soviet Union, the Palestine Liberation Organization, the Basque terrorist organization ETA, *Tupamaros* from Uruguay, and *Montoneros* from Argentina. The Sandinistas have set up a 25,000-man regular army plus around 50,000 men in active reserve or militias; together they are the largest and best equipped armed force in all Central America, much larger than Somoza's army. Also, in September 1983 the Council of State, a nominal parliament controlled by the FSLN, enacted a law for military conscription. From the Soviet bloc, directly or through proxies, Nicaragua has received tanks, anti-aircraft equipment, helicopters, artillery, ground-to-air missiles, and military transports, while Nicaraguan pilots are trained in Bulgaria.

Besides the military build up that is taking place in the country, there are other aspects of the relations between the Soviet Union and Nicaragua that suggest a growing interest by the Soviets in consolidating Sandinista power. During a visit to Moscow in May 1982, a Nicaraguan delegation headed by Interior Minister Tomás Borge signed an agreement with the Soviet government by which the Nicaraguans will receive credits amounting to $200 million. Under the terms of the agreement, parts of the Soviet fleet in the Pacific will receive maintenance in Nicaraguan ports. The Soviet Union will provide the necessary facilities and train the Nicaraguans in the appropriate fields of expertise. Also, according to the agreement, 300 Soviet physicians were supposed to start working in Nicaragua in 1983, and a 400-bed hospital was to be donated to Nicaragua by the Soviet Union. This agreement bears a striking resemblance to the Soviet policies toward Cuba in the early 1960s, the first years after the revolution.

Nicaragua is being used as a training camp for guerrilla activities in neighboring El Salvador and Guatemala. Some initial outbursts of violence in Costa Rica and Honduras have been traced back to origins in Nicaragua, according to a report from the US State Department presented before a Senate subcommittee on December 14, 1982. The report says that weapons coming from Cuba and other communist countries have been channeled through Nicaragua to the Salvadoran guerrillas.

This situation prompted a shift in US policy from a wait-and-see attitude toward the Sandinista government to a policy of suspension of all aid and, later, to direct economic and military support for rebel groups fighting the regime—an ironic turnaround, since the US and other nations (mainly Latin American and Western European) had been generous in helping the initial stages of the regime. The $1.3 billion foreign debt inherited by the Sandinistas from Somoza was easily renegotiated. According to a March 1983 report issued by the opposition Democratic Revolutionary Alliance (ARDE) based on official data, since 1979 the Sandinistas obtained additional loans totaling $3 billion, while donations amounted to $1 billion. Privately-owned businesses still account for a high percentage of the total economy, but despite assurances they have received from the regime, they depend on the government-controlled credits and are subject to harassment by groups with official sanction.

The Sandinistas have adopted much more hostile actions, against the independent political and social groups, reflecting an apparent design to become the sole controllers of all sources of power and action. The original pluralistic junta has been transformed and controlled by the FSLN. Political freedom has been more restricted for independent groups, and most of them have had to choose between exile, a mere nominal presence in Nicaragua, or armed struggle. Despite calls for internal negotiations, the regime has consistently rejected the option. For months in 1982 the so-called Patriotic Revolutionary Front, controlled by the Sandinistas, agreed to a dialogue with the Democratic Coordination, the only opposition coalition allowed to function in Nicaragua. But by October the Coordination's main leader, Adán Fleites, called off the talks after the FSLN refused even to consider lifting the state of emergency and press censorship. In December of the same year, former junta member Alfonso Robelo and former Sandinista commander Edén Pastora, who had set up the Democratic Revolutionary Alliance (ARDE), asked the Sandinistas for immediate and open talks with the aim of paving the way for elections by mid-1983. The answer was a heated and sharp diatribe against both "traitors." In January 1983 the Nicaraguan Democratic Force (*Fuerza Democrática Nicaragüense*—FDN), the rebel group fighting from Honduras with CIA backing, also called for negotiations, but there was no answer from the Sandinistas. By the end of July a new opposition group appeared: *Rescate* (Rescue), a group composed of former officials of the Sandinista regime defined as just a political—not military—entity in contact with social-democratic parties in Europe and Latin America. *Rescate* asked Managua to start a dialogue for implementing the original plan of the revolution. Again, refusal was the answer. The only promise the FSLN has made regarding a possible political solution has been to conduct elections by 1984.

However, on repeated occasions, members of the nine-man National Directorate have said those elections will not determine who will hold power in Nicaragua, because the people already "voted" for the FSLN during the war against Somoza. On January 14, 1984, the FSLN issued more conciliatory signals by announcing that elections will be held in 1984 for President, Vice President and a 90–man Congress that will write a Constitution during the first two years of a six-year term. The FSLN has also promised "guidelines" for the elections. The key question now is to what extent the totalitarian apparatus built by the Sandinistas in Nicaragua will be dismantled to allow a free electoral process, and whether outside observers will be allowed to monitor the process.(Attacks by US-backed *Contra* rebels are now being cited by the regime as an excuse to postpone elections.)

Not only political parties but other institutions, such as labor unions and the Catholic Church, have been constantly harassed by the regime. At a meeting with the governing junta in November 1983, after many affronts to priests and churches, the Nicaraguan bishops spoke out against military conscription and ideological pressures on the population and asked for the independence and non-alignment of the Nicaraguan revolution.

All these facts lead to the conclusion that the military actions conducted against the Sandinista regime by rebels with US support are to a great extent the consequence of political decisions taken by the FSLN. Had the Sandinistas demonstrated a true interest in pluralism, then the FDN (which counts some former National Guard officers as members), the ARDE led by former Sandinista supporters Alfonso Robelo and Edén Pastora, and the Nicaraguan Revolutionary Armed Forces (*Fuerzas Armadas Revolucionarias Nicaragüenses*—FARN) allied to the FDN would have been acting in a political vacuum. On the contrary, the inflexibility of the regime has been a main reason for the establishment of these opposition groups, although certainly their effectiveness depends to a great extent on external support, particularly from the United States and the other Central American countries.

So, if there is not a change by the FSLN toward some sort of political solution, the alternative will be either the consolidation of a totalitarian Marxist dictatorship or an intensification of violence leading to war.

4.5 EL SALVADOR

Prospects for stability and peace are not promising in war-torn El Salvador. Although the large voter turnout for the constitutional elections in March 1982 demonstrated—despite a leftist boycott—the people's opposition to violence and guerrillas and their commitment to democratic and peaceful solutions, the outcome was neither a stable new government to replace the ruling junta nor an end to internal war.

An alliance of the Salvadoran Army and the Christian Democrats, supported by the United States, had given the government by the end of 1979 the strength to nationalize basic exports in February of 1980 and, one month later, decree agrarian and financial reforms, despite guerrilla warfare and rightist opposition. Agrarian reform consisted of three phases. In the first one, almost completed, the largest farms have been expropriated and turned into peasant cooperatives. Phase two called for turning farms from 250 acres to 1,250 acres into cooperatives, but it has not yet started because of pressure by the owners and fears of a drop in agricultural output. Phase three, known as "land to the tiller," is already developing despite strong opposition from rightist groups; it provides for landless farmers to apply for claims up to 17 acres that they have been working as renters or sharecroppers. Financial reform took national banking and credit institutions from control of traditional families and business groups by limiting the amount of shares in each holder's hands and giving the state a 51 percent control.

Much of the campaign for the March 1982 elections dealt with these topics and the problems created by guerrilla and death-squad violence. Though the centrist Christian Democrats got the largest share of the votes and the largest group of deputies (24) of the 60–member Constitutional Assembly, they could not gain control. The extreme-right National Renewal Alliance (*Alianza Renovadora Nacional*—ARENA) got 19 seats which, when added to 14 held by the traditional rightist National Conciliation Party (*Partido Conciliacion Nacional*) and one by the Popular Salvadoran Party (*Partido Popular Salvadoreño*—PPS), gave them a majority and installed former army major and extreme-right leader Roberto D'Abuisson, twice accused of plotting coups in 1980, as

President of the Assembly. The other minority party, with 2 seats, center-right Democratic Action (*Acción Democrática*—AD), not allied with ARENA, could not influence the balance in favor of the Christian Democrats.

The outcome was a new phase of the power struggle which, after strong military and US pressure, resulted in the appointment of the moderate technocrat Alvaro Magana as president of a new government, with a cabinet made up of members from different parties. The rightists immediately started a campaign against reforms. The government showed itself incapable of dealing with the acute problems of the country, mainly due to its heterogeneous composition, lack of presidential power, and conflicts inside the armed forces. Facing this precarious situation, President Magana asked for an agreement among all political parties, which led to the Apaneca Pact in August 1982. The five parties represented in the Assembly agreed to a set of basic actions and principles, among them the promulgation of a new Constitution by March 1983 and general elections one year later; reaffirmation that there will be no negotiation of power sharing with Marxist guerrillas, who instead should participate in the electoral process with full guarantees; establishment of a "political commission" led by President Magana for coordinating factions in government and making it less fragmentary; establishment of human rights and peace commissions, the first aimed at improving individual rights and the second to look for peaceful solutions to the problems of the country; and declaration of an amnesty for guerrilla fighters.

Through this pact President Magana got more support for handling power. The pact also produced an important secondary effect: shortly thereafter, there was an internal crisis in the PCN, which led to the departure of several deputies, including AD's two, thus changing the balance in the Constitutional Assembly in favor of centrist positions. The cabinet was also reshuffled, and in November 1982 seven conservative army officers close to D'Abuisson were retired. Although President Magaña, reform-minded military officers, and Christian Democrats and other centrist groups gained greater leverage, violence by guerrillas and their refusal to become involved in the democratic process, plus rightist inflexibility, continued to obstruct political, economic, and social programs.

In January 1983 a garrison officer, Colonel Sigifrido Ochoa, rebelled against Defense Minister José Guillermo García, a general known for his support of reform but also criticized for alleged corruption and inefficiency in handling military affairs. Six days later Ochoa backed down and was transferred to a diplomatic post in Washington. By then it had come to light that there were severe strains inside the military. In April, after more internal quarreling, Garcia resigned and was replaced by a moderate, General Eugenio Vides Casanova, director of the National Guard. Vides has been prominent in efforts to change military tactics in the war against Marxist guerrillas from large units operating out of garrisons to small and highly mobile groups ready to chase the guerrillas in their own territory. The 50–odd US military advisors stationed in El Salvador, plus military instruction provided to Salvadoran troops by the US in Puerto Castillo, Honduras, have put strong emphasis on this tactic to regain the initiative. Applying Vietnam-style tactics, the Salvadoran army also is combining military with civilian actions in rebel strongholds. The tactic was first applied in the eastern department of San Vicente, but despite some advances, there is still strong criticism, even on the part of US officers, for what is considered lack of motivation and poor management among the Salvadoran military.

A major setback for the Salvadoran guerrillas' public image took place in April 1983, confirming suspicions of Nicaragua's involvement in the internal strife of El Salvador. On April 6 Melinda Anaya Montes ("Ana María"), number two leader of the guerrilla group known as the Popular Liberation Force (FPL) and member of the governing directorate of the Farabundo Marti coalition (FMLN), was killed in Managua by members of a faction led by the best known Salvadoran guerrilla leader, Cayetano Carpio. On April 12, Carpio was reported to have committed suicide in Managua in sorrow over Melinda Anaya's death. There were hints, though, that he too had been assassinated. Some observers shared the belief that these events had to do with power struggles within the guerrilla groups, and that the upper hand was being gained by the factions most subservient to the Soviet Union.

The guerrillas are less effective now in their fighting

than in 1981 and 1982. But they have managed to keep visible, control some important territories, and conduct sabotage against energy supply sources, transportation, and crops—in other words, economic terrorism, with severe economic consequences. Also they have consistently refused to become a peaceful political force and participate in the electoral process. This attitude can be traced back at least to 1979, after the young officers' coup that deposed General Carlos Humberto Romero. The first ruling junta, with a pluralistic composition, issued a proclamation calling on the guerrillas to join in the political process. As proof of its intentions, it lifted the state of siege and martial law on October 23, 1979, and on November 1 announced an amnesty for political prisoners and ordered an investigation into the fate of missing persons. Marxist groups, however, persisted in the struggle, and within days of the coup they launched a major offensive which clearly was an effort to prevent the moderate officers from solving the volatile situation peaceably. This violent course served to strengthen the most reactionary members of the junta and the military, who found in the guerrillas' intransigence a justification for shelving reforms.

The guerrillas' tactic was clearly exposed by Joaquín Villalobos, a commander of the Revolutionary Army of the People (*Ejército Revolucionario del Pueblo*—ERP) and now one of the main leaders of the Farabundo Martí National Liberation Front (*Frente Farabundo Martí de Liberación Nacional*—FMLN), in an interview published by the Mexican newspaper *Excélsior* on March 6, 1980: "Regardless of the good intentions of the individuals composing the first junta, our policy consisted in applying constant pressure in order to force the military sector that had the real power to defend the plans worked out by the imperialists, the oligarchy and their allies."[6]

One of the members of that first junta was Guillermo Ungo, leader of the small socio-democratic party National Revolutionary Movement (*Movimiento Nacional Revolucionario*—MNR), affiliated with the Socialist International. Ungo, together with representatives from other opposition leftist groups, organized in April 1980 the Democratic Revolutionary Front (*Frente Democrático Revolucionario*—FDR), which later became the political branch of the FMLN, an umbrella organization made up of three guerrilla groups and the Salvadoran Communist Party—a manifestation of the "unity" tactic advanced by the Cubans. Besides the Communist Party, the FMLN's other members are Villalobos' ERP, the Armed Forces for National Resistance (*Fuerzas Armadas de la Resistencia Nacional*—FARN), and the Popular Liberation Forces (*Fuerzas Populares de Liberacion*—FPL).

In the case of El Salvador, the strategy of "unity" plotted in Havana has not succeeded in attracting important sectors of the population. However, due to Ungo's connections with the Socialist International, the FDR-FMLN coalition has gained some measure of international legitimacy, despite the fact the Ungo and other non-Marxist elements inside it have no real power, and that the coalition depends on radical groups supported by Cuba and devoted to Marxist totalitarianism.

Besides the danger posed by Marxist armed groups, the Salvadoran democratic sectors also confront serious perils coming from the extreme right. Due to ARENA actions in the Constitutional Assembly, the project for a new constitution (which, according to the Apaneca Pact, should have been ready by March 1983 and have led to general elections in March 1984) has followed a slow pace. Major confrontations emerged over reforms decreed by the former junta which the Christian Democrats want to place in the document. The constitution was finally approved on December 18, 1983, after some compromising. Presidential elections were scheduled for March 25, 1984, with congresssional and municipal elections two years later. During October and November 1983, there was an upsurge in the activities of extreme right death-squads, with the assassination of politicians, labor leaders, and peasants' leaders, and a wave of threats against independent news media and church groups, which the government appeared incapable of controlling.

Continuation of violence, questions about the efficiency of the armed forces, rightist opposition to agrarian reform, and the slowness of judicial processes involving the murder of US citizens have again undermined the commitment of the US Congress to military aid to El Salvador. This aid amounted to $82 million in 1982 and $136.3 million in 1983; the administration has requested $86.3 million for 1984. In October 1983, however, reacting to the situation in El Salvador, the House Foreign Operations Subcommittee voted to cut President Reagan's military assistance request and to strengthen the human rights conditions on both military and economic aid to El Salvador. (The economic aid was $178.5 million in 1982 and $227.1 million in 1983; requests for 1984 amount to $195.5 million).

If, as it appears, Marxist guerrilla groups maintain their refusal to get involved in the electoral process unless they first get a share of power, and the government and legitimate political parties persist in refusing to yield power to a militant group that would not participate in the March 1982 elections, any political solution will depend on the ability of both the government and democratic sectors to create a legitimate institutional framework and conduct democratic elections with enough guarantees for all competitors, whether the Marxist opposition takes part or not. The leftist guerrillas and extreme-right groups are the main obstacles in this precarious path, which is also endangered by a lack of democratic tradition, social and economic backwardness, and the view among many sectors that to compete for power means becoming irreconcilable enemies, not pragmatic adversaries.

4.6 GUATEMALA

The last three decades of civil strife in Guatemala have increasingly eroded the position of moderate elements in the political spectrum. It has led to an increasing polarization of political and social action, with a saga since the beginning of the 1960s, of guerrilla warfare, urban terrorism, political criminality, and the emergence of the military as the ultimate source of power—which they have controlled directly or indirectly, in alliance with a closed political and economic elite, for almost 30 years. The March 23, 1982 coup against the corrupt government of General Fernanco Romeo Lucas, which came immediately after the elections in which General Angel Aníbal Guevara was declared the winner by the government, culminated in the presidency of the born-again Christian General Efraín Ríos Montt (see Chapter 1). He too was later removed, by a group led by Defense Minister Oscar Mejías Víctores on August 8, 1983. All this appears to have paved the way for some sort of change in the political framework, with constitutent assembly elections announced for mid-1984.

In the 1960s, when Castro was involved in his first phase of foreign intervention through guerrilla groups, his main Guatemalan client was the Revolutionary Armed Forces. Although both this and other minor groups managed to create a virtual internal war during the civilian government of Julio César Méndez Montenegro (1966–70), they were almost annihilated by the repressive regime of Colonel Carlos Arana Osorio (1970–74), who successfully applied counterinsurgency techniques.

Both guerrilla warfare and urban terrorism continued at a relatively low level during General Kjell Eugenio Laugerud's administration (1974–78), but began to regain strength by 1978, especially in the capital, when his successor, General Lucas, came to power. As the candidate of a self-proclaimed "wide" political front, he promised both social and political reform combined with strong military action against subversive groups. Social reform was aimed at eroding potential support for Marxist guerrillas, especially among rural and Indian populations. Political reform was tailored to flexible rules and procedures, so that new groups could become involved in a process traditionally controlled by a handful of parties, most of them rightist, and subject to inflexible rules. Social reform was minor and soon collapsed due to official corruption and oligarchic opposition. On the political side, while the administration certainly opened more possibilities for emerging groups—even from the democratic left—to become organized political parties, right-wing death squads started a process of annihilation of their leaders. So frustration grew among moderate and reform-minded sectors, and guerrilla warfare and terrorism became more heated. Marxist guerrillas were strong in the northeastern sector of the country, while rightist criminal gangs were most active in Guatemala City. By the end of General Lucas' government, Guatemala's four main guerrilla groups—the Guerrilla Army of the Poor (*Ejército Guerrillero de los Pobres*—EGP), the Organization of the Armed People (*Organización del Pueblo en Armas*—ORPA), the Armed Rebel Forces (*Fuerzas Armadas Rebeldes*—FAR) and the Guatemalan Workers Party (*Partido Guatemalteco del Trabajo*—PGT)—became united and established the Guatemalan National Revolutionary Unity, with Fidel Castro acting as mediator and pusher.

When elections were held at the beginning of March 1982, violence was at its height. Moreover, there were divisions inside both the traditional economic elite and the military. So a declaration of victory for Lucas' hand-picked successor, General Angel Aníbal Guevara, who lacked popular suppport, made a military coup almost unavoidable. When it occurred, the extreme-rightist National Liberation Movement (*Movimiento de Liberación Nacional*—MLN) initially appeared to be its main beneficiary; however, it led instead to a rather reform-oriented three-man junta that included General Ríos, who became president in June of that year.

Ríos, who, according to most accounts, had been defrauded of his victory as presidential candidate of the Christian Democratic Party in 1974 in favor of General Laugerud, was highly erratic during his government. On the one hand he liberalized labor and political activity in favor of previously marginal groups, hunted down government corruption, decreed minor social and economic reforms, and seemed to be really interested in providing guarantees for a democratic transition of power. But on the other he was very imprecise on a timetable for democratization; he established the death penalty and special courts, was reluctant to enter into a dialogue with political groups, and mixed religion with state affairs. He was very effective, however, in controlling the violence of both the guerrillas and the right-wing death squads. Against the former he combined a harsh military campaign in the northeastern departments of the country with civic action that provided jobs, shelter, and food to peasants. And the deputation of internal security forces was a severe blow against criminal political gangs in the cities.

By the time Ríos was deposed on August 8, 1983 by his Defense Minister, General Mejías, he had alienated himself from the most influential sectors, including strong branches in the military and the economic elite, who opposed a tax reform decreed on August 1, 1983. General Mejías, with better relations with the economic elite and traditional military sectors, decided to keep the main provisions of the reform, abolished special courts and martial law, and started negotiations with political parties for hastening elections; at the same time, in contrast to his predecessor, he became more involved in Central American affairs and tried to improve relations with the United States. In October 1983, Guatemala became the host country for the meeting in which the Central American Defense Council was reactivated. Also, after two years of providing no military aid to the counry, the Reagan Administration asked Congress for $10 million for 1984. However, an upsurge in political violence and an accusation of involvement of the security corps in violations of human rights has jeopardized the prospects for both military and economic aid.

As part of his promise for restoring democracy, General Mejías has guaranteed elections for organizing a Constitutional Assembly in July 1984. The offer was well received by established political parties, from the rightist MLN to the centrist Christian Democrats. However, emerging political groups worry that the time for organization will be very short. They are also concerned by Mejia's decision not to organize a new registration system to replace one that has been unable to guarantee honest electoral results.

Guatemala is now in a better position than during Lucas' regime to overcome what has led to polarization and violence in the last three decades. The traditional military-economic elite understanding, upon which most authoritarian governments had been based, has been weakened. Democratic political parties—both established and new—are more active, and the need for socio-economic change is recognized among them and even among wide sectors in the armed forces. However, many dangers still persist. Marxist guerrillas, although decimated, are still active and supported by Cuba, and may try, as in El Salvador, to obstruct any process of democratization. Extreme-right groups are still very powerful, and may resort to violence if they think their position is in severe danger. Social and ethnic problems have not been adequately faced. And, by the end of 1983, a new wave of political violence was under way. In this context external pressure, such as from the United States, could be of great importance, but it should be applied promptly and wisely in order to confront the military danger of Marxist guerrillas and to promote democracy and reform.

4.7 HONDURAS

The political situation in Honduras is one of the most stable, yet fragile, in Central America. After a popularly elected assembly approved a new constitution on April 20, 1981, the government of General Policarpo Paz García conducted general elections in November of the same year, and a civilian, Roberto Suazo Córdoba of the centrist Liberal Party assumed office in January 1982. His main opponent for the presidency, center-right Nationalist Party leader Ricardo Zuñiga, had discreet support from most of the military. Thus Suzao's election was seen as proof of the armed forces' commitment to democratic transition, and showed to what extent the more flexible political environment of Honduras differed from the polarization in El Salvador and Guatemala. The military, however, still hold considerable power vis-à-vis political institutions, and the success and consolidation of democracy depend to a great extent on the understanding and support of the armed forces.

Honduran democracy is confronted with many sources of strain besides the military influence in politics: it abuts both El Salvador and Nicaragua, and must contend with internal terrorist activities, the influx of anti-Sandinista groups and Salvadoran guerrillas, and severe strains on relations with the Nicaraguan regime.

Since the Sandinistas took power, Nicaraguan and Honduran governments have exchanged constant accusations of intervention in the internal affairs of each other and of violating their respective territories. Tensions created by these accusations have been inflamed by several factors: a series of border clashes; the entry into Honduras of thousands of Nicaraguan refugees, most of them Miskito Indians uprooted by the Sandinista government; and activities of the US-backed Nicaraguan Democratic Force (FDN) in Honduran territory, which is involved in guerrilla war and sabotage in Nicaragua. Although this group has considerable mobility and some control in areas of northern Nicaragua, its headquarters and main support center is in Honduras.

In June 1983, due to the US Congress' denial of more military advisors to El Salvador and the lack of funds for increased training of Salvadoran forces in the United States, the Reagan Administration announced the establishment of a camp in Honduras for training hundreds of Salvadoran troops in counterinsurgency tactics. According to official information, forces from Honduras and Guatemala could also be trained in that facility. Weeks later, US and Honduran forces started military maneuvers near the Nicaraguan border, designed to continue for months into 1984. Although there have been protests alleging serious US military involvement in the country, incursions from Nicaragua have decreased since the start of those maneuvers. More recently, in January 1984 a US helicopter was shot down near the border with Nicaragua and the pilot killed by Nicaraguan gunfire.

The Nicaraguans, on their part, seem to have been involved in promoting guerrilla activity in Honduras. In August 1983 the armed forces presented to the press three defectors from the Honduran guerrillas, who said they had entered the country with other rebels from Nicaragua and received training both there and in Cuba. According to the military, the guerrilla group would consist of 300 men, based in the eastern department of Olancho.

Even before the guerrilla presence was denounced, there was a wave of terrorist activities affecting Honduran interests. This came at the same time that the Salvadoran FMLN denounced Honduras for sending troops to joint counterinsurgency maneuvers with Salvadoran forces along their border, traditionally used as a conduit for the smuggling of guerrilla supplies from Nicaragua into El Salvador and as retreat territory for the FMLN. Among those terrorist acts, the Honduran airline offices in San Jose, Costa Rica, were bombed on July 3, 1982. Three weeks later, its offices in Guatemala City were also bombed. In July there was sabotage against energy lines in Tegucigalpa, the Honduran capital, and both there and in the industrial city of San Pedro Sula authorities seized terrorist hideouts. All those acts, precisely at the time when Salvadoran guerrillas had denounced Suazo's government, strongly suggest that there is a coordinated effort between subversive groups from both countries, with Nicaraguan support. Even more, in May 1983, at a press conference in Mexico, a Marxist commander identified as "Manuel Federico" announced the formation of a National United Directorate (*Dirección Nacional Unida*) by Honduran guerrilla groups and described the movement's main purposes as being related not so much to

Honduran internal problems as to the government's attitude towards Salvadoran guerrillas and the Nicaraguan regime.

Trapped because of its geographic position in a virtual regionalization of conflict in Central America, the civilian government is not only menaced from outside by Marxist intervention, but has also been forced to yield more power than is desirable to the military. In November 1982 the Honduran Congress approved a constitutional amendment by which the armed forces were granted greater independence from the executive branch. According to the amendment, the president was deprived of his post as commander-in-chief of the armed forces and was named instead Supreme Chief, but without clear powers. General Gustavo Alvarez Martínez, up to that point the chief of the armed forces, was named commander-in-chief. The country also faces acute social and economic problems, and the two traditional parties, the National and Liberal, although both with strong popular following, are facing some internal quarreling. And the greater the extent of foreign conflict—either with Nicaragua or with the regional network of terrorists—the greater the internal threat to democratic institutions. This is why the future of Honduran democracy depends so much on the establishment of stable democratic regimes in Nicaragua and El Salvador, a fact not clearly recognized in the United States.

4.8 PANAMA

It was almost ten years after the military coup of 1968 that Panama started a slow advancement toward democratic rule amid obvious obstacles and contradictions. In 1977, previous to a referendum on the treaties on the Panama Canal negotiated by General Omar Torrijos and President Carter, the government allowed a greater degree of freedom of expression and the return of political exiles, among them deposed President Arnulfo Arias. In 1972 a new constitution was approved, as an effort to institutionalize a controlled political system in which the president was elected by the nominal parliament. Panama's security force, the National Guard, was allowed a paramount role by the constitution.

General Torrijos stepped out of the political limelight

in 1978 and Aristides Royo was picked as president. After his indirect election, political parties were allowed to undertake normal activities, and all restrictions to freedom of expression were lifted.

All this, however, has been fraught with mixed signals, ambiguities, and accidents. The internal contradictions, both in the government and in the National Guard (so far the main source of power), have been reflected in foreign policy, an area in which Panama has been shifting between "neutralist" and pro-Western positions, but with an evident concern for Nicaragua and Cuba and a tendency to mediate in the Central American conflict, a role that it plays together with Colombia, Mexico, and Venezuela in the Contadora Group.

The death of Omar Torrijos on July 31, 1981 triggered a political struggle among factions in power. President Royo resigned one year later, presumably under pressure by the National Guard. His successor, Vice President Ricardo de la Espriella, echoed his commitment to democratic principles.

In April 1983 the constitution was reformed, limiting the power of the National Guard and making provisions for direct elections in May 1984. With Panama's first presidential election in 12 years only four months away, Espriella—who was not a candidate—abruptly resigned on February 13, 1984. He was replaced by Vice President Jorge Illueca, who is also President of the UN. General Assembly.

General Rubén Darío Paredes, commander-in-chief of the National Guard since March 1982, resigned his post in August 1983 with the aim of becoming the presidential candidate of a coalition led by the official Democratic Revolutionary Party (*Partido Revolucionario Democrático*—PRD). However, he refused to seek nomination one month later, after the nominal parliament approved, almost in secrecy, a law restoring to the National Guard a high degree of political power. Thus Paredes' successor as commander-in-chief, General Manuel Antonio Noriega, became a sort of strongman capable of jeopardizing the real power of any elected president. So the opposition almost immediately launched a campaign to reform the new law.

The apparent power struggle has developed in peace, and Panama, which enjoys a better economic situation than the rest of the Central American countries, has so far been free of the kind of turbulence and violence that afflicts the other countries. However, if the transition to democracy is interrupted by guerrilla groups or the National Guard splits into warring factions, both peace and stability will be in serious jeopardy.(The resignation of President Ricardo de la Espriella will present a new factor in the elections scheduled for May 1984.)

4.9 COSTA RICA

The current economic situation, characterized by a huge foreign debt and a drop in production output, plus the threat of subversion and violence from Nicaragua and, more recently, from internal terrorist groups, pose the greatest challenges to Central America's oldest democracy. President Luis Alberto Monge, of the social-democratic National Liberation Party (*Partido de Liberación Nacional*—PLN), acceded to the presidency in May 1982. His main task was to get hold of a deteriorating economic situation. A governmental stabilization program supported by the International Monetary Fund led to restructuring most of the country's foreign debt, dropping inflation from 85 percent in 1982 to an estimated 15 percent in 1983, and resuming the influx of foreign funds. In the last two years, Costa Rica has received an estimated $470 million in direct economic assistance, most of it from the United States. However, despite successes in stabilization, the country has not been able to start economic recovery, and hugh government deficits expected for 1984 have put financial and monetary stability in danger. Unfortunately the stringent economic measures adopted have produced some protests. However, Marxist groups continue to be an electoral minority, and general political stability and democracy have remained alive amidst violence in Central America. This does not mean that the country is free of political and military hazards. Costa Rica's involvement in the war against Somoza seems to have opened the nation's doors to communist-backed subversive groups and terrorists. From 1979 to 1981 the country was used by those groups mainly as a center of support, political mobilization, and propaganda.

By the end of Rodrigo Carazo's administration (1978–82), Costa Rica had become a target for actions from several activist groups. Foreign-trained commandos have been captured while infiltrating the country. Terrorist gangs have organized kidnappings and sabotage, frustrated most of the time by citizens and police. And an international campaign denouncing alleged human-rights violations and the country's close dependence on the United States has been organized abroad by communist groups. Also, Costa Rica has had sharp differences with Nicaragua over a border treaty, and while the Sandinistas have denounced Costa Rican authorities for their lack of concern over, and even cooperation with, Nicaraguan rebels supposedly acting from its territory, the Costa Rican government has denied the allegation and denounced incursions and violations by Sandinista forces.

According to a report issued in May 1981 by a special commission of the Legislative Assembly that studied arms traffic in Costa Rica, both former President Rodrigo Carazo and his security minister at that time, Juan José Echeverría, permitted during the war against Somoza, an enormous influx of weapons from Cuba, Panama, and Venezuela to Costa Rica, destined for the Sandinistas. There are no guarantees that all those arms really went to Nicaragua—and, in fact, it is presumed that important numbers of them were channeled to Salvadoran guerrillas and leftist groups operating now in Costa Rica.

President Monge has repeatedly denounced Marxist activities against his country and has held the Sandinistas and local communist groups responsible for several subversive actions.

Instability in the area and the government's preoccupation with dangers coming from Nicaragua have made the country very sensitive to peace efforts in Central America. "Neutrality" toward armed conflicts in the area was officially proclaimed in November 1983. However, Costa Rica has maintained the belief that the establishment of democratic governments is the only way of achieving true and durable peace in Central America. This position has produced repeated diplomatic confrontations with Nicaragua.

Costa Rica's policy toward the area, and especially toward Nicaragua, has not benefited from cohesive support within its own government. On the contrary, former Foreign Minister Fernando Volio had to confront strong opposition to the firm way in which he was conducting relations with Nicaragua, and after a series of actions by President Monge and other government officials, he resigned his post in November 1983. That raised a question: to what extent is a change under way in the country's international policy affecting its alliance with the United States, which views Costa Rica as the prime example of how democracy can work in Central America?

The mixture of a possible shift in foreign policy, the prospects against economic stability in 1984, and the proximity of Nicaragua cast some doubts over the country's future.

4.10 BELIZE

Grossly neglected by those interested in Central American problems, this former British colony, independent since 1981, has so far managed to stay relatively isolated from the political and military crises of the area, although it has absorbed a limited number of Salvadoran refugees.

Contrary to what some observers had expected, its independence has not reflected Cuban influence. On the contrary, the government headed by George Price appears to be following a moderate course. Although the British seem to desire a lesser role for themselves and a greater US involvement in Belize, they are still the country's most important foreign partner, maintaining a military garrison as a buffer against Guatemala's territorial claims, and providing economic aid.

Premier Price's Peoples United Party (PUP), which has been in power since the British conceded self-government in 1964, controls 13 of the 18 seats in Parliament. The rest are held by the United Democratic Party (UDP), led by Don Lido and oriented to the right of the PUP.

Though free of the kind of acute social problems faced by other countries in the areas, and blessed with internal political peace, economically poor Belize may not remain immune to the Central American crisis. So far, refugees are its main problem, but not a very acute one, due to the country's agricultural resources. However, even though Guatemalan territorial claims over the country have eased, tensions between both countries could be exacerbated.

So far, because of its colonial past and also as a way

of keeping its isolation from the area's problems, Belize has had closer relations with the English-speaking Caribbean countries than with Central America. But its geographic situation may force the government of Belize to relate more to its neighbors in the not-too-distant future.

4.11 CONCLUSION

The preceding analysis indicates that most of the Central American countries find themselves enveloped in political violence as left- and right-wing groups reject democracy as a way of advancing their interests and purposes. Instead these groups have resorted to violent means, leading to polarization and endangering efforts for reform and democratization.

Legitimate socioeconomic grievances have provided fertile ground for violence in an area where democratic traditions are weak. This has encouraged Cuban and Soviet attempts at gaining a new sphere of influence by supporting radical revolutionary movements, not with the aim of improving people's lives but of advancing strategic and ideological purposes. In Nicaragua the Sandinistas have established a Marxist government responsive primarily to Cuba, and are rapidly developing military and economic ties with the Soviet Union; at the same time they act as suppliers of support to guerrillas in the area. The Sandinistas are well on the way to destroying the remains of political pluralism in Nicaragua.

While Panama, Costa Rica, and Honduras continue to have governments generally responsive to the needs of their people, the latter two have begun to experience challenges from extreme leftist groups, while Panama is in a process of apparent power struggle. Guatemala and El Salvador continue to be in the grip of civil wars. The fact that there is such a polarization of ideologies in El Salvador and Guatemala makes any political solution very difficult. However, there are strong indications that violence is not supported by the people as a way to resolve conflicts. It is in this context that those who advocate an electoral solution gain relevance in the search for peace and democracy.

NOTES

1 "Report of the Special Committee to Study Resolutions I, II and VII of the Eighth Meeting of Ministers of Foreign Affairs on the First Afro-Asian-Latin American Peoples Solidarity Conference and its projections." Classification number OEA/SER G/IV e-i-769 (English), Rev-Volume I & II, January 1966.

2 Mentioned by Carlos Alberto Montaner, "Centroamérica, el mapa de la subversion," lecture before the Inter-American Press Association XXXVIII General Conference, Chicago, October 1982.

3 US Information and Cultural Service, "Politica de los EUA en Centroamérica. 1 Vista general." Distributed in October 1983.

4 This program, a detailed account of proposals, was interpreted as a main source of compromise by the FSLN.

5 Francisco Urcuyo, "Solos, Las últimas 43 horas en el bunker de Somoza," Guatemala: Editorial Académica Centroaméricana, 1974.

6 Mentioned by Gabriel Zaid, "Colegas enemigos" Mexico: Vuelta magazine, number 56, July 1981, pp. 10–11.

7 See Note 3 above.

CHAPTER 5
BASIC ELEMENTS OF A PROGRAM FOR ACTION

5.1 INTRODUCTION

The preceding chapters present an overview of the political, economic, and social conditions in Central America. From these analyses emerges a disturbing picture of nations beset by severe negative factors, both internal and external, which have implications for both the short and long term. The consensus is clear: these factors pose almost insurmountable difficulties for Central American nations trying to solve their problems by themselves with their own limited resources and capabilities. Thus a major conclusion is that they need help—*a concerted assistance program* from other nations—coupled with proper changes in their own policies and production apparatus.

In designing a program to assist Central America, it must be kept in mind that the complexity and fluidity of the situation in that region demands a long-range effort, coupled with short-term actions. Some time will elapse before appreciable results are achieved, though some beneficial results could be obtained during the first stages of the program.

Another prerequisite for the success of an assistance program is the firm commitment of Central American leaders to supporting the actions required and helping to bring positive changes through a democratic process. Further, a program aimed at improving the conditions of the Central American people cannot fully succeed if the destabilizing effects of violence and terrorist activity in the region continue. For the success of the plan, all external support of terrorism and insurgency must cease— a difficult condition in view of the polarization and diversity of all the external factors involved.

The magnitude of the effort, in terms of capital and resources, and the nature of structural changes required to redress social grievances and improve economic conditions are well beyond the capabilities of each country alone. Therefore, an assistance program must ensure a strong influx of capital resources and technical know-how from outside the region, through both bilateral and multilateral channels, such as the Inter-American Development Bank (IDB), World Bank (IBRD), Development Assistance Committee (DAC), etc. The success of this program, then, requires a concerted, participatory, international effort in which common objectives are shared.

A consensus can probably be achieved among the nations willing to participate in a multilateral effort for economic and social development of Central America. However, a consensus is apparently more difficult to attain in the political area in relation to the consolidation of democratic institutions and the eradication of violence.

Another important requirement is that any assistance program must be carried out in close coordination with the governments of the region, fully respecting each nation's integrity and sovereignty.

5.2 CONDITIONS FOR CHANGE

Before defining the basic elements of an assistance program aimed at achieving change in Central America, there are some facts that must be understood and agreed upon by the participants in any such effort.

Experience has shown that whenever certain minimum conditions have existed in the region (political stability, good investment climate, favorable external economic conditions), relatively rapid economic development can be attained; such growth occurred in Central America during the 1960s and early 1970s prior to the oil crisis and the stagnation of the CACM. Although social change occurred alongside economic development, neither kept pace with the aspirations and needs of the people, except in Costa Rica and Panama. And what little progress was achieved during this period was eventually eroded by political instability and external economic conditions, combined with a large rate of population growth. Furthermore, actual declines in per capita income have been recorded recently in all the Central American countries.

The challenge for those who wish to reach a democratic solution in Central America is to create the necessary conditions for the development of a pluralistic, just, open, and democratic social system. Such a system must address the essential political, social, economic, and spiritual needs of all.

One of the conditions which encourages the democratic process is the existence of social institutions based on the society's cultural values and sustained by the proper economic and social environment.

An important component of a democratic system is the existence and participation of diverse political groups. Given the present conditions in Central America, the achievement of social justice, economic development, and political stability within a democratic environment is not a simple task. In fact, the aim of the more radical factions (from both the right and the left) is to exacerbate the current conditions until power is attained by force. The reform process, then, is bound to be slow, but it must be carried out firmly in a series of well-planned steps.

A vital component of success must be the determination of the leaders in Central America, both civilian and military, to bring about change within a truly democratic environment. This determination must come primarily from the leading groups (politicians, businessmen, labor leaders, intellectuals, and the military), who must realize that they share the responsibility to lead their countries to a consolidation of democratic institutions and economic and social reforms. This commitment requires stability, dedication, and sacrifice.

As previously indicated in this chapter, another constraint upon any reform plan is that the necessary resources, both financial and material, cannot all be generated internally. This is due to the present economic problems in the region and to external factors such as the severe drop in the terms of trade, the current relatively low rate of growth of the developed world, the high real interest rate for foreign debt, and the effects of international terrorism and external political interference. Therefore, a concerted financial effort from outside sources is absolutely essential. Such an effort must be far greater than anything heretofore initiated to assist the developing Third World—a program more massive and effective than, for instance, the Alliance for Progress. Training teachers and paramedics, modernizing agricultural techniques, improving sanitary conditions and housing, expanding the educational system, and above all, revitalizing the economy are objectives which demand considerable internal and external resources to be effective within a reasonable time. It is very important that increased external investment be stimulated, markets for Central American products be guaranteed, and preferential treatment of Central American exports be granted from all involved in the assistance program. In this connection the Caribbean Basin Initiative (CBI) (Appendix 2) and the recommendations of the Kissinger Commission on Central America (Appendix 1) offer a unique opportunity for the Central American nations to revitalize their economies, improve their productive structure, and approach the US market aggressively, while implementing much-needed social programs. Trade and fiscal cooperation among Central American nations and with the North and South American nations must be strengthened.

5.3 OBJECTIVES OF AN ASSISTANCE PROGRAM

Given the premises above, we focus next on outlining the objectives of a program designed to help the Central American nations. It appears that the program must contemplate two major objectives, one political and the other socioeconomic—both of which must be dealt with in a coordinated manner.

The political objective must focus on promoting a rapid and orderly transition to democratic systems of government while ensuring active, direct participation of the people in that process. This means, among other things, the establishment and/or consolidation, through popular vote, of systems in which political and human rights are recognized and respected and democratic institutions function effectively. Terrorism would then be perceived as unjustifiable and would be rejected by the people of Central America.

The socioeconomic objective must be to adopt measures and establish a coordinated plan to improve economic conditions in the short run, concurrently with measures to correct social imbalances and to establish economic programs that will assure an adequate quality of life to all sectors of the population over the long run. Such a plan must guarantee the implementation of a fundamental structural change in the countries to stimulate an important increase in productivity, so that their internal resources can be allocated in a more efficient manner and the countries can assume responsibility for, and later self-sustain, the socioeconomic development initiated with the external assistance.

5.4 BASIC ELEMENTS OF A POLITICAL ASSISTANCE PROGRAM

The basic aim of a political assistance program should be to promote democratic systems or, until that is achieved, military-civilian coalitions that break traditional power alliances and open the way to democratic institutionalization. In addition, the political plan must include measures to reduce violence in the region. To attain such objectives, the plan should contemplate the aspects outlined below.

5.4.1 Establishment of Democratic Systems. The objective is to establish or consolidate democratic governments and institutions in *all* countries of the region, and democratic procedures by which the people freely choose their governing bodies and can achieve some sort of input in the decision-making process. This proposal involves organizing political parties, guaranteeing freedom of association, promoting the free interplay of political ideas, and holding fair elections, as well as educating people for democracy. In cases such as Costa Rica, and to a lesser degree Honduras, these measures do not warrant external action and can be carried out from within. However, the situation is more complex in the other Central American countries.

Most of those countries held elections at the beginning of the 1980s: Honduras on November 29, 1981; Guatemala on March 7, 1982; and Costa Rica on February 7, 1982 for president, Congress and local governments; and El Salvador on March 28, 1982, for a Constitutional Assembly, and with presidential elections in March 1984. Elections in Panama are scheduled for May 1984. The Sandinista government of Nicaragua has indicated that elections will take place on November 6, 1984, but for the time being, political parties have a precarious and limited existence, with many of their members in exile.

Elections in Costa Rica were held in a peaceful climate and resulted in transfer of power to the opposition. In Honduras elections were supervised by observers from several countries and private groups, including a team sent by the Organization of American States (OAS), and the general consensus is that the elections were fair; results were accepted by all political parties, the president took the oath of office, and Honduras now has an opportunity to consolidate a democratic system. Elections in El Salvador and Guatemala, however, were held in more difficult environments and produced less clear-cut results. In El Salvador there was substantial popular turnout at the polls, in spite of threats by guerrillas, and results were acknowledged by most political parties and observers as fair and corresponding to the will of the people. However, they have been followed by a very difficult political process, in which polarization has not been overcome. In Guatemala the elections were called fraudulent. This contention provoked the coup d'etat of March 23, 1982, in which a junta was installed. On June 10 the junta was replaced by a strongman, General Efraín Ríos Montt, who in turn was deposed by his Defense Minister, General Oscar Mejías Víctores on August 15, 1983. In Panama, President Aristides Royo resigned on July 30, 1982, alleging health reasons, and according to the Constitution, was replaced by Vice President Ricardo de la Espriella, who in turn resigned on February 13, 1984, and was replaced by Vice President Jorge Illueca. These events show that, important as they are, elections are not the only ingredient needed for achieving peace, real democracy, and stability in the region.

Thus, to accelerate the process of democratization in Central America, the following measures should be adopted:
A. Individual and collective statements by all Western democracies in support of the electoral process as the most viable procedure toward democratic systems of government. A provision should be included within these statements to the effect that present governments will take the necessary steps to ensure honest elections and participation of all political parties, and that the popular decision expressed at the polls will be respected. The OAS could be a potential forum for such collective expression.

When desirable, elections might be supervised by an

international organization such as the OAS, or by a group of countries agreed upon by the voting country's government. This latter option has been consistently exercised by Costa Rica, and recently by El Salvador and Honduras. In addition, technical assistance to help plan and organize the elections could be provided to those countries requesting such assistance. In October 1982 the Forum for Peace and Democracy held in San Jose, Costa Rica, agreed to establish an institution for advising and supporting electoral processes in Central America, and this could be very helpful to the process of adopting fair electoral laws and organizing reliable registration procedures for citizens—both vital steps in making elections legitimate and fair.

At the Eleventh General Assembly of the OAS, held in Santa Lucia in December 1981, a resolution was adopted (DOC AG/doc. 1456/81 rev. 1) in support of the electoral process in El Salvador, repudiating violence and terrorism and accepting in principle El Salvador's positive indication for outside observers to watch the elections. This clearly illustrates the potential for other countries to support the democratic processes in Central America. Both the Contadora Group composed of Mexico, Colombia, Panama, and Venezuela (Appendix 3) and the Kissinger Commission Report have emphasized their support for a democratic electoral process in Central America (Appendix 1).

In countries facing severe polarization and violence, steps should be encouraged for conducting some sort of dialogue and even negotiations for establishing political and electoral rules acceptable to a majority of groups, without that implying power-sharing prior to elections, a point that has also been recommended in Kissinger's report. It is especially important to guarantee that once elections are held, the winners will respect the opposition and vice versa, that power will be administered according to democratic rules and principles.

B. An appeal should be made through the inter-American system or by other means to all political parties and civic groups in Central America to contribute to conditions which will permit orderly, democratic transitions of power. A high-level meeting of democratic political leaders of the region could be convened to discuss the problems and issues and to design a strategy in accordance with the suggestions made in point A. Perhaps representatives from the Contadora Group and the US could be invited to participate as observers (the US involvement has been sugested in the Kissinger Report). Also, meetings of representatives of workers, students, peasants, women, businessmen, and other echelons of society should be promoted in order to strengthen a "civil society" upon which democracy and stability should be based.

International associations of political parties, such as the World Christian Democratic Union, Socialist International, Liberal International and the recently established International Democratic Union, should support their counterparts in the democratization efforts in the area. All of them, however, should view Central America not as a forum for ventilating their political differences and testing schemes rejected at home, but for promoting the basic value they all claim to support: democracy. The Socialist International in particular, which has been supporting alliances dominated by Marxist guerrilla groups, should seriously consider the dangers of such alliances and direct its assistance to more genuinely democratic groups.

C. A return to democratic pluralism in Nicaragua is essential, not only for the people of the country, but also for the achievement of peace throughout Central America. The recent bill prepared by the Nicaraguan government as a law for the operation of political parties does not assure political pluralism, and has been objected to by all independent political leaders. This poses an uncertain future for democracy in Nicaragua. Efforts should be made to convince the Nicaraguan government to take the necessary steps for effective return to democratic pluralism, which goes beyond promising elections and allowing international supervision of this process.

D. The Contadora Group should be supported in its efforts to attain peace and democracy in the area. However, democratic governments and political sectors should reject any kind of agreement that considers only the conflicts between states and ignores the conflicts within them, since that may result in a call for peace at the price of democracy. Any peace agreement, therefore, should be based on political pluralism, and on effective compromises and actions in favor of democracy by *all* involved.

E. Military leaders should be convinced of the desirability

and the urgency of an ordered transition toward democratic systems, and urged to support such efforts. This is an area in which the Inter-American Defense Board College, and needless to say the United States, should play a leading role by fostering the military's support for civilian governments based on popular consensus and not on domination by self-appointed groups.

F. Orientation and information programs directed at businesses and academic communities, labor unions, civic and religious groups, and the general public of Central America should be instituted both regionally and in each country. Such programs could help to organize meetings and seminars to teach effective use of the mass media in order to mobilize public opinion in favor of truly democratic solutions and against the use of violence and terrorism. Also, special programs should be developed at the municipal and town levels to involve more sectors of the population in the democratic process (election of local councilmen for education, health, public works, etc.) and local socioeconomic programs (schools, health services, transportation, food, and housing). Countries with genuine democratic systems, along with professionals from the social and political sciences, could contribute significantly to this effort, which should also be aimed at promoting relations among Central American democratic groups. In this respect the members of the Contadora Group and the US might consider the establishment of an international peace corps.

G. A public information campaign should be carried out in the United States, Europe, and Latin America. This program, through a realistic presentation of the Central American crisis, could effectively counteract the communist propaganda now clouding the image of Central America. This Marxist propaganda aims at undermining non-communist institutions by distorting the issues, manipulating ignorance about the area in the Western democracies, and preparing people psychologically to accept Marxist regimes or Marxist-controlled coalitions. It is the responsibility of the Central American countries committed to democracy to pool their resources to change public misconceptions about the area.

H. The United States, given its influence and responsibility to the area, should, as the Kissinger Commission has recommended, effectively respond to both the Cuban-

Soviet-Nicaragua military threat *and* the internal crisis of Central America.

5.4.2 Elimination of Terrorism and Violence. A major objective of a political plan of action must be to stop violence and terrorism in the region. The use of violence should not be considered a legitimate mechanism for acquiring power within governments that have taken steps towards democratization. In fact, the 1982 and 1984 elections in El Salvador showed that terrorism has not prevented the people from seeking democratic solutions; conversely, democratic solutions have not necessarily deterred terrorism, especially in a polarized society. Therefore, further efforts must be made to convince or press guerrilla and terrorist groups to stop using violence and to participate in the democratic process. In return, the guerrillas must be granted adequate guarantees to assure their safety and participation in the political process.

An end to violence in Central America requires the following measures, most of which also appear in the Kissinger report:

A. Individual and collective statements should be issued by all Western democracies rejecting all factions in Central America which use violence and terrorism as a means to overthrow any government that has demonstrated its willingness to open the way to democracy. This rejection should be expressed as a refusal to recognize such groups as bona fide participants in the resolution of the Central American crisis and a refusal to hold dialogue with their representatives if it is aimed at sharing power without popular consultation.

B. An appeal should be made to all power groups (from both the right and the left), by individual countries and organizations such as the OAS and United Nations, to cease terrorist activities and to accept the democratic process of governmental change. International mediation and satisfactory guarantees for the full participation of all groups in the democratic process should be offered. The Contadora Group could play an important role in persuading opinion leaders in the area to become involved in such a process.

C. If the guerrillas totally reject such negotiations, assistance by Western democracies to Central American governments committed to democracy, should be increased to help carry out anti-terrorist and counter-insurgency campaigns. An appeal could also be made for all private organizations to end assistance to activist armed groups that reject the democratic process. The Nicaraguan regime should be pressed to stop supporting guerrilla movements in the area and to honor—with adequate supervision—its promises of political pluralism and non-alignment.

D. An intensive public information campaign must be launched to awaken the Central American people to the objectives of this strategy to end terrorism and violence in the region, thereby improving prospects for public support.

E. Central American armed forces should be trained not only to improve their military effectiveness and raise their morale, but also to make them aware of the importance of democracy and what their place should be in a democratic society. For this purpose external assistance is needed from the US and other countries such as Venezuela that have successfully combated terrorism and guerrillas.

5.5 BASIC ELEMENTS OF A SOCIOECONOMIC ASSISTANCE PROGRAM

As indicated earlier in this chapter, the main objective of a socioeconomic program for Central America should be to reactivate the economy in a sound and expeditious manner in the short run while creating the conditions for a self-sustained socioeconomic development over the long run. Although the specific conditions and the magnitude of the socioeconomic problems of each Central American country are different, the basic problems and economic difficulties identified in Chapters II and III are common at least to the five members of the CACM, and can be treated in a global way.

5.5.1 Structural Changes. The first step in a comprehensive economic program should be the design and gradual implementation of a number of structural changes and policies in vital areas of the economy. These include a renegotiation of the Central American Tariff Agreement and the Agreement on Tax Incentives for Industry and

Development, a restructuring of the public sector, and a more appropriate handling of the fiscal, tax, monetary, exchange rate, interest rate, and price policies, as well as a rationing of the subsidies granted to industry.

The level of tariffs should be reduced considerably and their application determined in a more general fashion, so that more competition is allowed and a better allocation of resources ensured. For these purposes, special studies should be undertaken with the assistance of experts from other countries and international organizations. It would be a mistake, however, not to announce the proposed changes within a reasonable period of time, for it would create uncertainty and discourage investment in this and other areas.

The size and composition of the public sector should also be revised. The amount of public expenditures in terms of GNP seems to be too high in some countries, and the respective governments have undertaken the support of too many activities. Some of these activities clearly belong to the private sector, or to government-owned enterprises that operate on the same basis as the private sector.

Fiscal and tax policies should be made consistent with the above objectives. Before undertaking new activities, officials should make sure that sufficient financial resources are available without unduly taxing the productive sector or increasing the burden of internal or external debt. This requires adequate banking credits to finance private investment, at interest rates consistent with real economic growth, as well as internal and external financial stability. In this way the private sector would be in a better position to generate job opportunities to absorb the increase in population. If, however, inflation continued due to other internal or external factors, interest rate policies should be flexible enough to ensure the maintenance of positive rates of growth in the long run.

5.5.2 The Short Term Objectives. As already indicated, restructuring the economy of Central America requires sound changes in the tariff structures, the role and size of the public sector, the tax system, and the fiscal, monetary, interest rate exchange, and price policies, together with strong incentives and assurances for the private sector. To support these changes a rapid increase of investments in strategic sectors is needed. Yet the present climate of violence and terrorism does not encourage private investment, but instead, a massive flow of capital out of the countries, with the obvious result of seriously reducing fixed capital stock and international capital reserves. Also it is almost impossible to maintain a minimum level of social expenditures given the present difficult situations in the balance of payments, public debts and public finances.

Reversing this outflow of capital must be a top priority of any economic plan. Implicit is the creation of domestic conditions that will attract capital investment, grant the appropriate guarantees, and ensure modification of present economic policies. Investment should be stimulated particularly in those sectors of the economy that can create new and stable jobs.

In this regard, President Reagan presented an important economic assistance program for the Caribbean at the OAS on February 24, 1982, designated as the Caribbean Basin Initiative or CBI (Appendix 2), which was approved by Congress in July 1983. This program basically includes trade concessions and opportunities, investment incentives, and financial aid. Similarly, the Kissinger Commission recommends in its Chapter 4 a series of programs to assist Central America in its economic recovery. Both will be referred to as the analysis of economic and social measures is elaborated upon in the following paragraphs. Specifically, in relation to overall economic policies, the first point of Reagan's CBI program—providing a one-way free trade area (duty-free treatment) over 12 years for exports from the area—is of particular importance,[1] especially since it coincides with increasing worldwide demands for protectionism and with the worst worldwide recession of the postwar period.

Next, a series of possible socioeconomic measures based on the recommendations offered in Chapters 2 and 3 will be examined.

5.5.2.1 Special Fiscal and Financial Incentives. The first step of an economic program should be to establish a special system of fiscal incentives, to stimulate new investment and exports, taking advantage of the CBI program and aimed primarily at the larger enterprises, both local and foreign. These incentives should be limited in duration, perhaps up to five years. This fiscal system would affect (a) property and income taxes, (b) depreciation of buildings and equipment, and (c) new investment in plants, equipment, housing, etc. However, the fiscal incentives should discourage acquisition of existing fixed capital.

Investments resulting from these proposed incentives would be self-financed, since the large enterprises have ready access to financial markets as well as their own capital resources. If desirable, the OAS Program of Public Finances or the United Nations Development Program (UNDP) could offer technical assistance to countries wishing to set up such a fiscal system to stimulate new investment. US tax credits for new investment in Central America are contemplated in the second point of Reagan's CBI program,[2] and these credits will surely help increase American corporate investment in the region. The Kissinger Commission also supports this kind of assistance by the US

As a complement to these actions, which are primarily domestic in nature, the United States could revise the Overseas Private Investment Corporation (OPIC) program, broadening and strengthening this mechanism for insuring private US investment in Central America (another recommendation by the Kissinger Commission). In addition, other countries whose companies have private investments in the region, such as Mexico, Venezuela, Colombia, Canada, and other members of the Organization for Economic Cooperation and Development (OECD), should establish similar insurance programs.

As indicated before, it is important that the Central American countries also modify interest rates to build up capital stock by attracting savers, as well as establish more realistic exchange rates, thereby stimulating domestic savings and exports and curtailing capital outflows.

5.5.2.2 Emergency Fund. Fiscal and financial measures should be complemented by a substantial amount of multilateral aid to finance and increase private and public investments. These resources should be made available to Central American nations through an Emergency Fund, financed by multilateral and bilateral mechanisms through supplementary appropriations, and should be used for the following purposes:

A. *Investments in Production and Service Sectors.* The Emergency Fund should finance working capital and fixed capital investment of external origin for local enterprises, particularly small and medium, in strategic sectors where moderate investment and working capital are sufficient to reactivate production, create jobs, and generate foreign exchange in a relatively short time. These sectors comprise agriculture, manufacturing, and some services. Local firms should contribute at least 20 percent of the total investment required.

The reason for emphasis on small and medium-sized enterprises is that these firms have been more severely affected by the present situation due to reduced working capital and limited access to the scarce domestic and external financial resources. On the other hand, small and medium-sized enterprises make up a very important sector of the economy in the Central American countries, and their rapid reactivation could yield prompt and tangible political and socioeconomic benefits.

B. *Social Expenditures.* The Emergency Fund could also be used to finance specific expenditures of the public sector which are currently used to implement programs aimed at correcting basic social imbalances and integrating marginated segments of the population into the economic system. Such programs should immediately optimize the use of existing infrastructures and appropriations in order to improve education, housing, health services, nutrition, and sanitary conditions with a high degree of effectiveness and at a relatively low cost. For example, schools could be used for more class sessions each day by hiring more teachers; education reforms could make formal training more relevant to the conditions of each country; hospitals and health centers could broaden their services by hiring more paramedics; and basic literacy, preventive health, and sanitation campaigns could be promoted. Each local government should contribute a substantial share to the cost of the plan. The support provided by the Emergency Fund would thus help to expand effective social services without significantly increasing public expenditures. These ideas are also incorporated in the Kissinger report. A more detailed discussion of some of these recommendations appears in Chapter 2.

To assist in the development of these programs, resources from the Emergency Fund could be coordinated with those available for the same activities from specialized United Nations agencies (FAO, UNICEF, UNESCO), regional agencies and specialized institutions (OAS, INCAP, PAHO), and private NGOs with particular competence in certain social areas. Efforts by these agencies and institutions can supplement those of local, bilateral, and international lending agencies by providing required technical inputs and expertise. The wide international experience of these institutions, their international standing, and the goodwill they generate can facilitate the establishment of specially targeted social development programs capable of rapid payoffs. These agencies and institutions can also play a leading role in designing long-term development strategies for the betterment of social conditions in Central America.

C. *Counterpart to Development Projects.* In addition, the Emergency Fund could supplement and reduce the national contribution to developmental projects in priority fields, such as energy and food production, which are carried out with external financing through multilateral financing agencies (Inter-American Development Bank, World Bank) and bilateral agreements (AID). These projects presently suffer from the difficult economic situation of the Central American countries. However, they are very important for the economic development of the countries over the long run. Special attention should be given to those projects with immediate economic impact and relatively short-term implementation.

This approach has already been adopted by Mexico and Venezuela through the oil facility accorded to Central America. Canada is considering similar assistance, and likewise the Reagan adminstration, in the fifth point of the CBI program, stated the intention of the United States to participate in this type of program. In Costa Rica and El Salvador local resources generated by the sale of food products under the PL-480 Title 1 have been used to finance counterpart funds for development projects partially funded by the IBRD and the IDB. This practice, which the Kissinger report also recommends, should be expanded and generalized whenever it is desirable.

D. Organization of the Emergency Fund. An effective Emergency Fund requires a multilateral mechanism to permit more efficient coordination of scarce resources and, at the same time, encourage additional donors to consider it in their interest to match contributions to the Fund made by others, so that the aid burden might be more equitably distributed. Also, the Fund must mobilize a significant amount of capital during a reasonable period of time and be managed in an efficient yet flexible manner, thereby adapting its operation to the needs of each country. For example, Costa Rica might wish to place more emphasis on using the Emergency Fund for working capital and matching funds, whereas Guatemala might be more interested in expanding social expenditures.

Accordingly, based on detailed analysis of the region's requirements and the capabilities of its member countries, it is proposed that the Fund should mobilize no less than $6 billion over a period of five years.[3] The Fund would consist of contributions from those countries in a position to assist the region, such as the United States, Canada, and other OECD nations, as well as other Latin American countries such as Venezuela, Mexico, and Colombia. The Central American nations should also contribute to the Fund on the order of 20 percent, or in some proportion related to their use of Fund resources.

President Reagan proposed, in the third point of his CBI program, to set up a supplemental appropriation of $350 million in 1982,[4] primarily to assist the Central American private sector in taking advantage of the trade opportunities and investment incentives within the CBI program. Further appropriations could constitute a first step toward the establishment of the Fund. The Kissinger Commission has recommended that the US provide $8 billion of financial assistance during the same period of five years.

The management of the Fund could perhaps be entrusted to a multilateral financing agency, such as the IDB or the IBRD, drawing additional technical support form the OAS, UNDP, and ECLA. Within each country, technical financial institutions, such as central banks or national development banks, should be responsible for administering resources drawn from the Fund. The creation of a multilateral Emergency Fund would not preclude the continuation of bilateral arrangements whenever they are desirable. However, the Kissinger Commission recommends the establishment of a special Central American Development Organization, composed of all Central American countries and the United States to manage the funds offered by the US; other countries would also be invited to participate.

Of course, the individual nation's decision concerning application of Fund resources rests with its government. To this end, each country should appoint a technical institution such as the central bank, a national development bank, or the national planning office, to promote the identification and preparation of projects for potential funding. Similarly, representation from each country within the established governing body (Executive Board) of the Fund is essential for decisions concerning the overall allocation of the resources.

An important provision of this economic plan is the member country's assurance that once the support from the Emergency Fund ceases, projects will continue to operate smoothly. A commitment to the continuation of projects after the initial interim support should be a requirement for obtaining Fund assistance.

5.5.2.3 Multilateral Development Assistance. Further, the countries contributing to the Emergency Fund should continue their economic support through multilateral financing institutions, such as IDB and IBRD, in order to increase the endowment of these institutions to cope with long-range Central American socioeconomic development needs. Moreover, these contributions should encourage the financing agencies to give special attention to requests from Central American countries compatible with their respective regulations. This matter is also emphasized in the fifth point of the CBI program and in the Kissinger report.

5.5.2.4 Bilateral Cooperation. In addition to the multilateral action proposed, it is very important that bilateral programs of technical and economic cooperation be continued and strengthened. This type of cooperation is contemplated in the fourth point of the CBI program, but it should be broadened and not limited to assistance for the private sector, since efficiency should be encouraged in the public sector as well.

Many bilateral programs of cooperation might involve the supplying of services, such as training programs and advisers, rather than—or in addition to—direct financial resources and economic aid. These services might include (a) teachers, paramedics, and other social workers in a sort of international Central American Peace Corps; (b) training of skilled workers, professionals, and managers; (c) low-cost and locally produced construction materials and the technical training to use them; (d) school and hospital equipment; (e) organization of community and municipal programs; (f) technical advice in a variety of fields, such as agriculture, industry, education, and health; and (g) fellowship programs for specialized training in other countries. This type of cooperation, in which many Latin American nations—particularly those participating in the Contadora Group (Colombia, Mexico, Panama, and Venezuela)—as well as the United States, could become involved (Appendix 3), requires a relatively modest effort to bring about major results.

Further, the armed forces in Central America should be stimulated, through proper training, to become active in all the civilian fields mentioned above, constituting a sort of national peace corps and thus creating a proper climate for cooperation between the armed forces and the civilian population in social and economic development projects.

5.5.3 The Long-Term Objective. The long-run objective of the economic plan should be to consolidate a more efficient production system and to create conditions over the next two or three years for developing large projects or programs with high rates of return, thereby allowing the Central American countries to transform the dimensions of their economies. Given these conditions, it is likely that these countries will be able to achieve high and self-sustained rates of economic growth.

An example of this type of project is the irrigation of the Tempisque Valley in Costa Rica. This region encompasses 120,000 hectares of very good soils and abundant water, and it has a basic socioeconomic infrastructure (roads, electricity, potable water, telephone, schools, and health centers). Furthermore, it already has the basic infrastructure for irrigation (basic waterway works and main channels). However, due to the difficult economic situation in Costa Rica, it has been impossible to accelerate the relatively minor works (primary, secondary, and tertiary channels) needed to put the 120,000 hectares under irrigation. These works can multiply crop yields three to four times and allow 2.5 crops a year instead of one low-yield crop a year.

If the Emergency Program contributes to developing at least one large project or program such as this for each country, the whole expectation and investment climate of the Central American countries is very likely to improve.

Since one of the critical aspects of Central America is the limited size of the national markets, an important component of an economic plan should be the restructuring and reactivation of the Central American Common Market, a point also recommended by the Kissinger Commission.

The expansion of social development efforts indicated in section 5.5.2.2B., together with the economic development activities proposed here, should be designed to help create employment opportunities in the region over the short and medium term. Job creation should be at the center of any Central American development program, given the high levels of unemployment and underemployment in the region. A substantial increase in productive employment will ameliorate many of these countries' problems. It will also lead to more dynamic and sustained economic growth through its impact on aggregate demand and other outside factors.

Tied to the employment issue is the agrarian question. A principal objective of a regional development program must be to seek more equitable access to farm land for the peasants and the provision of needed inputs to make the rural sector more productive. This process seems to be well under way in the region, except in Guatemala. A long-term social development program should also place priority on the population dynamics of the region (demographic growth and internal and regional migration). Needed activities in the areas of health, nutrition, and family planning are discussed in Chapter II.

5.6 SUMMARY

The proposed basic elements of an assistance program contemplate a series of actions to ease the critical economic, social, and political crisis of the Central American nations and to create conditions for stable and self-sustained development over the long run. The political component of the plan emphasizes the consolidation of democratic systems through a broad, collective, internal effort and the eradication of violence, for which considerable external support is required. The formation of the Central American Democratic Community by Costa Rica, El Salvador, and Honduras in January 1982 is a positive step toward solutions to the political imbalances and conflicts in the area. Guatemala has asked to be admitted into the Community. The short-term socioeconomic portion of the plan is aimed at the implementation of a fundamental structural change and the rectification of domestic economic policies by providing fiscal and financial incentives to increase domestic savings, investment, and exports in order to halt capital outflow and increase foreign exchange earnings. This part of the plan also is intended to increase external economic cooperation aimed at providing preferential trade treatment for products manufactured in Central America and tax incentives for direct external investment, coupled with an infusion of capital from an Emergency Fund to bolster private investment in the productive sectors and public expenditures in the social sectors. Another element of the short-run economic plan should be the strengthening of multilateral developmental assistance and bilateral cooperation. Over the long run, support should be given to programs and projects that could transform the dimension of the Central American economies and could create conditions for self-sustained socioeconomic development. A restructuring of the CACM would be a positive step in this direction.

The organization of a political, social, and economic plan with the basic elements described in this chapter requires common understanding among the governments of Central America and of the countries granting assistance. Informal discussions and consultations among the latter, as in the Cancun (Mexico) meeting of October 1981, should be carried out immediately. In fact, President Reagan linked his CBI program to the discussions at Cancun.

It is very encouraging that the governments of Central America have already been considering collective action in the economic sector. A meeting of Central American foreign affairs ministers was held in Tegucigalpa, Honduras, on August 15, 1981 to discuss the nature of the economic crisis and the international cooperation required, as well as the elements of a strategic economic program (See Doc. ECLA/Mex/1050). Although their program was considered independently of this report, the ideas they presented regarding the basic element of an economic plan of action are very similar to those advocated here. Also a meeting sponsored by the IDB was held in Brussels on September 12–15, 1983 to promote an extraordinary assistance to Central American countries with participation of DAC countries and international organizations.

NOTES

1 It has been estimated that the value of export increases for the CBI countries is 1 percent for the first year of the free trade area program, 2 percent for the second year, and 2.4 percent for future years. See Richard E. Feinberg and Richard S. Newfarmer, "The Economic Impact of the Caribbean Basin Initiative," prepared statement before the Committee of Foreign Relations of the US Senate, March 31, 1982.

2 A credit against its total tax liability for an amount equal to 10 percent of new investment in plant and equipment.

3 The amount recommended will allow approximately $200 million a year over the five year period for each Central American country. The drop in export prices over the last two years alone has reduced the region's export earnings by over $600 million. The Central American countries' net capital inflow needs were estimated at about $2.3 billion for 1982 (See Richard E. Feinberg and Richard S. Newfarmer). The Kissinger Commission has estimated that the cumulative net financing requirement of the Central American countries for the period 1984–90 is $24 billion. The breakdown by country is as follows: Costa Rica, $5.1; El Salvador, $5.5; Guatemala, $4.5; Honduras, $2.3; Panama, $3.2; Nicaragua, $3.4.

4 $243 million of the $350 million of the proposed emergency assistance package in the CBI program is earmarked for Central America.

COMMENTARY ON THE KISSINGER COMMISSION REPORT

By Paul E. Sigmund

On July 18, 1983, President Reagan appointed a bipartisan commission to study and make recommendations on US policy towards Central America. The commission had been suggested in a Senate resolution, proposed by Senators Henry M. Jackson, a Democrat, and Charles McC. Mathias, a Republican. It was headed by former Secretary of State Henry Kissinger and had eleven other members as well as an executive secretary, Harry W. Shlaudeman, former ambassador to Venezuela and Argentina, and was advised by eleven Senior Counselors ranging on the ideological spectrum from Congressman Jack Kemp and UN Ambassador Jeane Kirkpatrick to Congressman Michael Barnes of the House Subcommittee on Interamerican Affairs. Modeled on the Scowcroft Commission on nuclear weapons, the Kissinger Commission was an attempt to respond to the deep divisions in American public opinion and among political elites concerning Central American policy by appointing a broadly-based group of opinion leaders to evaluate current policies and, if possible, agree on policy recommendations for the future.

At the time of the appointment of the Commission, some argued that it would be nothing more than a cloak for administration efforts to escalate military aid to Central America at a time of escalating congressional criticism of continued US support for the military in El Salvador and of the not-so-secret covert operations of the CIA-backed *Contras* in Honduras and northern Nicaragua. Critics pointed to Kissinger's admitted ignorance of the area (as Kissinger put it, "The president has chosen the only man in the United States who knows nothing about Central America"), and to the conservative orientation of the Republicans and some of the six Democrats on the Commission, which seemed to indicate that a Commission recommendation in support of present policy was a foregone conclusion. Others noted, however, that this might be an opportunity for a fresh look at a complicated situation by a membership which, just because of its lack of previous involvement, might be able to consider innovative approaches.

HISTORICAL BACKGROUND

The Reagan administration has not always taken a bipartisan approach to Central America. During the 1980 campaign and at the outset of the new administration, Reagan advisers had been harsh in their criticisms of the Carter policies towards the area, blaming them for the triumph of the Sandinistas in Nicaragua, and arguing that support for authoritarian rulers was preferable to human rights-related pressures that could lead to the triumph of the Marxist left. In 1981, then-Secretary of State Alexander Haig made the defeat of the Marxist guerrillas in El Salvador a major priority of US policy, sending arms and advisers to the area, and even threatening to "go to the source"—Cuba—in an effort to stop the infiltration of arms to the Salvadoran insurgents. The media focused on Central America and publicized US involvement, heightening fears that the US was in the process of becoming involved in another Vietnam quagmire.

Yet there were political limits to what the administration could do. The opposition to an escalation of US military involvement was broad-based, and the administration announced a self-imposed limit on the number (75) and armaments (light sidearms) of the US advisers in El Salvador. Despite fierce opposition of the Salvadoran right and of US conservatives such as Senator Jesse Helms, the administration continued to support agrarian reform as a means to assuage peasant discontent in a country where land ownership was grossly inequitable. It also needed to persuade the Democratic majority in the House of Representatives as well as Republican moderates, such as Senator Charles Percy of the Senate Foreign Relations Committee, to vote for military assistance to El Salvador only a few months after right-wing death squads related to the Armed Forces had murdered four American women religious workers and two representatives of the AFL-CIO-sponsored American Institute for Free Labor Development.

To get a vote for military aid, the administration was obliged to accept a congressional requirement that every six months the president must certify that El Salvador was making progress in curbing human rights abuses, in redistributing land, in investigating and prosecuting the murderers of the Americans, and in preparing for free elections as a condition on continued military aid.

The support for free elections, however reluctant at first, turned out to be an important weapon against the guerrillas. In March 1982, a surprisingly large turnout of Salvadorans braved guerrilla threats to vote for a constituent assembly, despite a leftist boycott of the proceedings. The election seemed to demonstrate that Salvadorans wanted democracy and peace, not revolution, and that the rebel support among the general population was not as generalized as their apologists argued. Indeed, the strong showing of the right—especially of Roberto d'Aubuisson, who had been linked to political murders including that of the Archbishop of San Salvador and whose campaign speeches included threats to napalm the guerrillas—indicated that the Democratic Revolutionary Front/Farabundo Martí Movement (FDR/FMLN) did not have nearly as much support in El; Salvador as the Sandinistas had had in Nicaragua during the struggle against Somoza.

The emphasis on democracy and free elections had an added advantage for the Reagan administration: it provided an additional argument against the Sandinistas in Nicaragua, since they had postponed the date of the first Nicaraguan elections until 1985 (in February of 1984, the date of elections was advanced to November of that year) and had indicated that they might limit the competitive character of those elections when they were held.

When it became apparent that a quick military victory was not likely, the administration turned to other instruments to defeat the left in Central America. In February 1982, President Reagan announced the Caribbean Basin Initiative, a program of aid, investment credits, and tariff exemptions aimed at promoting the development of Central America and the Caribbean. (Despite its location on the Pacific, El Salvador became a part of the Caribbean Basin, and along with Jamaica and Costa Rica, was scheduled to receive a major portion of the economic assistance under the program.) The Congress removed the investment credit provision of the proposal and made some major exceptions to the duty-free entry, but later adopted the bulk of the proposal.

In addition to the military, political, and economic responses to the Central American crisis, the administration also followed the diplomatic route. This included efforts by Assistant Secretary of State Thomas Enders, to negotiate with Nicaragua in August 1981 and again in early 1982. Those efforts did not make much progress, and Enders was removed as Assistant Secretary in May 1983, partly because of his continued support for negotiations. Nevertheless, just before Enders' removal, the administration appointed former US Senator Richard Stone as Ambassador-at-Large to conduct conversations concerning possible diplomatic solutions with all those concerned, including the representatives of the Salvadoran guerrillas. His mandate also included coordination of US policy with the diplomatic efforts of the Contadora Group, who were attempting to work out negotiated solutions for the region.

In November 1981, President Reagan approved a CIA plan to arm the opponents of the Sandinista regime. Less than a year later, the Nicaraguan Democratic Front (FDN), based in Honduras and composed mainly of anti-Sandinistas who had opposed Somoza (although some ex-members of Somoza's National Guard commanded military units), opened up military operations in the northern part of Nicaragua. Shortly thereafter, Edén Pastora, *Comandante Cero* of the anti-Somoza uprising, also organized a smaller force in Costa Rica which may have received some indirect CIA support. The arming of the *Contras* was criticized as illegal (against the Neutrality Act) and counter-productive (providing the Sandinistas with a pretext to tighten controls on the country), and funding was cut off in the House but restored in the Conference Committee. CIA support for the *Contras* was also opposed by all the Democratic candidates for the 1984 presidential nomination.

Military aid for El Salvador also ran into trouble. Every six months, there was a new debate on the wisdom of supporting the Salvadoran military in the wake of presidential certifications of progress in the areas specified by Congress—even when there was little or no evidence of such progress. While the Commission was holding its hearings in late 1983, the issue was dramatized when President Reagan vetoed the congressional bill containing new certification conditions after Congress had gone into recess, thus denying Congress an opportunity to override his veto. At the same time, the administration also placed additional pressure on the Salvadoran military to improve their human rights record. That pressure included a special visit by Vice President George Bush with a reported list of military men with poor human rights records whom the US wanted removed.

The Commission thus had its work cut out. To do its job properly it would have to evaluate the administration's military, political, economic, and diplomatic policy in Central America (summarized—not too accurately—by a State Department spokesman as "defense, democracy, development, and dialogue"). More specifically, it would have to deal with the two policy questions on which there were the most significant differences between the Republicans and the Democrats—covert support for the anti-Sandinistas, and human rights conditions on military aid for El Salvador.

STRUCTURE AND ORGANIZATION OF THE COMMISSION

The members of the Commission were all busy people. They came from a wide variety of backgrounds—and seem to have been chosen more because of their constituencies than for any foreign policy expertise and, even less, a specialized knowledge of Central America. Only one member was a Latin Americanist—Professor Carlos Diaz Alejandro of the Economics Department of Yale University, who was a Visiting Professor at Columbia University during the Commission's meetings—and his research and writing had been devoted to other parts of Latin America. Richard Scammon was a political scientist, but his work was on elections, and he had also been a member of the US Delegation to the UN General Assembly. The constituencies of Lane Kirkland, president of the AFL-CIO, John Silber, president of Boston University, Robert Strauss, former chairman of the Democratic National Committee, Henry Cisneros, the Mexican-American mayor of San Antonio, and Wilson Johnson, president of the National Federation of Independent Business, were self-evident. Nicholas Brady was an investment banker who had been appointed Senator for New Jersey by its Republican governor when the seat became vacant because of the resignation of Harrison Williams (as a result of the FBI's Abscam investigations), while William B. Walsh was a medical doctor and founder of Project Hope. William Clements was a former Republican governor of Texas (joining the Texas "mafia" of Cisneros and Strauss), and Potter Steward was a retired Justice of the Supreme Court.

The Commission met for a total of 30 days in the fall of 1983, mostly in Washington. There they heard testimony from four presidents, four secretaries of state, members of Congress, and the Joint Chiefs of Staff, as well as many other Central American affairs experts. The Commission spent only six days in Central America and three days in Mexico and Venezuela, but during that time it heard from 300 people.

The trip to Central America was important in modifying some views. Conservatives were reported to have been shocked by the level of violence in El Salvador, while liberals were adversely impressed by the degree of coordination among the Sandinista government and Soviet intelligence, which was demonstrated in a government briefing given to them during their short visit to Managua.

Commission meetings created a certain camaraderie among Commission members, and Kissinger and the conservative majority created an atmosphere that promoted the development of consensus. In addition, the original mandate of the Commission to make recommendations on "a long-term United States policy that will best respond to the challenges of social, economic, and democratic development in the region, and to internal and external threats to its security and stability" was intended to discourage wrangling over specifics.

Nevertheless, as the Commission noted in a covering letter to its report, it was impossible to avoid making some short-term recommendations within the framework of the longer term approach. While there was some disagreement, especially on short-term issues, the amount of agreement the Commission achieved was well within the guidelines of the President's request that Commissioners advise him on the "means of building a national consensus on a comprehensive United States policy for the region."

The report is lengthy—131 pages—and comprehensive. It comprises eight chapters, two introductory statements, an historical overview, and chapters on "democracy and economic prosperity," "human development," security, and diplomatic and regional solutions, as well as a conclusion and "notes" which are in reality dissenting statements by individual commissioners. Each of the chapters is summarized below, followed by an overall summary of the report.

Introduction. The two introductory chapters lay out what will be a repeated set of themes in the report—the interrelatedness of the economic, social, political, and military aspects of the Central American problem and the fact that "the roots of the crisis are both indigenous and foreign." While the report asserts that "indigenous reform, even indigenous revolution, is not a security threat to the United States," it warns that "the intrusion of aggressive outside powers exploiting local grievances to expand their own political influence and military control is a serious threat to the United States and to the entire hemisphere."

While the introduction devotes considerable attention to economic and political themes—the regional economic crisis, and the crisis of legitimacy with democracy as its solution—it links these directly to security (i.e., military) considerations, asserting, "Just as there can be no real security without economic growth and social justice, so there can be no prosperity without security. The Soviet and Cuban threat is real."

Historical Overview. In the historical chapter, the report repeats that the causes of the crisis are both indigenous and foreign. It does not mince words about the retrograde character of the political and social systems of many Latin American countries. Somoza's Nicaragua is described as a "kleptocracy." The initial openings in the 1960s of the political systems of Nicaragua, El Salvador, Honduras, and even Guatemala ("after the United States helped bring about the fall of the [Jacobo] Arbenz government in 1954" and "politics became more divisive, violent and polarized than in the neighboring states") are described as subsequently moving in a politically retrogressive direction in El Salvador, Nicaragua, and Guatemala, just at the time that expectations had been raised as a result of a prolonged period of economic growth from World War II until the early 1970s. Costa Rica is seen as an exception to the political pattern of repression. But it, too, suffers from the regional economic crisis, with a drop of 18 percent in per capita income in the period from 1980 to 1982.

After noting the struggle between authoritarian and democratic tendencies in Central American politics, the report adds that a "third strain," socialism, began to appear in the 1930s and has remained ever since, "frequently mixed into both democratic (as in Costa Rica) and Marxist or even communist elements." Marxist guerrillas received Cuban support in Guatemala in the 1960s, but factional divisions, the counterinsurgency efforts of the Guatemalan army, and Castro's disillusionment with the effort to export revolution to Latin America led to Cuba's de-emphasis of the export of revolution until 1978 when "guerrillas were once again in the field in Guatemala; the elements of a promising insurgency were present in El Salvador; and above all a particularly inviting situation presented itself in Nicaragua where the Somoza dictatorship was beginning to crumble."

It was at this juncture that Castro became deeply involved in the coordination of the squabbling guerrilla groups, and the supply of arms to Central American insurgents. That support was especially evident, the report argues, during the Salvadoran guerrillas' unsuccessful "final offensive" in January 1981, and it continues through the provision of training and command-and-control facilities in Nicaragua—although some evidence indicates that arms shipments have been reduced in recent months.

The section of the historical chapter dealing with the US is frank in describing the repeated US interventions in the area and past US support for authoritarian governments, "thereby creating an identity between the US and dictatorship in Central America that lingers, independent of the facts, to this day." However, after detailing US interventionism, economic and political domination, and the questionable practices of American companies in the early years, the report describes US assistance to the area since World War II in housing, health, credit, and agricultural assistance. It criticizes the lack of US attention in the last two decades to the region's growing problems, "a far cry, however, from saying as the Sandinista National Directorate and others say that this nation's policies have been the principal cause of the region's afflictions."

The chapter concludes that US strategic and moral interests coincide in Central America, where for both reasons it should improve living conditions, support democracy, promote peaceful change, and "bar the Soviet Union from consolidating either directly or through Cuba a hostile foothold on the American continents."

Democracy and Economic Prosperity. Despite its title, most of the next chapter is devoted to recommendations on economic assistance. While the chapter recommends aid to Central American nations to strengthen their judicial and electoral systems and promote the development of free and democratic trade unions, almost all 28 pages of the chapter are devoted to economic development. However, the most innovative of the Commission's proposals—the establishment of a Central American Development Organization (CADO), links democracy and economic aid in important ways. The members of CADO would include the United States and the seven Central American countries (including Belize and Panama) with the possibility of associate member status for "any democracy willing to contribute significant resources to promote economic development."

Each country would send representatives of its trade union movement, business groups, and government. CADO would make regional recommendations on the allocation of aid funds to each country over a five-year period with a view to coordinating economic growth with social and political development. Social and political development is defined as personal and economic liberties, respect for human rights, an independent judiciary, and political pluralism with competitive elections, along with tax and land reform. All the members of CADO would renounce intervention in the affairs of their neighbors and limit arms by mutual agreement. Nicaragua would be encouraged to participate provided that it committed itself to political pluralism and economic and social development "in harmony with the rest of the region." One quarter of the US aid would be channeled through CADO in the form of quick disbursement balance-of-payment loans aimed at economic growth, the promotion of democratization, and the improvement of social conditions. CADO is said to be modeled on the independent review body associated with the Alliance for Progress, but the proposed tripartite structure is different from that of the Interamerican Committee for the Alliance for Progress (ICAP, or CIAP for the Spanish acronym).

For the short run, the report calls for an immediate increase in bilateral economic assistance aimed especially at promoting labor-intensive projects such as housing and roads, as well as new public credits for trade and to revive the Central American Common Market. The Commission recommends that the debt burden of Central American countries, especially Costa Rica, be rescheduled, and it proposes a number of other immediate measures including US affiliation with the Central American Integration Bank (CABEI).

The proposal of the Commission that received the most attention from the media was its call for the United States to provide $8 billion in economic assistance to the region over the next five years, preferably on a multi-year basis. This aid would mark an approximate doubling of present US economic assistance to the area, and would be accompanied by other forms of assistance such as the further extension of trade benefits such as the removal of import quotas and additional provisions for duty-free entry of area products. For their part, Central Americans would be asked to promote investment opportunities, carry out tax reforms, and accelerate agrarian development through a variety of programs including "where appropriate" agrarian reform involving "land for the landless."

The expanded aid program was criticized by Congress as involving a very high figure in a time of record government deficits in the US. The Commission recognized this, but argued that a long-term large-scale program of this magnitude was necessary to achieve economic recovery, social progress, and democracy in an area that had suffered sharp reductions in real per capita income over the last six years—35 percent in El Salvador, 38 percent in Nicaragua, 23 percent in Costa Rica, 14 percent in Guatemala, and 12 percent in Honduras.

Human Development. The next chapter in the report is devoted to education, health, and housing—areas of special concern for President Silber, Dr. Walsh, and Mayor Cisneros respectively. In the first area, the Commission states that a precondition for educational development is an effort to reduce malnutrition, especially among school children, through an expanded program of food aid and improved food distribution. Other recommended educational programs include the establishment within a greatly expanded Peace Corps program of a Spanish-speaking Central American Teacher Corps with the primary purpose of staffing a Literacy Corps both for direct teaching and for training of literacy instructors, the creation of 10,000 scholarships on the university and vocational-technical levels, 100 to 200 mid-career fellowships for public administrators, exchanges with Central American universities, assistance to strengthen their judicial and legal systems; and a program to subsidize the translation and publication of books in both languages.

In the health area, the report calls for the development of alternative systems in health care delivery, the resumption of AID (Agency for International Development) programs against malaria and dengue fever, and more targeting of free health programs to the indigent and the rural and urban poor. On the topics of population programs and family planning, there are only two sentences, which re-endorse current AID support in this area and describe overpopulation as a serious threat.

Housing is also seen as an urgent need in all the

Central American countries except Costa Rica. The combination of a high rate of urbanization with a lack of urban services has meant that half of all urban residences in Central America lack basic water supplies, and more than 60 percent lack sewage facilities—with the situation much worse in rural areas. A crash program in housing construction is recommended, partly assisted by the expansion of existing US government programs for housing guarantees, housing banks, and construction financing. Since, as the report points out, construction is a labor-intensive area, additional investment in urban construction would have the added benefit of employing large numbers of unskilled or semiskilled laborers.

Military Policy. Disagreements with the recommendations described so far are mainly technical—the lack of wherewithal on the part of the United States, and the lack of absorptive capacity by the Central American countries. The most controversial issues of the report, however, are not treated until Chapter Six, which is entitled "Central American Security Issues." Once again the chapter asserts that the struggle in Central America involves two separate conflicts—one between those seeking democratic government and those seeking oligarchical rule, and the other between those who seek to establish Marxist-Leninist states and those who oppose the establishment of such states. It reviews again the political, economic, and social causes of the Central American crisis, and the recent involvement of Cuba and the Soviet Union, using Nicaragua as a "crucial stepping stone."

The fine hand of Henry Kissinger is evident in the ensuing analysis of the adverse effect on the global balance of power of the further advance of Marxism-Leninism in the area. Specifically, the report mentions sharpening polarization, repression, and violence in the region, the diversion of resources to defend the southern approaches to the US, the threat to shipping lanes, the flow of refugees—"perhaps millions of them"—seeking entry to the US, and the decline in US credibility undercutting "the ability of the United States to sustain a tolerable balance of power on the global scene at a manageable cost." An additional Kissingerian note is struck later in the discussion of El Salvador: the report criticizes those who think that diplomacy and military operations are antithetical—while in fact, they are interrelated so that a political solution is made more likely only if the insurgents are convinced that they cannot win through force. This may appear to be an argument in favor of a military stalemate followed by negotiations. But the next paragraph seems to call for a "successful counter-insurgency effort"—presumably a victory over the insurgents—as "a necessary condition for a political solution."

In striking contrast to its earlier, specific discussion of levels of economic assistance, the report is vague about levels of military assistance. It does not go beyond calling for "significantly increased levels of military aid" to El Salvador, and noting that the Department of Defense estimates that approximately $400 million in US military aid would be needed in 1984 and 1985 in order to break the military stalemate. Yet from the point of view of the Reagan administration, this is the most important recommendation of the Commission—since it could be—and immediately was—put to use in arguing before Congress that a bipartisan commission favored a sharp increase in military aid for El Salvador.

The issue of military aid to El Salvador was linked to that of certification. Here a bit of interparty bargaining seems to have taken place, since in order to get the recommendation of increased aid, Kissinger and others who oppose conditionality accepted the Democratic-supported proposal that—as a condition of military aid to El Salvador—the Congress continue to require periodic reports of "demonstrated progress" toward free elections, freedom of association, the rule of law, the termination of death squad activity, and prosecution of those guilty of past crimes. (Absent from the list was one of the elements of the current certification legislation—progress in the area of agrarian reform.)

Kissinger and two other members of the Commission, John Silber and Nicholas Brady, filed a note to this recommendation which stated that while they "strongly endorse the objectives of the conditionality clause," it should not be interpreted by the president or Congress "in a manner that leads to a Marxist-Leninist victory in El Salvador, thereby damaging our vital interests and risking a larger war." The difference of their position from the more liberal members of the Commission on this point was illustrated in a New York *Times* op-ed article a few days later (January 18, 1984) by Carlos Diaz Alejandro, stating that if the Salvadoran regime ignores the goals of conditionality, "the United States must stand ready then to cut off its bilateral aid, seeking higher ground elsewhere in the region. The warning must be credible, otherwise death squads and electoral fraud will not be eliminated." Yet to all intents and purposes in the area of human rights certification, the appearance of the consensus that was hoped for by the president when he appointed the Commission was maintained.

The consensus was not maintained in the other major area of controversy between the Republicans and Democrats—covert aid to the opponents of the Sandinista government in Nicaragua. The main body of the report is ambiguous on the question. It notes that an adequate analysis would require discussion of classified information, and concludes that while "the majority" of the members believe that the Nicaraguan insurgency represents an incentive to persuade the Nicaraguans to agree to an overall negotiated settlement, the Commission had not come to a collective judgment on whether or how the US should support the insurgents.

In the notes at the end of the report, however, two of the members of the Commission take public positions opposing aid to the *Contras*. Henry Cisneros, the mayor of San Antonio, calls for a suspension of the aid to the insurgents pending Sandinista actions to fulfill their promise to hold free and fair elections, while Professor Diaz Alejandro describes the aid as strengthening the most intransigent sectors of the Sandinista leadership and making successful negotiations less likely. Diaz proposes that all support for the democratic opposition to the Sandinista government be overt, and channeled through the new National Endowment for Democracy—and thus be non-military in character.

A third major recommendation of the Commission in the area of security policy was controversial but unanimous—the proposal to end the prohibition on the training and support of law enforcement agencies in Central America. In 1974, after the revelation of torture and other abuses by Latin American police forces trained by the United States, Congress terminated police training in order to dissociate the US from such practices. The Commission argued, however, that if there is a desire to end human rights abuses in Central America, the US should be allowed to re-establish a relationship with police organizations in the area with a view toward the development of training programs that would promote a more professional and humane approach.

An additional argument for such aid was that Costa Rica's only armed force is the police, since it abolished its army in 1948. The police training proposal was attacked after the publication of the report on the grounds that the US would be less prone to control the actions of the recipients of its aid today than in the earlier period. And it seemed unlikely that Congress would reverse itself on the issue. (In the case of Costa Rica, ways seem to have been found to circumvent the ban by giving aid to the Civil Guard, which has some non-police functions, e.g., border patrols.)

Diplomatic Policy. The final chapter, except for a brief conclusion, is devoted to recommendations concerning the appropriate diplomatic strategy to be adopted by the US in Central America. Describing the principal objectives of US policy as ending the killing in El Salvador, creating conditions for a peaceful and democratic Nicaragua, and promoting democratic development throughout the area, the chapter reveals how important the promotion of democracy has become for administration policy. Democracy is seen as the key to a settlement in El Salvador, to a guarantee of the security of Nicaragua's neighbors, and to an overall regional settlement, complementing the efforts of the Contadora Group (Mexico, Panama, Colombia, and Venezuela).

In the section devoted to El Salvador, the Commission rejects the proposals of the Political Diplomatic Commission of the guerrilla FDR/FMLN alliance for negotiations on power-sharing. Citing a September 1983 FDR/FMLN document that states that "The Salvadoran people need a negotiated settlement between the government and the FDR/FMLN to bring about peace; they do not need elections," the Commission argues that it is not the lack of security guarantees that leads the left to refuse to participate in elections, but they do so because they wish to use power sharing as a way to replace the existing elected government and the armed forces with a provisional structure that the left could dominate. Power sharing, in the Commission's view, would inflate the strength of the insurgents and lead to a government not based on the consent of the governed. The Commission recommends instead the creation of a broadly representative Elections Commission to supervise the future elections, a cease fire on both sides, and a system of international electoral supervision. All this would be supported by the US with adequate levels of economic and military aid to produce the conditions for a politically negotiated end to the fighting.

The Commission thus makes an argument which is exactly the reverse of that of the administration critics who call for a cutoff of military aid in order to induce the Salvadoran government to negotiate with the rebels. It believes that support of the legitimately elected government there will finally persuade the insurgents to negotiate their future participation in the electoral process—for instance, in the congressional elections scheduled for March 1985 (although the report does not mention this date), where the social democratic MNR, former Christian Democrats, and other civilian politicians who are members of the FDR could hope to gain representation in the Salvadoran Congress.

The discussion of Nicaragua specifically mentions the intelligence briefing that the Commission received in Managua as leaving no doubt that Nicaragua is tied to the Cuban and Soviet intelligence network. Citing the expressed fears of Nicaragua's neighbors, the report asserts that the consolidation of a Marxist-Leninist regime would be seen by Nicaragua's neighbors as a permanent security threat. The Commission report argues that given the economic and military weaknesses of Nicaragua's neighbors, a containment strategy along the lines of postwar Europe would be costly and unstable. It calls instead for a comprehensive regional settlement along the lines of the 21 points proposed by the Contadora Group, although with more emphasis on the need for pluralism and free elections than in the Contadora proposals.

In addition to emphasizing democracy, the description of regional settlement envisaged by the Commission repeatedly mentions the need to continually verify compliance with the proposed prohibitions on arms transfers, and on bases and advisers from non-Central American countries. It also stresses the need to supervise the reduction of arms inventories. The United States and the Contadora Group would meet regularly with the Central American foreign ministers to review compliance and develop procedures for the resolution of conflicts among member states.

The report thus involves the Contadora Group but insists on US participation in any resulting settlement. While describing the work of the Contadora Group as constructive, the report notes that "the interests and attitudes of these four countries are not identical, nor do they always comport with our own." Yet we must work together, according to the report, because "the process works most effectively when the United States acts purposefully. When our policy stagnates, the Contadora process languishes. When we are decisive, the Contadora process gathers momentum." The Commission recommendations are thus seen not as an alternative to the Contadora process, but complementary to it, and giving it greater "concreteness"—presumably in the insistence on pluralism and free elections and the emphasis on "verification of compliance and penalties for violation."

The Commission rejects the argument that the only genuine threat to be forestalled is the establishment of Soviet bases in Central America. It clearly wishes to keep all forms of Soviet influence in the area to a minimum. In the case of Cuba, the effort would be to limit "Cuban adventurism" while remaining open to a broader settlement involving Cuban agreement to end its support for insurgency in exchange for the lifting of present US restrictions on Cuban trade and diplomatic relations. Only a single page is devoted to the role of Western Europe, and focuses mainly on encouraging the economic involvement of the Europeans in the region, while limiting their aid to the Sandinista regime until Nicaragua "fundamentally changes course."

EVALUATION

Most of the media coverage of the report was devoted to its recommendations for increased military and economic aid. The report was cited by the administration when it requested a large increase in military aid to El Salvador, and leading Democratic members of Congress expressed doubts about the size of the recommended US commitment to economic aid as beyond the absorptive capacity of Central America. Some media attention was given to the acceptance of conditionality on military aid and the Kissinger footnote on the subject, as well as to Cisneros and Diaz dissents on support for the *Contras*. The Commission's most innovative proposals such as the Central American Development Organization and the linkage of economic assistance and progress toward democracy went almost unnoticed. Perhaps because the media did not believe it was sincere, the report's praise for the Contadora Group and partial incorporation of its proposals provoked no comment by the media.

The ideological commentaries were predictable. *The Nation* (January 28, 1984) called the report "overblown, aggressive, palliative, superficial, and blind to the imperatives of history, revolution, and independence," and stated that in Central America "the revolutionary remedy has appeared as the only path to popular democracy and national independence." At the other extreme, *National Review* (February 24, 1984) gave a more complete and accurate summary, but followed it with the statement that "the criticism of random slaughter in Central America comes with minuscule grace from congressmen representing some of the most crime-ridden cities in urban civilization," and called for an increase in support for the Nicaraguan rebels because Nicaragua is the key "to the preservation of the constitutional option all the way to the northern Mexican border," and the collapse of Central America would produce a Mexican convulsion which in turn would mean withdrawal of our troops from Europe.

Expressing a point midway between these two extremes was *The New Republic* (January 30, 1984), which complained that the Commission did not seem to be able to distinguish among various kinds of Marxists, some of whom "might turn out to be democrats too," but concurred with the report that "the suspension of military aid, or the freezing of it at its present levels, would bring no relief to Salvadoran society; the Leninists who would come to power are not exactly thirsting for social justice. (And they would probably do with the likes of Guillermo Ungo [head of the FDR] what the Leninists in Nicaragua did with the likes of Edén Pastora.)"

Evidently the report can be viewed in a variety of different ways. Those who wish to stress the threat of Soviet and Cuban involvement in Central America will find ample support in its conclusions. But those who view Central American unrest as primarily related to the desires of the Central Americans for democracy, social justice, and an end to oppression will also find parts of the report sympathetic to their views. The important point that the report makes is that it is not a question of a choice of one or the other, since both assertions are true. Similarly, in its recommendations the Commission seems to be all things to all people, favoring democracy, economic aid, social reform, military aid to legitimate governments, the Contadora mediation proposals, and an overall regional settlement based on democracy and social justice. Most of its proposals are unobjectionable—but it is not clear how they would achieve the main goals of US policy outlined at the beginning of the document— an end to the killing in El Salvador, and the reintegration of Nicaragua into the Central American community.

Critics on the left, mainly in academia and the churches, have proposed a formula that responds to both these objectives—a cutoff of CIA support for the Nicaraguan exiles, and forcing negotiations on power-sharing with the Salvadoran rebels by the termination of US military aid to the present government. The second policy is firmly rejected by the Commission for reasons outlined above, and it is unlikely to receive congressional support. The first policy is evaded except in the Cisneros and Diaz notes, but it has considerably more congressional backing.

The report's insistence on democracy and pluralism as a condition for the receipt of economic aid and for the implementation of an overall regional settlement, may make it more difficult to come to some kind of understanding with the Nicaraguans. However, it does not, as William Leogrande charges (*World Policy Journal*, Winter 1984), give us "a brief for war" by proposals for negotiation that are "so unrealistic that they are doomed to fail." In the Salvadoran case the Commission proposals strongly support an electoral solution, and the example of Venezuela in the 1960s shows the elections can in fact lead eventually to a withering away of insurgency.

In the case of Nicaragua, the problem is vagueness about what changes the US should demand from the

Sandinistas. Would the proposals for guarantees to the opposition recently put forward by the Nicaraguan government in connection with the November 4, 1984 elections be sufficient to qualify it for inclusion in CADO—or are the report's authors really interested only in the overthrow of the Sandinistas? What other changes would be necessary in order to end US support for the Contras—support which is justified in the report only as an incentive for negotiation? The report is not clear on what the Nicaraguans must do in order to be "responsive to serious negotiations." Ominously, it says that "Nicaragua must be aware that force remains an ultimate recourse," but then it backs away by describing "discussion of the military option" as beyond its mandate, although it says that military intervention should only be "a course of last resort and only where there are clear dangers to US security."

The report's discussion of the issue on US support for the Contras implies, but does not use the word "symmetry"—which has come into increasing use in the search for a possible overall solution. The incentive for the Nicaraguans to cut off aid to the Salvadoran insurgents might indeed be a US agreement to cut off aid to the Nicaraguan insurgents. Supervised free elections with international observer teams—or even a multinational peace force—in El Salvador might be matched by supervised free elections under similar conditions in Nicaragua. Limits on US advisers in Honduras and El Salvador might be matched by limits on Cuban and Soviet advisers in Nicaragua. Limits on US advisers in Honduras and El Salvador might be matched by limits on Cuban and Soviet advisers in Nicaragua. And the Contadora Group with US and, possibly, European support, could be central in achieving and verifying such agreements.

This would probably mean the continued domination of Nicaragua by the Sandinistas but with much greater freedom of expression and an end to the use of Nicaragua as a staging area for subversion of its neighbors. However, it would also allow pressures for liberalization throughout the area to operate more freely—and make possible, one would hope, a gradual evolution towards more open and democratic societies throughout Central America.

The US is committed to avoiding leftist takeovers in Central America, but it is also constrained by public opinion and probably by the 1973 War Powers Act from committing US troops to effect that goal. The problem, then, is how to support the Salvadoran government as well as those of Honduras and Costa Rica—and to a lesser degree, that of Guatemala (which seems to need outside support less)—and at the same time pressure Nicaragua to accept limits on the Soviet and Cuban presence and to stop the movement toward the imposition of a centralized Marxist-Leninist state. The Commission has made some useful suggestions to achieve these goals. As Tom Farer said in testimony to the Commission, the US must work for "ends uncongenial to conservatives, by means unsettling to liberals, at a cost disproportionate to any conventional consideration of the national interest."

Liberals may turn out to be right that the report is nothing more than a rationale for increased military aid, and conservatives may be correct in arguing that the proposed levels of economic and social aid are unrealistic. Yet the implementation of this ambitious and innovative report may prove both groups wrong, by increasing American awareness of what is at stake in Central America, and by producing a long-overdue commitment by the US to encourage democracy and social justice in Central America—for Central America's own sake, and also as the best defense against subversion and Marxist-dominated insurgency.

APPENDIX 1
SUMMARY OF THE REPORT OF THE NATIONAL BIPARTISAN COMMISSION ON CENTRAL AMERICA
(JANUARY 14, 1984)

The Commission on Central America, presided over by Henry A. Kissinger, was established by President Reagan to define appropriate elements of "a long-term United States policy that will best respond to the challenges of social, economic, and democratic development in the region, and to internal and external threats to its security and stability." The Commission was also requested to give advice on "means of building a national consensus on a comprehensive United States policy for the region."

Perhaps one of the most important conclusions in the Commission's report is that the situation in Central America is of sufficient gravity as to become a matter of "national interest," well above partisan politics.

The report was released on January 14, 1984. It is very difficult to do justice in a short summary to such a comprehensive document. However, it is hoped that by concentrating on the recommendations, it will be easier to grasp the depth and breadth of the report. In what follows, the recommendations of the Commission are presented in the same order in which they appear in the report.

Chapter 1–Introduction. This chapter describes how the Commission learned about the crisis in Central America, what they learned and how they reached the conclusion that the matter is of national interest above political partisanship.

Chapter 2–A Hemisphere in Transformation. In this chapter the Commission elaborates on the economic and political challenges faced by the US in the region. In particular, the Commission states three principles to meet the challenges of the region.

TWO CHALLENGES: The report recognizes that the situation in Central America poses two challenges to the United States, one economic and the other political. These two challenges are common to all Latin America but are particularly acute in Central America. Also the two challenges are closely interlocked and cannot be dealt with independently.

THREE PRINCIPLES: *The report establishes three principles that should guide the hemispheric relations of the United States and that particularly apply to Central America.*

1. The first principle is democratic self-determination.

By this the report means political pluralism, freedom of expression, respect for human rights, an independent and effective system of justice and the right of the people to choose their destiny in free elections, without repression, coercion, or foreign manipulation.

2. The second principle is encouragement of economic and social development that fairly benefits all.

The report recommends encouragement of those incentives that liberate and energize a free economy.

3. The third principle is cooperation in meeting threats to the security of the region.

In this regard the report emphasizes the seriousness of the Soviet-Cuban threat in the region.

Chapter 3—Crisis in Central America: An Historical Overview. *This chapter briefly examines the geography of the region, the colonial legacy, the independence period, the rule by oligarchies, the quest for change, the political retrogression, the economic background of the crisis, the growth of communist insurgency, the nature of the present crisis, and the relations of the United States with Central America.*

US INTERESTS IN THE CRISIS IN CENTRAL AMERICA: *The report highlights the following specific strategic and moral interests of the United States in Central America:*

- To preserve the moral authority of the United States. To be perceived by others as a nation that does what is right because it is right is one of this country's principal assets.

- To improve the living conditions of the people of Central America. They are neighbors. Their human need is tinder waiting to be ignited. And if it is, the conflagration could threaten the entire hemisphere.

- To advance the cause of democracy, broadly defined, within the hemisphere.

- To strengthen the hemispheric system by strengthening what is now, in both economic and social terms, one of its weakest links.

- To promote peaceful change in Central America while resisting the violation of democracy by force and terrorism.

- To prevent hostile forces from seizing and expanding control in a strategically vital area of the Western Hemisphere.

- To bar the Soviet Union from consolidating either directly or through Cuba a hostile foothold on the American continents in order to advance its strategic purposes.

Chapter 4—Toward Democracy and Economic Prosperity. *As a result of meetings with leaders and ordinary citizens in Central America, the report concludes that economic growth in the region requires taking into account the following policy aspects:*

- Economic growth goes forward in tandem with social and political modernization.
- Indigenous savings are encouraged and supplemented by substantial external aid.
- The nations of the region pursue appropriate economic policies.
- In particular, these policies recognize that success will ultimately depend on the re-invigoration of savings, growth, and employment.

To address these issues the report recommends the following programs:

AN EMERGENCY STABILIZATION PROGRAM (SHORT TERM): *The program includes eight key elements:*

1. We urge that the leaders of the United States and the Central American countries meet to initiate a comprehensive approach to the economic development of the region and the reinvigoration of the Central American Common Market.

In particular the report recommends that the leaders of Central America consider a new multilateral organization to promote comprehensive regional development.

2. We encourage the greatest possible involvement of the private sector in the stabilization effort.

Specifically the report states that renewed investment and lending, higher production from existing facilities, more training, increased purchases of Central American goods, and other initiatives would provide immediate economic benefits.

3. We recommend that the United States actively address the external debt problems of the region.

Among the measures recommended is a rescheduling of external debt, both bilateral and multilateral.

Also, the United States and the governments of other creditor countries should urge private lenders, especially commercial banks, to renegotiate existing debt at the lowest possible interest rates. A task force of key public and private creditors as well as debtors could be established to facilitate these debt renegotiations and to encourage new lending.

4. We recommend that the United States provide an immediate increase in bilateral economic assistance.

Total commitments of US bilateral economic assistance to Belize, Costa Rica, El Salvador, Guatemala, Honduras, Nicaragua, and Panama in FY 1983 was $628 million; the request for appropriated funds for FY 1984 is $477 million. We recommend a supplemental appropriation of $400 million for the current fiscal year (1984).

5. We recommend that a major thrust of expanded aid should be in labor-intensive infrastructure and housing projects.

Central America suffers from pressing needs for [housing], rural electrification, irrigation, roads, bridges, municipal water, sewer and drainage construction and repair. Such construction projects, using labor-intensive methods, can quicky be initiated, with considerable economic benefit.

6. We recommend that new official trade credit guarantees be made available to the Central American countries.

A Trade Credit Insurance Program would provide US government guarantees for short-term trade credit from US commercial banks. Such a program could be administered by the Export-Import Bank.

7. We recommend that the United States provide an emergency credit to the Central American Common Market Fund (CACMF).

The Central American countries have asked for a credit to refinance part of the accumulated trade deficits among themselves which have contributed to the contraction of intra-regional trade. The United States should use part of the increased economic aid for this purpose.

8. We recommend that the United States join the Central American Bank for Economic Integration (CABEI).

The infusion of new resources [to CABEI] would help...the bank...[to] channel much-needed funds to small-scale entrepreneurs and farmers, provide working capital to existing private sector companies, and encourage the development of new industries.

A MEDIUM- AND LONG-TERM RECONSTRUCTION AND DEVELOPMENT PROGRAM: *The report recommends the following* medium-term objectives which are compatible with the interests of the United States:

• Elimination of the climate of violence and civil strife. Peace is an essential condition of economic and social progress. So too is elimination of the fear of brutality inflicted by arbitrary authority or terrorism.

• Development of democratic institutions and processes. *The United States should encourage the Central American nations to develop: (a)strong judicial systems, (b)free elections, and (c)free and democratic trade unions.*

• Development of strong and free economies with diversified production for both external and domestic markets....[T]he Central American economies need to grow at per capita annual rates of at least 3 percent in real terms, which...is necessary to absorb new entrants to the labor force each year.

• Sharp improvement in the social conditions of the poorest Central Americans. *The report refers in particular to improvement of health, education and social welfare.*

• Substantially improved distribution of income and wealth. *In particular the report recognizes the need to improve* rural incomes and living standards....Agrarian reform programs should continue to be pursued as means of achieving this.

The report recommends the following programs dealing with the nature of US development support:

1. We urge a major increase in US and other countries' financial and economic assistance for Central America.

The report stresses that unless economic recovery is accompanied by social progress and political reform, additional financial support will ultimately be wasted. By the same token, without recovery, the political and security prospects will be grim.

The report estimates that between now and 1990 as much as $24 billion for the seven countries as a group *will be needed (see 4.4).* The World Bank, the International Monetary Fund, the Inter-American Development Bank, other official creditors, private investors, and commercial banks are likely to provide at least half of these funds—especially if each Central American country follows prudent economic policies, if there is steady social and political progress, and if outside aggression is eliminated. The balance, as much as $12 billion, would have to be supplied by the United States.

2. We now propose that economic assistance over the five-year period beginning in 1985 total $8 billion.

We firmly believe that without such large-scale assistance, economic recovery, social progress, and the development of democratic institutions in Central America will be set back.

3. Because of the magnitude of the effort required and the importance of a long-term commitment, we further urge that Congress appropriate funds for Central America on a multiple-year basis. We strongly recommend a five year authorization of money, a portion of which would be channeled through the proposed Central American Development Organization...(see 4.3). The balance would support economic assistance programs administered by existing US government agencies.

4. What is now required is a firm commitment by the Central American countries to economic policies, including reforms in tax systems, to encourage private enterprise and individual initiative, to create favorable investment climates, to curb corruption where it exists, and to spur balanced trade. These can lay the foundation for sustained growth.

The increased economic assistance we propose should be used to promote democracy, renew economic growth, improve living conditions, achieve better distribution of income and wealth, encourage more dynamic and open economies, and develop more productive agriculture.

5. We recommend that the United States expand economic assistance for democratic institutions and leadership training.

Among the activities recommended are the development of community improvement organizations, producer cooperatives, USIS bi-national centers, and exchange and training programs for leaders of democratic institutions.

The following programs dealing with expanded trade opportunities are recommended in this section:

6. We encourage the extension of duty-free trade to Central America by other major trading countries.

The CBI [Caribbean Basin Initiative] is a landmark piece of legislation and we hope that other countries will be willing to extend similar benefits to Central America. *The report urges the European Community and other Latin American countries to extend similar trade benefits to Central America.*

7. We urge the United States to review non-tariff barriers to imports from Central America.

The report recognizes the international and domestic difficulties associated with this recommendation and encourages the President to use whatever flexibility exists in such agreements in favor of Central American producers.

8. We recommend technical and financial support for export promotion efforts.

US economic assistance should be used to provide technical and financial support for trading and export marketing companies and innovative export-oriented joint ventures between Central American and foreign entrepreneurs.

Recommended programs regarding improved investment conditions include the following:

9. We encourage the formation of a privately-owned venture capital company for Central America.

We recommend that a venture capital company—which might be called the Central American Development Corporation (CADC)—be established for Central America....CADC, capitalized by private sector investors, would use its capital to raise funds which, in turn, would be lent to private companies active in Central America....The US government could support the CADC initiative through a long-term loan as it has for similar initiatives in other areas of the world.

10. We recommend the expanded availability of OPIC insurance in the region.

Needed foreign investment could be encouraged through an expanded insurance guarantee program. The Overseas Private Investment Corporation [OPIC]... should have the resources and the mandate to provide such support.

11. We recommend the development of aid programs to nurture small businesses, including microbusinesses.

Economic aid programs specifically aimed at encouraging the growth and formation of such businesses would assist in putting more people to work and also give people a larger stake in their economies. Such programs should include such incentives as seed capital, loan guarantees, and technical assistance.

With regard to accelerating agricultural development, the report mentions several programs that Central American countries and regional institutions should adopt. The following are some of the programs suggested:

- Provide long-term credit...to make possible the purchase of land by small farmers.

- Improve title registration and the defense of property rights of farmers.

- Provide short- and medium-term credit to finance the harvesting and storage of crops, the purchase of fertilizers and other inputs, and the acquisition of machinery and equipment.

- Follow pricing policies for agricultural commodities that protect farmers against unnecessary price fluctuations and unfair marketing practices....

- Where appropriate, initiate programs of agrarian reform—of "land for the landless"—in order to distribute more equitably the agricultural wealth of the country.

- Expand the network of rural feeder roads, storage facilities, and rural electrification.

- Sharply increase rural research and extension services....

In particular, the report makes the following recommendations:
12. We recommend that the financial underpinnings of the efforts to broaden land ownership be strengthened and reformed.

In programs of land reform, ways should be found to ensure that the redistribution of land provides the new owners with a valid title....
13. We recommend the provision of financial resources to supplement credit and investment programs.

A key thrust of US bilateral assistance should be to supplement national and regional agriculture credit programs; this is an element of AID's program which should be expanded in the future.
14. We recommend increased economic support for cooperatives.

We recommend that the United States increase its support for such organizations as part of its bilateral aid program.

ORGANIZING FOR DEVELOPMENT. *In analyzing the requirements for development in Central America, the report offers these considerations:*

- The development of Central America should be a cooperative program, with involvement of the United States and other democracies willing to participate and to provide assistance.
- The program should promote the development of Central America in all its dimensions—economic prosperity, social change, political modernization and peace.
- The assessment of progress should be conducted by representatives of participating nations who have access to a broad range of information and experience from both public and private sources. Private groups and institutions in donor and recipient countries should be drawn fully into the deliberative process.
- The ultimate control of aid funds will always rest with the donors. But a multilateral body including eminent Central Americans can most effectively...assess progress, evaluate program objectives, and measure external resource needs.
- The structure must be established on a sufficiently permanent basis to demonstrate the long-term commitment of both the United States and the Central American countries to the coordination of economic development with social and political development.

The structure proposed to carry out this program is the Central America Development Organization (CADO), mentioned above:

Membership in CADO, as we envision it, would initially be open to the seven countries of Central America—Belize, Costa Rica, El Salvador, Guatemala, Honduras, Nicaragua and Panama—and to the United States. Associate member status would be available to any democracy willing to contribute significant resources to promote regional development. We would hope that the other Contadora countries would participate actively, as well as the nations of Europe, Canada and Japan. The organization's Chairman should be from the United States with an Executive Secretary from Central America. *Representation in CADO would include the private sector, trade unions, and the government.*

Central American participation in the program should turn on acceptance of and continued progress toward:

- The protection of personal and economic liberties, freedom of

expression, respect for human rights, and an independent system of equal justice and criminal law enforcement.
• Political pluralism, and a process of recurrent elections with competing political parties.
• ...A commitment to preserve peace, independence and the mutual security of Central American member nations....
• The establishment and maintenance of sound growth policies in the various countries....
• The development of the human resources of the region....

CENTRAL AMERICAN FINANCIAL NEEDS. *In estimating the financial needs (defined as a country's balance-of-payment current account deficit plus minimal foreign reserve build up) of the region between 1984 and 1990, the report considers that four requirements will be met: peace, improved economic policy, increased economic assistance, and improved global economic environment.*

The estimates are the following:

EXTERNAL FINANCING REQUIREMENTS (IN BILLIONS OF US$), 1984 - 1990

Costa Rica	$ 5.1
El Salvador	5.5
Guatemala	4.5
Honduras	2.3
Panama	3.2
Sub-total	20.6
Nicaragua [no current US aid]	3.4
TOTAL	$ 24.0

Chapter 5–Human Development. *The report affirms that a comprehensive effort to promote democracy and prosperity among the Central American nations must have as its cornerstone accelerated "human development."*

The report then states that the following are ambitious yet realistic objectives for the 1980s:

• The reduction of malnutrition.
• The elimination of illiteracy.
• Universal access to primary education.
• Universal access to primary health care.
• A significant reduction of infant mortality.
• A sustained reduction in population growth rates.
• A significant improvement in housing.

The following programs related to human development are recommended in the report:

DEVELOPING EDUCATIONAL OPPORTUNITIES:

1. We recommend that the United States increase food aid on an emergency basis.

Although the permanent solution to the problem lies in accelerated agricultural development, the United States and other donors—including members of the European Community—can help in the short run by providing additional food aid. The United States now provides about $100 million annually to Central America in such aid through the PL 480 program. This should be expanded....

2. We recommend that the Peace Corps expand its recruitment of front line teachers to serve in a new Literacy Corps.

A Literacy Corps of qualified volunteers should be created to engage in direct teaching and also to train Central Americans *to teach their compatriots.*

3. We recommend that Peace Corps activities be expanded at the primary, secondary, and technical levels in part by establishing a Central American Teacher Corps, recruited from the Spanish-speaking population of the United States.

We believe that other democracies in Latin America should be encouraged to undertake similar programs, and that the countries themselves should dramatize the education effort by seeking local volunteers.

4. We recommend an expanded program of secondary level technical and vocational education.

Although both the public and private sectors are already active in this area, there is a substantial need for additional training programs matched to real jobs. We particularly urge that business and labor unions develop apprenticeship programs.

5. We recommend expansion of the International Executive Service Corps (IESC).

The IESC is a private, voluntary organization of retired American business executives. An expanded IESC effort in Central America, perhaps with some support from the US Government, should give particular attention to training managers of small businesses.

6. ...[W]e recommend a program of 10,000 government-sponsored scholarships to bring Central American students to the United States.

The United States should provide 5,000 four to six year university scholarships and 5,000 two to four year vocational-technical scholarships. Admittedly, this is an ambitious program compared both to current efforts and to the 500 scholarships anticipated under the CBI.

We suggest that such a program involve the following elements:

• Careful targeting to encourage participation by young people from all social and economic classes.

• Maintenance of existing admission standards—which has sometimes been a barrier in the past—by providing intensive English and other training as part of the program.

• Mechanisms to encourage graduates to return to their home countries after completing their education, perhaps by providing part of the educational support in the form of loans and linking forgiveness of loans to their return.

• Arrangements by which the Central American countries bear some of the cost of the program.

• The availability of at least 100 to 200 of these scholarships to mid-career public service officials and a further 100 for University faculty exchanges.

7. We recommend that the United States, in close partnership with

the Central American governments and universities, develop a long-term plan to strengthen the major universities in Central America.

The principal thrust of this assistance effort should be to help improve the quality of Central American universities. A balanced program of assistance would include:

- Technical assistance to provide immediate improvements in undergraduate teaching and curriculum.
- Selective investments in improving libraries, laboratories, and student facilities.
- An innovative effort to recruit and train junior faculty and young administrators.
- A complimentary program of refresher training and upgrading of existing faculty and administrative staff.
- An expanded program of pairing of US and Central American colleges and universities.
- A significant expansion of opportunities for faculty, students, and administrators to visit the United States for periods which may range from a few weeks to several years.

8. We recommend that the United States help strengthen Central American judicial systems.

Specifically, we recommend the use of US economic assistance to:

- Enhance the training and resources of judges, judicial staff, and public prosecutors' offices.
- Support modern and professional means of criminal investigation.
- Promote availability of legal materials, assistance to law faculties, and support for local bar associations.

9. We recommend a greatly expanded effort, subsidized by the US Government through the National Endowment for the Humanities, to train high level translators, to support translations of important books from both languages, and to subsidize their publication so as to make them generally available.

The National Endowment could make an important contribution to US-Central American understanding through such a center.

A REGION'S HEALTH: *The report states that* the Central American people suffer from extremely poor health conditions, although there are sharp differences among countries. But the report also recognizes that considerable effort has been made by the governments of Central America in the support of primary health care, environmental sanitation and population control.

The recommendations of the report with regard to health issues are the following:

1. In order to meet this need, [for health services] we recommend that existing technical assistance programs supported by AID should be expanded.

...[C]oncentration should be placed upon health care systems, management health care planning and health economics. *Training of Central Americans for these specialties* should be carried out in an integrated manner. A regional center for such training should be considered in either Costa Rica or Panama.

2. We recommend a resumption of the AID-sponsored program to eradicate vector-borne diseases such as malaria and dengue fever.

An AID-sponsored vector control program was suspended five years ago. However, Belize, Guatemala, Honduras and El Salvador are currently experiencing a serious resurgence of malaria and dengue fever. The mosquito knows no frontiers and Nicaragua, Costa Rica and Panama will soon suffer equally unless drastic measures are taken to eradicate the breeding grounds of the mosquito.

3. We recommend that the United States support an expansion of programs of oral rehydration and immunization so as to reduce dramatically the incidence of childhood disease and mortality in Central America during the next five years.

...[T]he experience of UNICEF, AID and others indicates that...[most diseases] of early childhood can be virtually wiped out in a very short time by well administered programs of oral rehydration and immunization.

4. We recommend the continuation of the population and family planning programs currently supported by the Agency for International Development.

Overpopulation presents a serious threat to the development and health of the region. Attempts must be made through education and family planning to reduce the birth rate to a more moderate level.

5. We recommend that Central American educational institutions be encouraged to increase their concentration on the training of primary health care workers, nurses, dental assistants and personnel in the allied health skills.

The United States, through AID, should provide funds for expanded programs in these areas to be supervised and administered by appropriate divisions of AID, by the Peace Corps, or by private voluntary organizations.

6. We recommend that the nations of Central America be urged to develop methods which would integrate public and private financing of health services.

In this effort state investment should be focused on primary health care services for the rural and urban poor and on environmental services for all.

United States corporations, active in the region, have a particular responsibility to provide leadership in creating safe and healthy conditions, as well as to introduce appropriate standards of environmental pollution control in their own operations.

HOUSING: *The report recognizes that* urbanization throughout Central America is rapidly transforming the character of the region...*and that*...housing and the development of urban services are critical needs, affecting as much as three-quarters of the population, primarily the poor.

The report indicates two areas where US assistance should be concentrated.

1. First, we recommend an enlarged housing and infrastructure construction program.

It is essential that such a program rely heavily on the private sector for both design and implementation. There is considerable unused capacity in both the US and Central American construction industries that could be harnessed to expand the production of shelter and related infrastructure.

2. Second, we recommend US government support for accelerated education and training of professionals in public administration.

Improved public sector management—through better trained managers—is critical to addressing the housing and shelter problems of the region in both the short and medium term. This should occur both through scholarship and exchange programs in the United States and by providing resources to national and regional public administration institutes.

HUMANITARIAN RELIEF: The tragedy of the more than one million displaced persons in Central America—driven from their homes by violence and fear of violence—is well known....These nations, whose economies have been seriously disrupted, cannot by themselves provide adequate care or relief for these people. The refugee camps and overcrowded cities to which they have fled become breeding grounds for discontent and frustration.

1. We recommend expanded support for adequate relief efforts through the Agency for International Development and the Department of State refugee program.

Chapter 6—Central America Security Issues. *The report begins by recognizing that the conflicts that ravage the nations of Central America have both indigenous and foreign roots. The report goes on to analyze the path of insurgency, external intervention, the totalitarian outcome, the Cuban-Soviet connection, the strategic implications for the United States, and the problems of guerrilla war. Next the report examines the situation in El Salvador, Guatemala, and other parts of the region. The report then makes recommendations in two areas: military assistance and human rights.*

MILITARY ASSISTANCE: *The report considers specifically the military assistance to El Salvador, which is where the situation is more critical, and identifies some military requirements of that country to carry out its campaign against the guerrillas:*

• Increased air and ground mobility, to enable the government forces to reach and assist static positions under attack and, eventually, to seek out and engage the guerrillas.

• Increased training to upgrade the forces tactically and to generalize further the use of modern, humane, counterinsurgency methods, including civic action as such.

• Higher force levels, to enable the government forces both to protect important installations and to carry the war to the guerrillas....

• Greater stocks of equipment and supplies to support a consistent war effort.

• Improved conditions for the troops in order to retain trained personnel, particularly by providing medical evacuation....

The report recognizes the US Department of Defense estimate that $400 million in US military assistance in 1984 and 1985 are *needed* to break the military stalemate and allow the National Campaign Plan *(pacification plan) to be carried out. The report then makes the following recommendations:*

1. The Commission recommends that the United States provide to El Salvador—subject to the conditions we specify later in this chapter—significantly increased levels of military aid as quickly as possible, so that the Salvadoran authorities can act on the assurance that needed aid will be forthcoming.

2. The Commission believes the administration and the Congress should work together to achieve greater predictability [in funding military assistance]. That could be most effectively achieved through multi-year funding.

3. We believe the National Security Council should conduct a detailed review of these [following] issues:

- The length of the service of tours of our military people in El Salvador.
- The development of greater area expertise by selected US military personnel.
- Organization and command structure in the Pentagon and the field.
- Prospects for closer cooperation among the nations of Central America in defense matters.
- The possibility of a strengthened role for the Inter-American Defense Board.

HUMAN RIGHTS: *The report recognizes that* the question of the relationship between military aid and human rights abuses is both extremely difficult and extremely important, *given the present conditions in the region.*

The report also states that the United States Government has a right to demand certain minimum standards of respect for human rights as a condition for providing military aid to any country, *and recommends the following:*

1. With respect to El Salvador, military aid should, through legislation requiring periodic reports, be made contingent upon demonstrated progress toward free elections; freedom of association; the establishment of the rule of law and an effective judicial system; and the termination of the activities of the so-called death squads, as well as vigorous action against those guilty of crimes and the prosecution to the extent possible of past offenders. These conditions should be seriously enforced.

2. As an additional measure, the United States should impose sanctions, including the denial of visas, deportation, and the investigation of financial dealings, against foreign nationals in the United States who are connected with death-squad activities in El Salvador or anywhere else.

It is the Commission's judgment that the same policy approach should be employed in the case of Guatemala.

Chapter 7—The Search for Peace. *The report states that* US diplomacy toward Central America can be neither conducted nor considered in a vacuum. It must reflect the larger realities of the hemisphere and of the world. *In that context, the report suggests that* a successful political strategy in Central America...requires:

• Significant resources to promote economic progress.
• Vigorous efforts to advance democracy and social reform.
• Other inducements and penalties, short of force, to reinforce our diplomacy.

The report emphasizes that peace cannot successfully be attained by sharing power with guerrillas without a due democratic electoral process.

Specifically, with regard to El Salvador, the report makes the following recommendations:

The Salvadoran Governemnt would invite the FDR/FMLN to negotiate mutually acceptable procedures to establish a framework for future elections.

As part of this framework a broadly representative Elections Commission would be established, including representatives of the FDR/FMLN.

Violence should be ended by all parties so that mutually satisfactory arrangements can be developed among the government, pro-government parties, the different opposition groups and insurgent groups for the period of campaigning and elections.

A system of international observation should be established to enhance the faith and confidence of all parties in the probity and equity of arrangements for elections.

Regarding Nicaragua, the report states that the Commission encountered no leader in Central America, including democratic and unarmed Costa Rica, who did not express deep foreboding about the impact of a militarized, totalitarian Nicaragua on the peace and security of the region. Several expressed the view that should the Sandinista regime now be consolidated as a totalitarian state, their own freedom, and even their independence, would be jeopardized.

The report does not enter into details about how to deal with the Sandinista regime in Nicaragua. However, it states that the Commission believes...that whatever the prospects seem to be for productive negotiations, the United States must spare no effort to pursue the diplomatic route....With specific reference to the highly controversial question of whether the United States should provide support for the Nicaraguan insurgent forces opposed to the Sandinistas now in authority in Managua, the Commission recognized that an adequate examination of this issue would require treatment of sensitive information not appropriate to a public report. However, the majority of the members of the Commission, in their respective individual judgments, believe that the efforts of the Nicaraguan insurgents represent one of the incentives working in favor of a negotiated settlement and that the future role of the United States in those efforts must therefore be considered in the context of the negotiating process.

The report establishes principles for a comprehensive regional settlement:

- Respect for the sovereignty, independence, and integrity of all Central American countries.
- A broad and concrete commitment to democracy and human rights.
- A verifiable commitment by each nation not to attack its neighbors; nor to transfer arms overtly or covertly to any insurgents; nor to train the military personnel of a Central American country; nor to practice subversion, directly or indirectly, against its neighbors.
- A verifiable commitment by each country not to possess arms that exceeded certain sizes, types, and capabilities. The total permissible scale of military forces in each nation could be stipulated as not to exceed an agreed level substantially lower than now. No military forces, bases, or advisers of non-Central American countries would be permitted.
- United States respect for and cooperation with the agreement. This would include a readiness to support the Central American military and security arrangements, and a commitment to respect whatever domestic arrangements emerge from legitimating elections, as long as there is continuing adherence to the basic principles of pluralism at home and restraint abroad.
- Commitments by all countries to pluralism, to peaceful political activity, and to free elections in which all political parties would have a right to participate free of threat or violence. Particularly, the pledges by Nicaragua of July 1979 to the OAS, and reaffirmed by the Contadora group, would be fulfilled. All insurgent groups would stop military activity.
- Permanent verification. The United States would be prepared to offer technical assistance to ensure effective verification. The Contadora countries could play a major role.
- The Central American nations that are parties to the agreement could invite other countries to be associated with it. They could also request that others in the hemisphere undertake mutual pledges of non-interference.
- Adherence to the agreement would be a condition for participating in the development program outlined in Chapters 4 and 5. The Central American Development Organization would, as suggested there, maintain a continuing audit and review of compliance with the commitments to nonintervention abroad and democratization at home.
- Foreign and other ministers of the Central American members, together with the United States, Mexico, Panama, Colombia, and Venezuela as observers, would meet regularly to review the arrangement and compliance with it. The council would develop procedures for conflict-resolution among member states.

The chapter is concluded with an expression of gratitude toward and support of the efforts of the Contadora Group.

APPENDIX 2
CARIBBEAN BASIN INITIATIVE
(Excerpts of President Reagan's Proposal,
February 24, 1982)

On February 24, 1982, President Reagan proposed, before the Council of the Organization of American States, a broad plan of trade and incentives designed to improve the economic conditions of the Caribbean area through trade, private investment, and technical assistance to the private sector. The plan covers six basic points.

The first point and "centerpiece of the program is free trade for Caribbean basin products exported to the United States....Exports from the area will receive duty-free treatment for 12 years," a period long enough to encourage private investment. The only exceptions are textile and apparel products, which are covered by other international agreements.

Secondly, because of the high risk in the area, "significant tax incentives" are to be offered to any who invest in the area. In addition, the United States is prepared "to negotiate bilateral investment treaties with Basin countries."

Third, "a supplementary fiscal year 1982 appropriation of $350 million" was to be requested to assist those countries which are particularly hard hit economically. Much of this aid will be concentrated on the private sector, to assist in "taking advantage of the trade and investment portions of the program."

Fourth, "technical assistance and training to assist the private sector in the Basin countries" is to be offered, including "investment promotion, export marketing, and technology transfer." The American business community was invited to take active participation in this undertaking. Also, the Peace Corps in the region will be reinforced with volunteers who have skills in developing local enterprises.

Fifth, the United States "will work closely with Mexico, Canada, and Venezuela," which already have aid programs in the region, "to encourage stronger international efforts" to coordinate developmental assistance, with a potential participation by Colombia. European allies, Japan, and multilateral development institutions will be encouraged to increase their assistance to the region.

Sixth, the United States "will propose special measures to insure that Puerto Rico and the Virgin Islands" also will benefit and prosper from this program.

Besides the economic and trade assistance program, President Reagan elaborated on the critical situation in El Salvador; the dangers posed to the region by the communist regime in Nicaragua; and the intervention of the Soviet Union in the area directly and covertly, using Cuba as a proxy.

The US Congress approved in July 1983 the programs proposed in the Caribbean Basin Initiative. Several US agencies (NSF, AID, NAS) are charged with their implementation.

APPENDIX 3
RECOMMENDATIONS OF THE CONTADORA GROUP
(Colombia, Mexico, Panama, and Venezuela)

The members of the Contadora Group(named after the resort island off the Pacific coast of Panama where the group first gathered) have met several times, inviting on some occasions representatives of the Central American governments, with which they maintain close consultations. At the meeting held during September 7–10, 1983, the Group adopted the following document that forms the basis for continued negotiations and defines the objectives for a peaceful settlement of the region.

DOCUMENT OF OBJECTIVES

CONSIDERING:

The situation prevailing in Central America, which is characterized by an atmosphere of tension that threatens security and peaceful coexistence in the region, and which requires, for its solution, observance of the principles of international law governing the actions of states, especially:

The self-determination of peoples;

Non-intervention;

The sovereign equality of states;

The peaceful settlement of disputes;

Refraining from the threat or use of force;

Respect for the territorial integrity of states;

Pluralism in its various manifestations;

Full support for democratic institutions;

The promotion of social justice;

International cooperation for development;

Respect for and promotion of human rights;

The prohibition of terrorism and subversion;

The desire to reconstruct the Central American homeland through progressive integration of its economic, legal, and social institutions;

The need for economic cooperation among the states of Central America so as to make a fundamental contribution to the development of their peoples and the strengthening of their independence;

The undertaking to establish, promote, or revitalize representative democratic systems in all the countries of the region;

The unjust economic, social, and political structures which exacerbate the conflicts in Central America;

The urgent need to put an end to the tensions and lay the foundations for understanding and solidarity among the countries of the area;

The arms race and the growing arms traffic in Central America, which aggravate political relations in the region and divert economic resources that could be used for development;

The presence of foreign advisors and other forms of foreign military interference in the zone;

The risks that the territory of Central American states may be used for the purpose of conducting military operations and pursuing policies of destabilization against others; [and]

The need for concerted political efforts in order to encourage dialogue and understanding in Central America, avert the danger of a general spreading of the conflicts, and set in motion the machinery needed to ensure the peaceful coexistence and security of their peoples;

Declare their intention of achieving the following objectives:

1. To promote detente and put an end to situations of conflict in the area, refraining from taking any action that might jeopardize political confidence or prevent the achievement of peace, security, and stability in the region;

2. To ensure strict compliance with the aforementioned principles of international law, whose violators will be held accountable;

3. To respect and ensure the exercise of human, political, civil, economic, social, religious, and cultural rights;

4. To adopt measures conducive to the establishment and, where appropriate, improvement of democratic, representative and pluralistic systems that will guarantee effective popular participation in the decision-making process and ensure that the various currents of opinion have free access to fair and regular elections based on the full observance of citizens' rights;

5. To promote national reconciliation efforts wherever deep divisions have taken place within the society, with a view to fostering participation in democratic political processes in accordance with the law;

6. To create political conditions intended to ensure the international security, integrity, and sovereignty of the states of the region;

7. To stop the arms race in all its forms and begin negotiations for the control and reduction of current stocks of weapons and on the number of armed troops;

8. To prevent the installation on their territory of foreign military or any other type of foreign military interference;

9. To conclude agreements to reduce the presence of foreign military advisers and other foreign elements involved in military and security activities, with a view to their elimination;

10. To establish internal control machinery to prevent the traffic in arms from the territory of any country in the region to the territory of another;

11. To eliminate the traffic in arms, whether within the region or from outside it, intended for persons, organizations, or groups seeking to destabilize the governments of Central American countries;

12. To prevent the use of their own territory by person, organizations, or groups seeking to destabilize the governments of Central American countries, and to refuse to provide them with or permit them to receive military or logistical support;

13. To refrain from inciting or supporting acts of terrorism, subversion, or sabotage in the countries in the area;

14. To establish and coordinate direct communication systems with a view to preventing or, where appropriate, settling incidents between states of the region;

15. To continue humanitarian aid aimed at helping Central American refugees who have been displaced from their countries of origin, and to create suitable conditions for the voluntary repatriation of such refugees, in consultation with or with the cooperation of the United Nations High Commissioner for refugees (UNHCR) and other international agencies deemed appropriate;

16. To undertake economic and social development programs with the aim of promoting well-being and an equitable distribution of wealth;

17. To revitalize and restore economic integration machinery in order to attain sustained development on the basis of solidarity and mutual advantage;

18. To negotiate the provision of external monetary resources which will provide additional means of financing the resumption of intra-regional trade, meet the serious balance-of-payments problems, attract funds for working capital, support programs to extend and restructure production systems and promote medium- and long-term investment projects;

19. To negotiate better and broader access to international markets in order to increase the volume of trade between the countries of Central America and the rest of the world, particularly the industrialized countries, by means of a revision of trade practices, the elimination of tariff and other barriers, and the achievement of price stability at a profitable and fair level for the products exported by the countries of the region;

20. To establish technical cooperation machinery for the planning, programming and implementation of multi-sector investment and trade promotion projects.

APPENDIX 4
RESOLUTION AG/551/(XI-0181) OF THE GENERAL ASSEMBLY OF THE ORGANIZATION OF AMERICAN STATES
(Santa Lucia, December 1981)

This resolution expresses a hemispheric consensus in relation to the situation in El Salvador and is an example of how it is possible to mobilize the political will of the countries in the region.

SITUATION OF EL SALVADOR

THE GENERAL ASSEMBLY,

HAVING SEEN:

The provisions of articles 3 and 16 of the Charter of the OAS, which refer to the principle of solidarity of the American States with a political organization on the basis of the effective exercise of representative democracy, to respect for the fundamental rights of the individual, and to the principle of free determination of the peoples; and

Resolution AG/RES. 510 (X-0/80), which provides that the democratic system is the basis for the establishment of a political society where human values can be fully realized;

HAVING HEARD:

The statements made by heads of delegations in the course of the debates of the General Assembly; and

CONSIDERING:

That the Government of El Salvador has expressed its intention to find, through the democratic process, the political solution to the violence affecting its country and that, to that end, it has scheduled the election of a National Constituent Assembly for March 1982;

That the Government of El Salvador has announced that the political electoral process of El Salvador is in progress; and

That the Government of El Salvador has invited other governments to observe the elections,

RESOLVES:

1. To express the wish that the people of El Salvador attain peace, social justice, and democracy within a pluralist system that will enable its citizens to exercise their inalienable rights.

2. To express the hope that all Salvadorans will attain an atmosphere of peace and harmony through a truly democratic electoral process.

3. To suggest to the governments that wish to do so that they consider the possibility of accepting the invitation extended by the Government of El Salvador to observe its election proceedings.

4. To repudiate violence and terrorism and any act that constitutes a violation of the principle of non-intervention.

5. To reiterate that, in accordance with the principle of non-intervention, it is up to the Salvadoran people alone to settle their internal affairs.

INDEX

A

Acción Democrática (Democratic Action)
  in El Salvador, 174
  in Venezuela, 31
Account deficits, 103
Act of Independence, 15
AD. See Democractic Action
AFL-CIO, 28
African slaves, 13
Agency for International Development (AID), 28, 207
Agrarian Reform Law of 1962 in Honduras, 28
Agreement on Tax Incentives for Industry and Development, 202-203
Agriculture in Honduras and Panama, 90
AID. See Agency for International Development
Alianza Popular Revolucionaria Americana (APRA) of Peru, 31
Alianza Renovadora Nacional (National Renewal Alliance, or ARENA), 23, 173, 174, 177
Alliance for Progress, 21, 99, 115, 194
Alonso, Marcelo, ix
Alvarez Martinez, Gustavo, 184
American Department of Cuban Communist Party, 167
American Revolution, 14
"Ana Maria" (Melinda Anaya Montes), 175
Anarcho-syndicalist movement, 14
Anticlericalism, 15
Apaneca Pact, 23, 174, 177
APRA. See Alianza Popular Revolucionaria Americana
Arana, Francisco, 25
Arbenz, Jacobo, 25, 159
ARDE, See Democratic Revolutionary Alliance
Area statistics, vi
Arellano, Oswaldo Lopze, 28
ARENA. See Alianza Renovadora Nacional
Arevalo, Juan Jose, 25
Argentinian Montoneros, 169
Arias, Arnulfo, 30, 184
Armas, Carlos Castillo, 25
Armed Forces for National Resistance (Fuerzas Armadas de la Resistencia Nacional, or FARN), 177
Armed Rebel Forces (Fuerzas Armadas Rebeldes, or FAR), 179

Assistance
  economic. *See* Economic assistance
  multilateral development, 209
  political, 196–202
  socioeconomic, 202–211
Association of Stockmen and Farmers, 21
Authentic Constitutional Party (PAC), 21

B

Balance of payments, 92, 102–103
  See also Trade
  in Costa Rica, 103
  deficits of, 101, 103, 113, 114, 119
  in Panama, 102
Bananas, 13, 15, 104
Banking, 93
Baraona, Paz, 28
Barrios, Justo Rufino, 24
Basque terrorists, 169
Bay of Pigs, 159
BD International, ix
Belize
  area of, vi
  political conflict in, 188–189
  population of, vi
Bilateral cooperation, 207, 209–210
Biomass, 118
Bipartisan Commission on Central America. *See* Kissinger's Commission
Birth control, 43, 65
Birth rates, 42
Bonachea, Rolando, x
Borge, Tomás, 169, 170
"Brain drain," 45
Brazilian investments, 109
Broad Opposition Front (FAO), Nicaragua, 207

C

CABEI. *See* Central American Bank for Economic Integration
Cacao, 13
CACD. *See* Central American Democratic Community
CACM. *See* Central American Common Market
Calderon, Rafael, 31
Cambodia, 2
Canada, 205, 207, 208
Canals
  Panama. *See* Panama Canal
  transisthmian, 19
Capitalism, 15
Captaincy General of Guatemala, 12, 14
Carazo, Rodrigo, 186, 187
Carias, Tiburcio, 28
Caribbean, 16
  transisthmian canal linking Pacific Ocean with, 19
Caribbean Basin Initiative (CBI), xiii, 121, 164, 165, 195, 204, 205, 207, 208, 209, 212, 253
Carpio, Cayetano, 175
Carter, Jimmy, 5, 29, 30, 31, 166, 167, 184
Castaneda, Rolando, ix
Castro, Fidel, 159, 179, 180
Castro, Juan Alberto Melgar, 28
Catholic Church, 13, 15, 166, 172
CBI. *See* Caribbean Basin Initiative
CDS. *See* Sandinista Defense Committee (Nicaragua)
Central American Agreement on Tax Incentives, 120
Central American Bank for Economic Integration (CABEI), 106
Central American Clearing House, 106
Central American Common Market (CACM), 91, 92, 93, 95, 97, 99, 100, 101, 102, 106, 107, 115, 122, 193, 202, 211, 212
  restructuring of, 120
  withdrawal of Honduras from, 107
Central American Defense Council, 165, 181
Central American Democratic Community (CACD), 162, 165, 212
Central American Development Organization, 209
Central American Institute of

Public Administration (ICAP), 107
Central American Institute of Technological and Industrial Research, 106
Central American Peace Corps, 210
Central American Tariff Agreement, 202
Central Banks, 94, 108
Central Intelligence Agency (CIA), 25, 28
CEPAL. See Economic Commission of Latin America
Chamber of Commerce and Industry, 21
Chamorro, Pedro Joaquín, 166, 167
Chiari, Roberto P., 30
Christian Democratic Party (PDC), 5, 21, 23, 27, 30, 158, 173, 174, 177, 180, 181
Christopher, Warren, 168
CIA. See Central Intelligence Agency
Coffee, 13, 96, 104
Coffee Growers Association, 21
Coffee plantations, 20
Cold War, 159
Colombia, 6, 34, 161, 163, 205, 208
　and Contadora Group, 162, 210
　independence of Panama from, 29
Colonial period, 12, 13
COMECON. See Council for Mutual Economic Assistance
Communist Party, 27, 177
　Cuban, 161, 167, 168
　Department of the Americas of, 161
　in El Salvador, 177
　Political Bureau of Secretariat of in Cuba, 161
Communists
　in Cosa Rica, 159
　vs. democracy, 1
　in Guatemala, 27, 159, 179
　involvement and tactics of, 158–161
　vs. oligarchic-military regimes, 7
Compensatory Financing Facility, 114

Conditionality in IMF agreements, 114
Conquistadores, 12
Conservation, 99
　of energy, 118
Conservatives, 15
Constituent Assembly
　in El Salvador, 23
　in Guatemala, 27
　in Honduras, 29
Contadora Group, xiii, 164, 165, 185, 198, 199, 200, 201, 210, 255
　and Colombia, 162, 210
　and Costa Rica, 163
　and El Salvador, 163
　and Guatemala, 163
　and Honduras, 163
　and Mexico, 162, 210
　and Nicaragua, 163
　and Panama, 162, 210
　and Venezuela, 162, 210
Contra rebels, 172
Cordova, Roberto Suazo, 29, 182
Costa Rica, 3, 5, 6, 7, 12, 13, 14, 17, 19, 34, 62, 93, 95, 107, 193, 196
　area of, vi
　birth control in, 43
　and Central American Democratic Community, 162, 212
　communists in, 159
　and Contadora Group, 163
　debt in, 93, 112
　economic growth in, 96, 115
　education in, 56, 57, 93
　elections in, 33, 196, 197, 198
　emergency funds in, 207
　employment in, 100
　ethnic composition of, 40, 41
　exports of, viii, 104, 112
　farmland access in, 51
　financial market in, 108
　fiscal deficits in, 93, 112
　foreign trade of, 106
　and Forum for Peace and Democracy, 162
　and FSLN, 166
　GDP of, 94, 97, 98
　health conditions in, 58, 59
　housing in, 61, 67
　hydroelectricity in, 100
　and IMF, 113, 114

Costa Rica (*cont.*)
  income distribution in, 55, 56
  industry in, 101
  inflation in, 97, 114
  interest rates in, 109
  investments in, 109, 110
  irrigation in Tempisque Valley in, 210
  land concentration in, 50
  land reform in, 53, 54, 65
  major industries of, viii
  National Liberation Party in, 16
  non-agricultural labor in, 46, 49
  nutrition in, 60
  oil imports in, 105
  payroll taxes in, 92
  per-capita GDP in, 95
  political conflict in, 186–188, 189
  political development of, 31–32
  population of, vii, 42
  ratio of external debt service to value of exports in, 112
  real GDP in, 97
  and Somoza downfall, 168
  terrorism in, 165, 187
  TFR in, 42, 43
  trade deficits in, 103
  unemployment in, 48, 92, 100, 101
  unions in, 158
  US economic assistance to, 186
  violence in, 165, 170, 187
Council for Mutual Economic Assistance (COMECON), 103, 112
Credit policies, 91, 93
Cruz, Ramon Ernesto, 28
Cuba, 5, 8, 13, 34, 158, 161, 165, 177, 181, 183, 189
  influence of, 2, 3, 6, 188
Cuban Communist Party, 168
  American Department of, 167
  Political Bureau of Secretariat of in, 161
Cuban revolution, 159
Customs duties, 91

D

D'Abuisson, Roberto, 23, 173, 174
DAC. *See* Development Assistance Committee of OECD

Death rates, 42
Debt, 93, 94, 103, 111, 112
Deficits
  of balance of payments, 101, 103, 113, 114, 119
  fiscal. *See* Debt
De la Espriella, Ricardo, 30, 185, 186, 197
De Lesseps, Ferdinand, 29
Democracy vs. communism, 1
Democratic Action (*Acción Democrática*, or AD)
  in El Salvador, 174
  in Venezuela, 31
Democratic Coordination, 171
Democratic pluralism in Nicaragua, 199
Democratic reconstitution in Honduras, 4
Democratic Revolutionary Alliance (ARDE), 170, 171, 172
Democratic Revolutionary Front (*Frente Democrático Revolucionario*, or FDR), 176, 177
Democratic Revolutionary Party (*Partido Revolucionario Democrático*, or PRD), 30, 185
Department of the Americas of the Communist Party, 161
Depression of the '20s, 20
Devaluation of exchange rate, 93
Development
  assistance in, 209
  regional, 211
Development Assistance Committee (DAC) of OECD, 112, 113, 193, 213
Development financing, 108–114
Diaz-Briquets, Sergio, ix
Diaz, Julio Lozano, 28
Dictatorship, 2, 3, 4
Dirección Nacional Unida (National United Directorate), 183
Direct investment, 110–111
Diseases, 13
Domestic investment, 116–117
  gross, 108, 109
Domestic product structure, 98–99
Domestic savings, 108, 116–117
Dominican Republic, 161
Duarte, Jose Napoleon, 22, 23

E

Earthquake in Guatemala and Nicaragua, 96
Echeverrila, Juan Jose, 187
ECLA. See Economic Commission of Latin America
Economic assistance, 113
  to Costa Rica from US, 186
  to El Salvador, 178
Economic Commission of Latin America (ECLA), 55, 208
Economy, 90, 91, 94, 115
  in Costa Rica, 96, 115
  in Guatemala, 90, 96
  in Honduras, 90, 95, 96
  in Nicaragua, 95, 96, 115
  in Panama, 95, 115
Education, 56–58, 62, 63
  in Costa Rica, 56, 57, 93
  in El Salvador, 57
  in Guatemala, 56, 57
  in Panama, 56, 57
EGP. See Ejército Guerrillero de los Pobres Ejército Guerrillero de los Pobres (Guerrilla Army of the Poor, or EGP), 179
Ejército Popular Sandinista (Popular Sandinist Army), 169
Ejército Revolucionario del Pueblo (Revolutionary Army of the People), 176
"El Brujo" (General Martinez), 20
Elections
  in Costa Rica, 33, 196, 197, 198
  in El Salvador, 8, 23, 33, 36, 196, 197, 198
  in Guatemala, 33, 196, 197
  in Honduras, 29, 33, 196, 197, 198
  in Nicaragua, 196
  in Panama, 196
  supervision of, 197
Electrical energy, 100
El Nuevo Diario, 19
El Salvador, 3, 4, 5, 7, 8, 12, 14, 16, 34, 62, 95, 107, 165
  area of, vi
  birth control in, 43
  and Central American Democratic Community, 162, 212
  Communist Party in, 177
  Constituent Assembly election in, 23
  and Contadora Group, 163
  Cuban mediation, in 161
  debt in, 93, 112
  economic aid to, 178
  education in, 57
  elections in, 8, 23, 33, 36, 196, 197, 198
  emergency funds in, 207
  emigration to United States from, 46
  employment in, 47, 100
  ethnic composition of, 41
  farmland access in, 51
  fiscal deficits in, 93, 112
  food output of, 99
  and Forum for Peace and Democracy, 162
  GDP of, 94, 95, 96, 97, 98
  geothermal plants in, 100
  health conditions in, 58
  housing in, 61
  hydroelectricity in, 100
  illiteracy rates in, 57
  and IMF, 113, 114
  imports of, 105
  income distribution in, 55
  Indians' and peasants' insurrection in 1932 in, 159
  industrial output in, 99
  inflation in, 97, 98
  investment coefficient in, 109
  land concentration in, 49
  land reform in, 53, 54, 65, 66
  "Land to the Tiller" law in, 51
  military aid to, 178
  Nicaragua as training camp for guerrilla activities in, 170
  nutrition in, 60
  oil imports in, 105
  per-capita food output of, 99
  per-capita GDP of, 95
  political conflict in, 173–178, 189
  political development of, 20–23
  population of, vi, 42, 44, 90
  real GDP in, 96, 97
  rebellion in, 4, 158
  Revolutionary Junta in, 23
  and SDR, 114
  size of, 90
  terrorism in, 201

El Salvador (*cont.*)
  trade of, 106
  unemployment in, 48, 101
  US military aid to, 177
  US negotiations with, 164
  war between Honduras and. See "Soccer War"
Emergency fund, 205–209
Emigration to United States, 45, 46
Employment, 93, 100–101, 117, 211
  See also Unemployment
  in Costa Rica, 100
  in El Salvador, 47, 100
  in Guatemala, 47
  in Honduras, 100
  in Panama, 100
  structure of, 46–49
Encyclopedists, 15
Energy, 99–100
  conservation of, 118
  crisis in, 105
  geothermal, 118
  hydroelectric, 99, 118
  policies on, 117–118
English intervention in 18th century, 17
EPS. See Popular Sandinist Army
ERP. See Revolutionary Army of the People
Escuintla, 24
Estrada, Armando Ulises, 167
ETA (Basque terrorist organization), 169
Ethnic composition, 40–42
European public information campaign, 200
Excelsior, 176
Exchange rates. See Money
Exports, 92, 95, 101, 102, 104, 107, 117, 195
  [See also] Trade
  in Costa Rica, 104
  in El Salvador, 104
  in Honduras, 104
  ratio of external debt service to value of, 112
External debt service ratio, 112
External financing, 111–114
External sector, 101–107

F

FAO. See Broad Opposition Front (Nicaragua)
FAR. See Armed Rebel Forces
Farabundo Martí National Liberation Front (*Frente Farabundo Martí de Liberación Nacional*, or FMLN), 175, 176, 177, 183
Farmland access, 51, 211
FARN. See Armed Forces for National Resistance
FDN. See Nicaraguan Democratic Force
FDR. See Democratic Revolutionary Front (El Salvador)
Federalism, 15
Federation of United Provinces of Central America, 14
Federico, Manuel, 183
Fertility rates, 42, 43
Figueres, Jose, 31
Financial incentives, 204–205
Financial market in Costa Rica, 108
Financial policies. See Money
Financing
  development, 108–114
  external, 111–114
Fiscal deficits. See Debt
Fiscal incentives, 204–205
Fiscal policies. See Money
FITRE. See Florida Institute of Technology Research and Engineering
Fleites, Adán, 171
Flores, Gonzalez, 31
Florida Institute of Technology Research and Engineering (FITRE), ix
FMLN. See Farabundo Martí National Liberation Front
Food output of El Salvador and Nicaragua, 99
Foreign assistance, 121–122
Foreign exchange shortage, 119
Foreign investment, 118
  direct, 110–111
Foreign trade. See Trade
Forum for Peace and Democracy, 162, 165, 198

FPL. *See* Popular Liberation Forces
FPN. *See* National Patriotic Front (Nicaragua)
French Revolution, 14, 15
Frente Democrático Revolucionario (Democratic Revolutionary Front), 176, 177
Frente Farabundo Martí de Liberación Nacional (Farabundo Martí National Liberation Front, or FMLN), 175, 176, 177, 183
FSLN. *See* Sandinista Front of National Liberation
Fuentes, Miquel Ydigoras, 26
Fuerza Democrática Nicaragüense (Nicaraguan Democratic Force), 171, 172, 182
Fuerzas Armadas de la Resistencia Nacional (Armed Forces for National Resistance, or FARN), 172, 177
Fuerzas Armadas Rebeldes (Armed Rebel Forces), 179
Fuerzas Armadas Revolucionarias Nicaragüenses (Nicaraguan Revolutionary Armed Forces), 172, 174, 177
Fuerzas Populares de Liberación (Popular Liberation Forces), 175, 177
"Fundamental Statute" in Nicaragua, 169

G

Galvez, Juan Manuel, 28
Garcia, Jose Guillermo, 175
Garcia, Policarpo Paz, 28, 182
GDP. *See* Gross Domestic Product
General Assembly, Organization of American States, ix
General Treaty on Central American Economic Cooperation (SIECA), 106
Geopolitical configuration of Central America, 12
Geothermal energy
 in El Salvador, 100
 resources in, 118
GNP. *See* Gross National Product

Gross domestic investment, 108, 109
Gross Domestic Product (GDP), 90, 94–95
 in Costa Rica, 94, 95, 98
 in El Salvador, 94, 95, 96, 98
 Growth rates in, 95
 in Guatemala, 94, 95, 98
 in Honduras, 94, 95, 96, 98
 in Nicaragua, 94, 95, 96, 98
 in Panama, 94, 95, 98
 per-capita, 94–95, 96
 real, 96, 97
 regional, 95, 98, 111
Gross National Product (GNP), 203
 and gross domestic investment, 108, 109
Group of Twelve, 166, 168
Guardia, Jorge, ix
Guatemala, 3, 4, 12, 13, 14, 33, 62, 95, 107
 area of, vi
 brith control in, 43
 Captaincy General of, 12, 14
 and Central American Democratic Community, 162, 212
 communists in, 159
 Constituent Assembly of, 27
 and Contadora Group, 163
 Cuban mediation in, 161
 debt in, 93, 112
 eqrthquake in, 96
 economy of, 90, 96
 education in, 56, 57
 elections in, 33, 196, 197
 employment in, 47
 ethnic composition of, 40
 exports of, viii, 112
 fiscal deficits in, 93, 112
 foreign trade of, 106
 GDP of, 94, 95, 98
 health conditions in, 58, 59
 housing in, 61, 62
 illiteracy rates in, 57
 imports of, 105
 income distribution in, 55
 Indians in, 24, 41
 inflation in, 97
 investments in, 109, 110
 Labor Code of, 25
 land concentration in, 49
 land reform in, 53, 54
 language problems in, 41

Guatemala (*cont.*)
   merchandise trade surplus in, 102
   National Assembly of, 25
   Nicaragua as training camp for guerrilla activities in, 170
   non-agricultural labor in, 49
   nutrition in, 60
   oil imports in, 105
   per-capita GDP of, 95
   petroleum in, 99
   political conflict in, 178–181, 189
   political development of, 24–27
   population of, vi, 90
   ratio of external debt service to value of exports in, 112
   terrorism in, 165, 179
   TFR in, 43
   unemployment in, 48
   urban population of, 90
   voter registration in, 27
Guatemala City, 27
Guatemalan Institute of Social Security, 25
Guatemalan National Revolutionary Unity, 179–180
Guatemalan Workers Party (*Partido Guatemalteco del Trabajo*, or PGT), 27, 179
Guerrilla activities in El Salvador and Guatemala, 170
Guerrilla Army of the Poor (*Ejército Guerrillero de los Pobres*, or EGP), 179
Guevara, Angel Anibal, 26, 178, 180
Guevara, Ernesto "Che," 161

H

Hay-Bunau-Varilla Treaty, 29, 30
Health conditions, 58–59, 62, 63–64, 67, 93
Hernandez, Maximiliano, 20
Herrera, Thomas, 29
Honduras, 3, 8, 12, 13, 14, 17, 34, 95, 107, 196
   Agrarian Reform Law of 1962 in, 28
   agriculture in, 90
   area of, vi
   birth control in, 43
   and Cenral American Democratic Community, 162, 212
   Constituent Assembly in, 29
   and Contadora Group, 163
   Cuban mediation in, 161
   debt in, 93, 112
   democratic reconstitution in, 4
   economy of, 90, 95, 96
   elections in, 29, 33, 196, 197, 198
   emigration to United States from, 45
   employment in, 100
   ethnic composition of, 41
   farmland access in, 51
   fiscal deficits in, 93, 112
   foreign trade of, 106
   and Forum for Peace and Democracy, 162
   GDP of, 94, 95, 96, 98
   health conditions in, 58
   housing in, 61
   Hurricane Fifi in, 96
   and IMF, 113
   imports of, 105
   income distribution in, 55
   investment in, 110
   land concentration in, 49, 50
   land reform in, 52, 53, 65
   Liberal Party in, 28, 182, 184
   liberals in, 5
   military confrontation between El Salvador and. *See* "Soccer War"
   Nationalist Party in, 28, 182
   National Party in, 184
   non-agricultural labor in, 49
   nutrition in, 60
   oil imports in, 105
   per-capita GDP of, 95, 96
   political conflict in, 182–184, 189
   political development of, 27–29
   population of, vi
   public health in, 93
   terrorism in, 165
   TRF in, 43
   unemployment in, 48
   unions in, 28
   urban population of, 90

violence in, 165, 170
war between El Salvador and. See "Soccer War"
withdrawal of from CACM, 107
Housing, 61–62, 66–67
Hurricane Fifi in Honduras, 96
Hydroelecric resources, 99, 118
  in Costa Rica, 100
  in El Salvador, 100

I

IBRD. See International Bank for Reconstruction and Development
ICAITI. See Central American Institute of Technological and Industrial Research
ICAP. See Central American Institute of Public Administration
IDA. See International Development Agency
IDB. See Inter-American Development Bank
Ideological polarization, xiii
IFC. See International Finance Corporation
Illiteracy rates, 57
Illueca, Jorge, 185, 197
IMF. See International Monetary Fund
Imports, 91, 92, 101, 102
  See also Trade
  in Costa Rica, 105
  in El Salvador, 105
  in Guatemala, 105
  in Honduras, 105
  in Nicaragua, 105
  oil, 105
  in Panama, 105
INCAP. See Institute of Nutrition in Central America and Panama
Incentives, 204–205
Income distribution, 54–56, 66, 108
Independence, 15
  of Panama from Colombia, 29
  from Spain, 14
Indians
  in Guatemala, 24, 41
  insurrection of in El Salvador, 1932, 159

Indigo, 13
Individual rights, 3
Industrial production
  in El Salvador, 99
  in Nicaragua, 99
  stagnation of, 107
  See also specific industries
  in Costa Rica, 101
Inflation, 93, 94, 97–98, 115, 120
  in Costa Rica, 97, 114
  in El Salvador, 97, 98
  in Guatemala, 97
  in Nicaragua, 97
Injustice, 2, 3, 4
INRA. See Instituto Nacional de Reforma Agraria (Nicaragua)
Institute of Nutrition in Central America and Panama (INCAP), 207
Inter-American Defense Board College, 200
Inter-American Development Bank (IDB), ix, 113, 117, 118, 193, 207, 208, 209, 213
Interest rates, 96, 108, 203
  in Costa Rica, 109
  on external debt, 112
  policies on, 93
International associations of political parties, 199
International Bank for Reconstruction and Development (IBRD, World Bank), 48, 113, 117, 118, 193, 207, 208, 209
International Democratic Union, 199
International Development Agency (IDA), 113
International Finance Corporation (IFC), 113
International Labor Organization, 48
International Monetary Fund (IMF), 113, 114, 115, 119, 122, 186
  conditionality in agreements with, 114
  and Costa Rica, 113, 114
  and El Salvador, 113, 114
  and Honduras, 113
  and Nicaragua, 113
  and Panama, 113, 114

269

INDEX

International Socialist Movement (Social Democrats), 21, 31, 158
Intra-regional trade, 107
Investment, 108, 109, 204, 205
 in Brazil, 109
 coefficient of, 109
 in Costa Rica, 109, 110
 domestic, 108, 109, 116–117
 foreign, 110–111, 118
 gross domestic, 108, 109
 in Guatemala, 109, 110
 in Honduras, 110
 incentives for, 117
 in Nicaragua, 110
 in Panama, 109, 110
 in Peru, 109
 private, 110–111, 204
 by US, 118, 119
 in Venezuela, 109
Irrigation in Tempisque Valley, Costa Rica, 210

J

Jamaica, 161
Joint Programming Mission, 106

K

Kaplan, Morton A., xii
Kissinger's Bipartisan Commission on Central America, viii, xiii, 111, 113, 121, 164, 165, 195, 198, 200, 201, 204, 205, 209, 211, 215–235, 237–251
Korea, 169

L

Labor Code of Guatemala, 25
Labor movement of 19th century, 14
Labor unions. See Unions
Laissez-faire capitalism, 15
La Nacion, ix
Land
 concentration of, 49, 50
 redistribution of, 66
 underutilization of, 50

Land reform, 54, 66, 211
 in Costa Rica, 53, 54, 65
 in El Salvador, 53, 54, 65, 66
 in Guatemala, 53, 54
 in Honduras, 52, 53, 65
 in Nicaragua, 52, 65
 in Panama, 65
Land tenure, 49–54
"Land to the Tiller" law in El Salvador, 51
Language
 in Guatemala, 41
 Spanish, 13
La Prensa, 166
Latin American public information campaign, 200
Latin American Solidarity Organization (OLAS), 160
Laugerud, Kjell Eugenio, 26, 179, 180
Lemus, Jose M., 20, 21
Liberal International, 199
Liberal Party
 in Honduras, 28, 182, 184
 in Panama, 30
Liberals, 15
 Honduran, 5
Liberation theologists, 16
Lido, Don, 188
Loans, 111
Lucas, Fernando Romeo, 4, 26, 178, 179, 181

M

Magaña, Alvaro, 23, 174
Managua, 44, 166, 171
Manufacturing output, 99
Martí, Augustin Farabundo, 20
Martinez, General ("El Brujo"), 20
Marxist-Leninists, 158
Measles, 13
Mejias Victores, General, 180, 181
Melendez family, 20
Merchandise trade, 103–107
 balance of, 102
 surplus of, 102
Mexican Revolution, 18
Mexico, 6, 14, 19, 34, 105, 106, 161, 163, 205, 208
 and Contadora Group, 162, 210

and Forum for Peace and Democracy, 162
anf FSLN, 166
and Somoza downfall, 168
Migration, 44–46
Military aid to El Salvador, 177, 178
Military confrontation between El Salvador and Honduras. See "Soccer War"
Military-economic alliance, 3
Military occupation of Nicaragua by US, 17
Miskitos in Nicaragua, 41
Missile crisis of 1962, 159
MLN. See National Liberation Movement
MNR. See National Revolutionary Movement
Molina, Arturo, 22
Money
 cost of, 120
 exchange rate for, 93, 117, 120, 121, 203
 policies on, 108, 116, 119–120, 203
 printing of, 93
Monge, Luis Alberto, 31, 186, 187, 188
Montane, Jesus, 161
Montenegro, Julio Cesar Mendez, 179
Montes, Melinda Anaya ("Ana Maria"), 175
Montoneros of Argentina, 169
Montt, Efrain Rios, 26, 27, 178, 197
Morales, Ramon Villeda, 28
Morazan, Francisco, 14
"Mosquito Kingdom," 17
Movimiento de Liberación Nacional (National Liberation Movement), 180, 181
Movimiento Nacional Revolucionario (National Revolutionary Movement), 21, 176
Multilateral efforts, 161–165, 193, 209

N

National Action Party (PAN), 21

National Assembly of Guatemala, 25
National Bipartisan Commission on Central America. See Kissinger's Commission
National Conciliation Party (*Partido Conciliacion Nacional*, or PCN), 21, 22, 23, 173, 174
National Directorate in Nicaragua, 172
Nationalist Democratic Union (UDN), 21
Nationalist Party in Honduras, 28, 182
National Liberation Movement (*Movimiento de Liberación Nacional*, or MLN), 180, 181
National Liberation Party (*Partido de Liberación Nacional*, or PLN), 16, 27, 31, 186
National Party in Honduras, 184
National Renewal Alliance (*Alianza Renovadora Nacional*, or ARENA), 23, 73, 174, 177
National Revolutionary Movement (*Movimiento Nacional Revolucionario*, or MNR), 21, 176
National savings rates, 108
National United Directorate (*Direction Nacional Unida*), 183
Natural resources, 90, 92
NGOs, 207
Nicaragua, 1, 4, 5, 8, 12, 13, 14, 17, 34, 62, 93, 95, 107, 165
 area of, vi
 birth control in, 43
 and CACD, 162
 and Contadora Group, 163
 debt in, 93, 112
 democratic pluralism in, 199
 earthquake in, 96
 economic growth in, 95, 96, 115
 elections in, 196
 emigration to United States from, 45
 ethnic composition of, 41
 exports of, 112
 farmland access in, 51
 fiscal deficits in, 93, 112
 food output of, 99

Nicaragua (cont.)
   foreign trade of, 106
   and Forum for Peace and Democracy, 162
   "Fundamental Statute" in, 169
   GDP of, 94, 95, 96, 98
   health conditions in, 58
   and IMF, 113
   imports of, 105
   income distribution in, 55
   industrial output in, 99
   inflation in, 97
   investment in, 110
   land concentration in, 50
   land reform in, 52, 65
   merchandise trade surplus in, 102
   Miskitos in, 41
   National Directorate in, 172
   non-agricultural growth rates in, 46
   oil imports of, 105
   per-capita food output of, 99
   per-capita GDP in, 95
   political conflict in, 165–172
   political development of, 17–19
   population of, vii, 44, 90
   ratio of external debt service to value of exports in, 112
   real GDP in, 96
   size of, 90
   "strategic unity" in, 161
   as training camp for guerrilla activities, 170
   unemployment in, 48
   urban population of, 90
   US military occupation of, 17
   US negotiations with, 164
Nicaraguan Democratic Force (*Fuerza Democrática Nicaragüense*, or FDN), 171, 172, 182
Nicaraguan Revolutionary Armed Forces (*Fuerzas Armadas Revolucionarias Nicaragüenses*, or FARN), 174, 177
Non-agricultural labor, 47, 49
Noriega, Manuel Antonio, 185
North Korea, 169
North Vietnam, 169
Nutrition, 59–61, 62

O

OAS. *See* Organization of American States
Ochoa, Sigifrido, 175
ODECA. *See Organizacion para el Desarollo Economico de Centro America*
Odio, Rodrigo Carazo, 32
OECD. *See* Organization for Economic Cooperation and Development
Oil, 105, 118
   imports of, 105
   worldwide prices of, 114
OLAS. *See* Latin American Solidarity Organization
Oligarchic-military vs. communist-totalitarian regimes, 7
OPEC, 112
OPIC. *See* Overseas Private Investment Corporation
Opposition National Union (UNO), 22
Organizacion del Pueblo en Armas (Organization of the Armed People), 179
Organization of American States (OAS), 6, 21, 113, 159, 164, 167, 197, 198, 201, 204, 207, 208
   General Assembly of, 259
   Program of Public Finances of, 205
Organization of the Armed People (*Organizacion del Pueblo en Armas*, or ORPA), 179
Organization for Economic Cooperation and Development (OECD), 112, 205, 208
ORPA. *See* Organization of the People in Arms (Guatemala)
Osorio, Carlos Arana, 179
Osorio, Oscar, 20
Out-migration from rural areas, 50
Overseas Private Investment Corporation (OPIC), 110–111, 119, 205

P

PAC. *See* Authentic Constitutional Party (El Salvador)

PAHO, 207
Palestine Liberation Organization (PLO), 169
PAN. See National Action Party
Panama, 3, 5, 6, 13, 17, 19, 62, 96, 163, 193
  agriculture in, 90
  area of, vi
  and balance of payments, 102
  birth control in, 43
  Christian Democratic Party of, 30
  and Contadora Group, 162, 210
  debt in, 93, 112
  Democratic Revolutionary party of, 30
  economic growth in, 95, 115
  education in, 56, 57
  elections in, 196
  employment in, 100
  ethnic composition of, 41
  fiscal deficits in, 93, 112
  and FSLN, 166
  GDP of, 94, 95, 98
  health conditions in, 58, 59
  housing in, 61, 62
  and IMF, 113, 114
  imports of, 105
  income distribution in, 55
  independence of, from Colombia, 29
  investments in, 109, 110
  land reform in, 65
  Liberal Party of, 30
  merchandise trade surplus in, 102
  non-agricultural labor in, 49
  oil imports of, 105
  Panamanian Popular Party of, 30–31
  per-capita GDP in, 95
  political conflict in, 184–186, 189
  political development in, 29–31
  population of, vi, 42, 44, 90
  ratio of external debt service to value of exports in, 112
  Republican Party of, 30
  and SDR, 114
  Socialist Democratic Party of, 30
  and Somoza downfall, 168
  surplus in service account of, 102
  TFR in, 42, 43
  trade surplus in, 102
  unemployment in, 48, 100, 101
  urban population of, 90
Panama Canal, 16, 29, 41, 102, 184
Panamanian Popular Party of Panama, 30–31
Paredes, Ruben Dario, 185
Partido Conciliacion Nacional (National Conciliation Party), 21, 22, 23, 173, 174
Partido de Liberación Nacional (National Liberation Party, or PLN), 16, 27, 31, 186
Partido Guatemalteco del Trabajo (Guatemalan Workers Party), 27, 179
  See also Communist party
Partido Popular Salvadoreno (Popular Salvadoran Party, or PPS), 173
Partido Revolucionario Democrático (Democratic Revolutionary Party, or PRD), 30, 185
Pastora, Edén, 171, 172, 218
Patriotic Revolutionary Front, 171
Payroll taxes, 120
  in Costa Rica, 92
Paz, Octavio, 2
PCN. See National Conciliation party
PDC. See Christian Democratic Party
Peasant insurrection in El Salvador in 1932, 159
Peoples United Party (PUP), 188
Per-capita food output, 99
Per-capita GDP, 94–95
Perez-Lopez, Jorge, ix
Permanent Secretariat of the General Treaty of Central American Economic Integration (SIECA), 106
Peru, 13
  APRA of, 31
  investments in, 109
Petroleum in Guatemala, 99
PGT. See *Partido Guatemalteco del Trabajo* (Guatemala)

Plantations, 14
  coffee, 20
PLN. See National Liberation party (Guatemala)
PLO. See Palestine Liberation Organization
Pluralism, 199
Polarization, xiii
Political assistance program, 196–202
Political conflict, 158
Political parties
  See also specific parties
  international associations of, 199
Popular Liberation Forces (Fuerzas Populares de Liberación, or FPL), 175, 177
Popular Salvadoran Party (Partido Popular Salvadoreno, or PPS), 173
Popular Sandinist Army (Ejército Popular Sandinista, or EPS), 169
Population
  of Costa Rica, 42
  of El Salvador, 42, 90
  growth of, 42–44, 64, 115
  of Guatemala, 90
  of Nicaragua, 44, 90
  of Panama, 42, 44, 90
  size of, 42–44
  structure of, 42–44
  urban, 90
Population statistics, vi
PPS. See Popular Salvadoran Party
PRAM. See Revolutionary Party of April and May (El Salvador)
PRD. See Democratic Revolutionary Party
PREALC. See Regional Employment Program of Latin America and the Caribbean
Precolonial era, 12
Price
  of oil, 114
  policies on, 203
Price, George, 188
Private investment, 110–111, 204
PRN. See National Republican party (Costa Rica)
Production, 98
  stagnation of, 107

Professors World Peace Academy—US (PWPA-US), vii
Proletarian Tendency, 167
Prolonged Popular Struggle, 167
Protectionism, 91, 107
PRUD. See Revolutionary Party of Democratic Union (El Salvador)
Public health. See health conditions
Public information campaign, 200, 202
Public sector
  composition of, 203
  restructuring of, 203
  size of, 120, 203
PUN. See National Union Party (Costa Rica)
PUP. See Peoples United Party
PWPA-US. See Professors World Peace Academy—US

Q

Quezaltenango, 24
Quinonez, Alfonso, 20

R

Reagan, Ronald, xiii, 121, 164, 178, 181, 182, 204, 205, 207, 208, 212, 215, 216, 218, 219
Real GDP
  in Costa Rica, 97
  in El Salvador, 96, 97
  in Nicaragua, 96
Rebellion in El Salvador, 4, 158
Redistribution of land, 66
Regional development program, 211
Regional Employment Program of Latin America and the Caribbean (PREALC), 48
Regional GDP, 98, 111
  growth rates in, 95
Regionalization of violence, 8
Registration of voters in Guatemala, 27
Remon y Reyes, Victor, 18
Republican Party of Panama, 30

Rescate, 171
Resources, 90, 92
Restructuring of CACM, 120
Reunification of Central America, 14, 15, 24, 32
Revolution
  American, 14
  Cuban, 159
  French, 14, 15
  Mexican, 18
  Spanish, 15
Revolutionary Armed Forces (Guademala), 179
Revolutionary Army of the People (*Ejército Revolucionario del Pueblo*, or ERP), 176, 177
Revolutionary Junta in El Salvador, 23
Revolutionary Party of April and May (PRAM), 21
Revolutionary Party of Democratic Union (PRUD), 20
Rights of individuals, 3
Rios Montt, General, 180
Rivera, Julio Adalberto, 21
Rivero, Emilio Adolfo, ix
Robelo, Alfonso, 171, 172
Roman Catholic Church. *See* Catholic Church
Romero, Carlos Humberto, 4, 22, 176
Romero, Oscar Arnulfo, 22
Royo, Aristides, 30, 185, 197
"Rural Development Regions," 53
Rural out-migration, 50

S

Sacasa, president, 18
Salary situations, 93
Salvadoran Communist Party, 177
Sandinista Defense Committees (CDS), 169
Sandinista Front of National Liberation (FSLN), 166, 167, 168, 169, 171, 172
  and Costa Rica, 166
  and Mexico, 166
  and Panama, 166
  and Venezuela, 166
Sandinistas, 6, 16, 19, 52, 93, 161, 164, 167, 168, 169, 170, 171, 172, 182, 187, 189
Sandino, Cesar Augusto, 18
Savings, 109
  domestic, 108, 116–117
  rates of, 108
SDR. *See* Special Drawing Rights
Seasonal wage labor, 50
Services account, 102
Sex differentials in illiteracy rates, 57
Shuttle diplomacy, 167
SIECA. *See* General Treaty fo Central American Economic Integration
Slaves, 13
Smallpox, 13
"Soccer War" between El Salvador and Honduras, 21, 28, 107, 115, 165
Social Democrats, 21, 31, 158
Social expenditures, 206
Socialist Democratic Party of Panama, 30
Socialist International, 176, 177, 199
Socioeconomic assistance program, 201–211
Somoza, Anastasio, 4, 5, 6, 18, 32, 166, 168, 169, 170, 172, 186, 187
Somoza family, 3, 17, 18, 52
Somoza, Luis, 18
Somoza, "Tachito," 18
Somoza, "Tacho," 18
Soviet bloc, 19
Soviet Union, 2, 3, 6, 8, 16, 34, 158, 169, 170, 175, 189
Spanish colonial period, 12, 13
Spanish conquistadores, 12
Spanish language, 13
Spanish revolution, 15
Special Drawing Rights (SDR), 114
Stagnation of industrial production, 107
Stone, Richard, 164, 165
"Strategic unity," 161, 177
Structure
  changes in, 202–203
  inequalities in, 65–66
  of population, 42–44
Subsidies, 107, 108

Sugar cane, 13
Supervision of elections, 197

T

Tariffs, 91, 99, 107, 117, 120, 203
Task Force on Central America, viii, ix
Taxation, 108, 119–120, 203
　payroll, 92, 120
　reforms in, 66
Tegucigalpa, 44
Tempisque Valley irrigation in Costa Rica, 210
Terceristas (Third Force), 167
Terrorism, 7, 93, 95, 204
　Basque, 169
　in Costa Rica, 165, 187
　elimination of, 201–202
　in El Salvador, 201
　in Guatemala, 165, 179
　in Honduras, 165
　public information campaign on ending of, 202
TFR. See Total fertility rate
Theology of liberation, 16
Third Force (Terceristas), 167
Tinoco, Federico, 31
Torrijos, Omar, 30, 31, 184, 185
Total fertility rate (TFR), 42
Trade, 102, 106
　See also Balance of payments; Imports; Exports
　in Costa Rica, 103
　deficits in, 101, 103
　intra-regional, 107
　merchandise, 103–107, 122
　surplus in, 102
Transisthmian canal linking Caribbean with Pacific Ocean, 19
Tri-Continental Conference, 159, 160
Tupamaros of Uruguay, 169
Typhus, 13

U

Ubico, Jorge, 24, 25
UDN. See Nationalist Democratic Union

UDP. See United Democratic Party
Ulate, Otilio, 31
Ulibarri, Eduardo, viii, ix, 1
Underdevelopment, 2, 3, 4
Underemployment, 94
Underutilization of land, 50
UNDP. See United Nations Development Program
Unemployment, 48, 94, 100–101, 107, 120
　See also Employment
　in Costa Rica, 48, 92, 100, 101
　in El Salvador, 48, 101
　in Guatemala, 48
　in Honduras, 48
　in Nicaragua, 48
　in Panama, 48, 100, 101
UNESCO, 207
Ungo, Guillermo Manuel, 22, 176, 177
UNICEF, 207
UNIDAD (Unity), 31
Unions
　in Costa Rica, 158
　in Honduras, 28
United Democratic Party (UDP), 188
United Nations, 19, 113, 164, 185, 207
United Nations Development Program (UNDP), 113, 205, 208
United States
　emigration to, 45, 46
　Honduran emigration to, 45
　investments in Central America by, 118, 119
　negotiations between El Salvador and, 164
　negotiations between Nicaragua and, 164
　Nicaraguan emigration to, 45
　public information campaign in, 200
　Salvadoran emigration to, 46
United States aid, 113, 114, 186
　to Costa Rica, 186
　economic, 186
　to El Salvador, 177
　military, 177
Unity (UNIDAD), 31
"Unity" tactic, 161, 177
University of Chicago, 23
University of Costa Rica, ix

University of St. Louis, ix
UNO. *See* Opposition National Union
Urbanization process, 45
Urban populations, 90
Urcuyo, Francisco, 168, 169
Uruguay, 169

V

Venezuela, 6, 19, 34, 105, 106, 161, 163, 205, 208
   Acción Democrática of, 31
   and Contadora Group, 162, 210
   and Forum for Peace and Democracy, 162
   and FSLN, 166
   investments in, 109
   and Somoza downfall, 168
Victores, Oscar Mejias, 27, 178, 197
Vides-Casanova, Eugenio, 175
Vietnam, 169
Vietnam analogy, 2
Villalobos, Joaquin, 176, 177
Violence, xiii, 9, 158, 204
   See also Terrorism
   in Costa Rica, 170

elimination of, 201–202
in Honduras, 170
public information campaign on ending of, 202
regionalization of, 8
Volio, Fernando, Foreign Minister, 187
Voter registration in Guatemala, 27

W

Walker, William, 17
War between El Salvador and Honduras. *See* "Soccer War"
World Bank. *See* International Bank for Reconstruction and Development
World Christian Democratic Union, 199
World depression of '20s, 20
World oil prices, 114

Z

Zelava, President, 17
Zuniga, Ricardo, 182